MODERN SMALL ARMS

MODERN SMALL ARMS

IAN V. HOGG

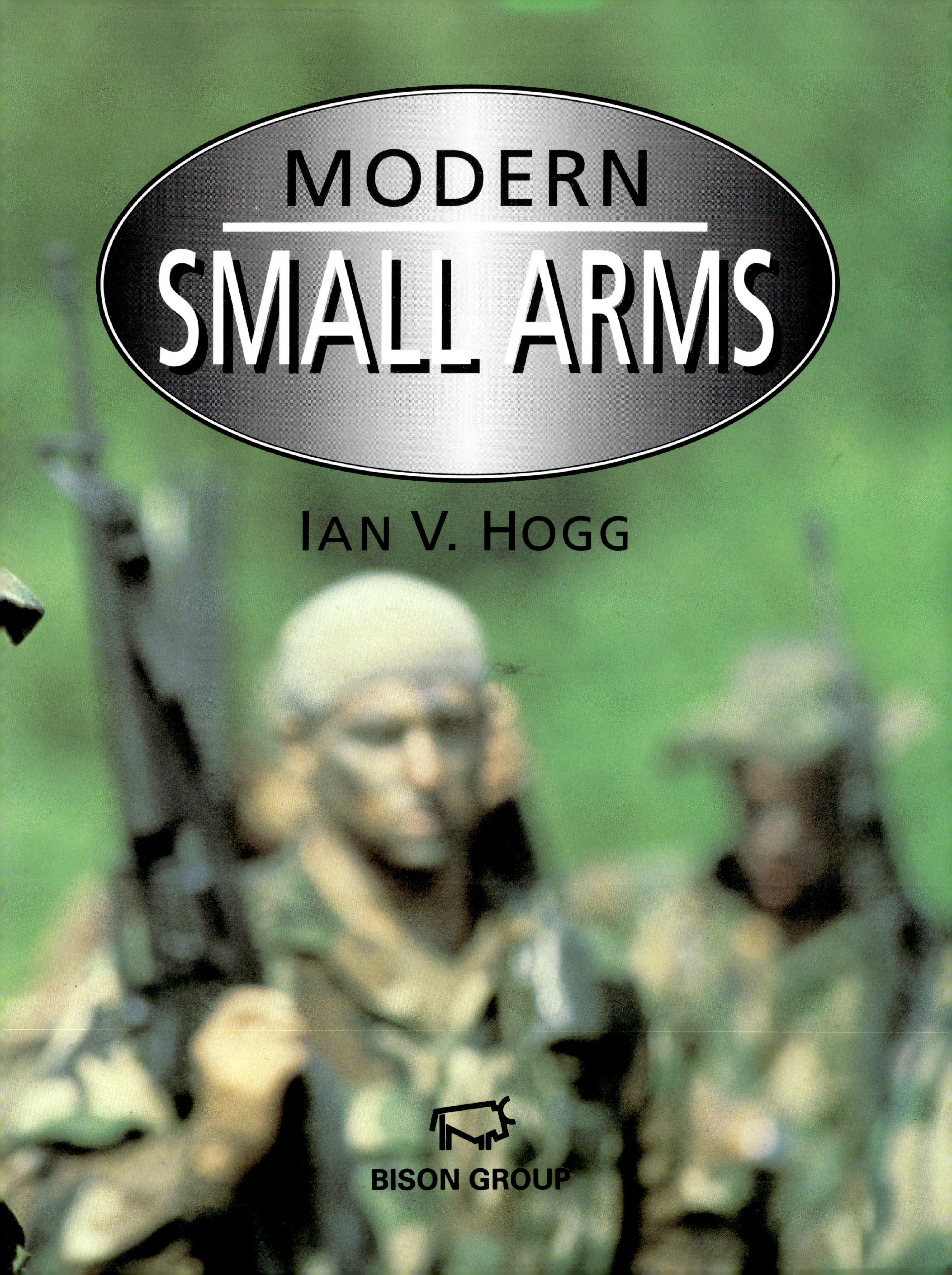

BISON GROUP

First published in 1994 by
Bison Books Ltd
Kimbolton House
117A Fulham Road
London SW3 6RL

ISBN 1-85841-075-4

Printed in Slovenia

Page 1: A pair of counter-revolutionary warfare specialists armed with automatic weapons.

Pages 2-3: A group of U.S. Navy Seals. The man in the foreground is armed with an M16A1 rifle with an underslung M203 grenade-launcher.

Right: Hunting with a Beretta automatic shotgun.

CONTENTS

INTRODUCTION

In the 12 years which have passed since the first edition of this book was published many new small arms designs have appeared, as might be expected. However, if a graph was drawn showing the number of designs against the passage of time, a downward trend would be revealed. The conclusion seems to be that small arms design has reached a level of technology which will be difficult to improve upon, both mechanically and economically. As will be seen in the text, the United States has spent several years in an attempt to find an Advanced Combat Rifle which would show a significant performance improvement over the current M16A2. The best brains in the firearms business were applied, the results were technically outstanding, but the desired improvement was not achieved, which indicates the size of the technical barrier standing in the way of significant design advances. The economic factor can also be seen in the cost of the program – some $350 million.

So far as military weapons go, the point has been reached at which any major improvement can only be achieved at a grossly disproportionate cost; a hunter might be persuaded to pay a 50 per cent increase for his next rifle, and $10,000 for a shotgun is not considered outrageous, but an army contemplating buying rifles by the hundred thousand is likely to balk at such a premium on excellence. The simple fact is that the current military rifle is generally more accurate than the man firing it, and it is as efficient as it needs to be, given a reasonable amount of training in its use. There is no point in laying out vast sums of money for a percentage increase in the probability of hitting the target with the first shot, which is what rifle improvement really means. And bear in mind that half the world is running round with Kalashnikovs, a 50-year-old design, not exactly at the cutting edge of technology, but one which, nevertheless, is killing very effectively.

On the commercial market, too, economics have made their impact. Since 1982 many long-established gunmakers have vanished; from the 1982 edition we have removed Harrington & Richardson, Iver Johnson, Renato Gamba, Benelli, High Standard, BSA, Stirling, Midland, Parker-Hale . . . all names which, in 1982, we thought would last for ever. Some have been absorbed into other companies, others have simply died, all victims of the economic climate of the 1980s. Fabrique National of Herstal and Heckler & Koch of Oberndorf, two pillars of the industry, have both been sold, the former to Giat Industries of France, the latter to Royal Ordnance of Britain. Other companies are in financial straits and may not see the century out. Small wonder, then, that new ideas and bold commercial ventures are thin on the ground.

One of the more interesting aspects of the past decade has been to see several ideas from the past being resurrected and the benefits of modern technology applied to them. The practice of using a revolving barrel to lock the breech of a pistol had vanished by 1982, the principal reason being the difficulty and expense of machining the necessary curved lugs on the barrel and corresponding grooves in the frame and slide; but the rapid growth in the

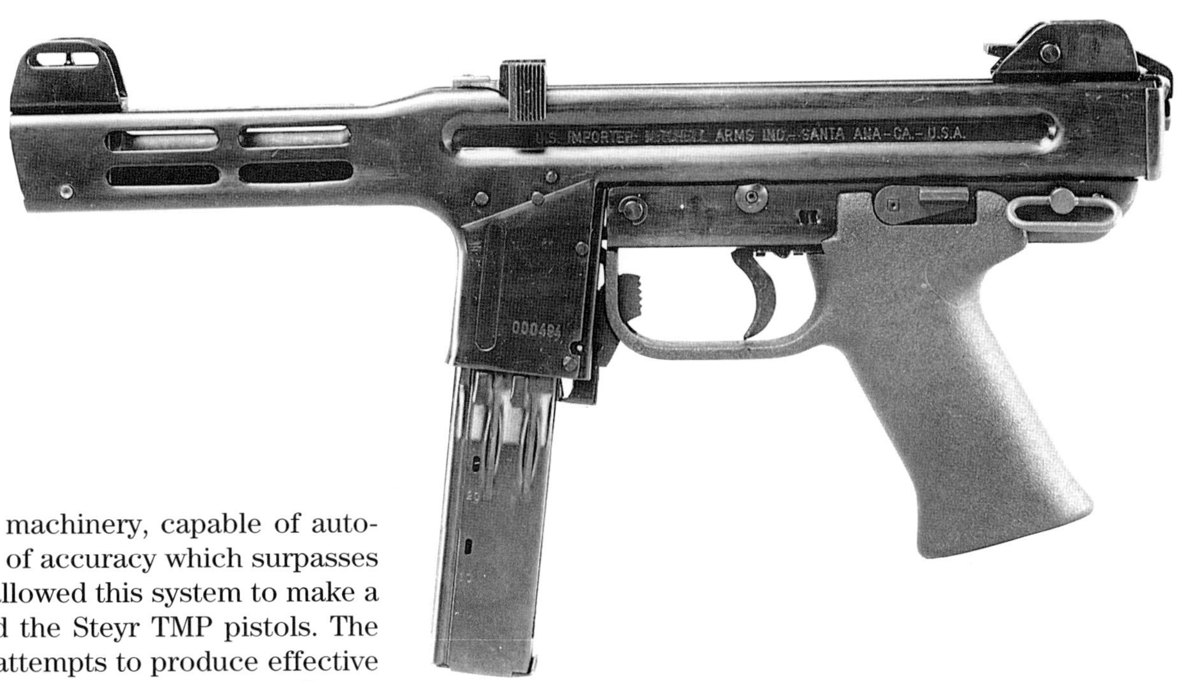

Previous pages: A Yugoslavian variant of a Kalashnikov.
Left: An Italian sniper with the Beretta M1 sniping rifle.
Top: Syrian special forces with AKM variants.
Right: The Spectre submachine gun.

use of computer-controled machinery, capable of automatically working to a level of accuracy which surpasses the best hand-worker, has allowed this system to make a return in the Colt 2000 and the Steyr TMP pistols. The 1950s and 1960s saw many attempts to produce effective fléchette rounds, cartridges in which the "bullet" was actually a finned dart capable of high velocity and hence flat trajectory and a better chance of a hit. The accuracy left a great deal to be desired, largely due to problems with the "sabot", the plastic collar which mated the thin dart with the much larger bore of the rifle, and as a result the fléchette fell from favor. It returned, however, in the American Advanced Combat Rifle program, vastly improved by the use of new materials, though still unable to unseat the traditional jacketed bullet from its place of dominance. Similarly, the Duplex bullet, tried in Vietnam and abandoned, also returned in improved form, while Heckler & Koch carried the caseless cartridge to its peak

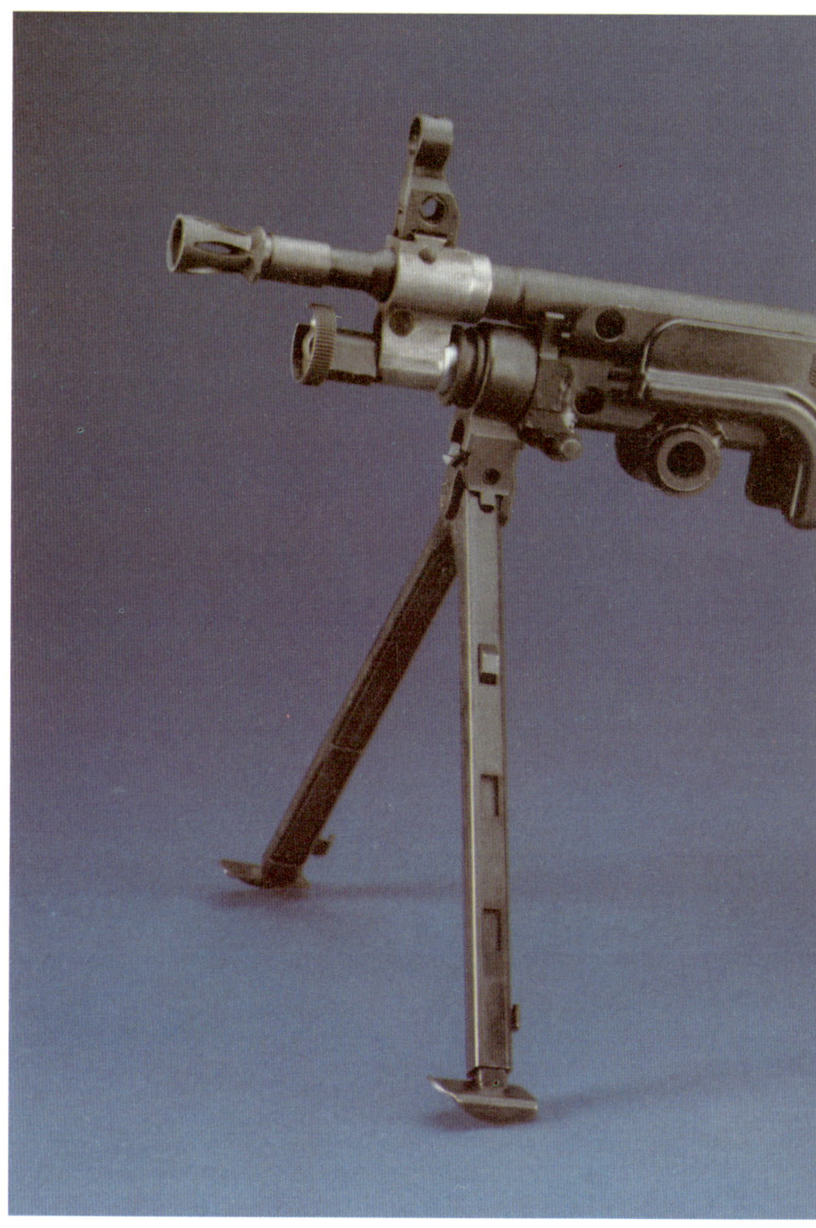

Above: Shiny new SA-80s undergoing trials with British paras.
Top: The Bushman Individual Defense Weapon.
Right: The FN Minimi machine gun.

by designing a machine gun to suit it.

There is, therefore, no shortage of designing talent in the world; unfortunately, all their designs are evolutionary rather than revolutionary, making marginal improvements upon existing foundations, rather than striking out in some totally new dimension. And since major firearms development is invariably military-stimulated, the stagnation in military circles makes itself felt in the commercial arena as well.

As and when the military designs make a quantum leap into the next generation (and it is unlikely to be in this century) it will still leave the commercial gun unaffected, because current military thinking is towards such things as directed-energy weapons – lethal lasers, electric propulsion systems, liquid propellants, plasma weapons – which are unlikely ever to become acceptable as sporting weapons; I find it difficult to visualize trap shooting with a laser beam. Another military aim is the "non-lethal" weapon (a contradiction in terms if ever there was one) which will render an opponent incapable of retaliation for sufficient time to move him to a conventional prisoner-of-war compound.

This brings us back to where we began; firearms have reached a peak from which it is going to take a long time to move, largely because moving is not going to be cost-effective. Nevertheless, there is still room for small improvements and fine-tuning; new cartridges will continue to be developed, usually by hand-loaders in the first instance, but soon taken up by commercial manufacturers if they show any promise. Experience shows that innovation does not necessarily sell guns; quality and reliability, accuracy and, of course, price sells guns, and as the following pages show, there is still sufficient diversity in the gun-making business to satisfy just about every demand of either the soldier, the hunter, or the target enthusiast.

In the sections which follow I have adhered to a standard format, and the facts presented are based upon the manufacturers' information wherever possible; otherwise, they are based on reliable reports or upon actual examination of the weapon. I have attempted to handle and fire as many of the presented weapons as possible. Opinions are my own, presented as constructive analysis.

Left: A Browning .50 M2 machine gun with blank firing attachment and laser simulator.
Right: A Spanish Ameli 5.56mm machine gun.
Below: British troops armed with the Enfield L85A1 rifle.

PIETRO BERETTA GARDONE V.T. – MADE IN ITALY
A08647X
PB

PISTOLS

ASP 9mm Auto Pistol

Manufacturer Armament Systems and Procedures, Appleton, WI 54911, U.S.A.
Type Semi-auto, locked breech, double-action
Caliber 9mm Parabellum
Barrel 3.25in (82.5mm)
Weight 24oz (680gm)
Magazine Capacity 7 rounds

Almost 20 years ago the clandestine services of the U.S. Government stated a requirement for a concealable but powerful automatic pistol, and the first response was a cut-down .45 M1911A1 Colt developed by the C.I.A. While this worked, it could hardly be said to be an elegant solution. It was noisy, had excessive muzzle flash, a magazine capacity of only four shots, and less target effect than the average .38 Special revolver. Another solution was sought, which was to be based on the 9mm Parabellum cartridge, and this led to the design which is now commercially available as the 'ASP', named for the company who make it.

The ASP is actually a re-manufacture. It begins life as a standard Smith & Wesson Model 39 which is then severely cut about. The butt, slide, slide stop and safety catch are all dimensionally reduced and lightening cuts are made in the slide so as to distribute the balance correctly. The barrel is shortened, throated and polished, the feed ramp smoothed and polished, and a custom-built barrel bushing pressed into the slide. New recoil spring and guide are fitted, every edge of the weapon hand-smoothed, and the entire surface coated with 'Teflon' to give a smooth, black, resistant finish. The butt plates are replaced with special models, with that on the left side having a transparent panel which allows the contents of the magazine to be checked. The trigger-guard is given a forward hook and the magazine floor given a finger rest, both aiding the holding of the pistol in combat mode. Finally a 'Guttersnipe' combat sight unit is fitted to the slide. This is a trough with the interior walls colored yellow, and if the sight picture is correct, the target can be seen within three equally-proportioned walls. If the aim is off, then the walls of the sight display an unbalanced picture which indicates the sighting error.

The resulting weapon is not cheap; it is necessary to buy the Model 39 first and then add $350 for the conversion. But for those whose life could depend upon quick and accurate firepower, the price is immaterial and the ASP promises to be the right answer.

Previous pages: A pair of Beretta 92 SB Compact pistols.

Right: The ASP 9mm combat pistol, displaying the visible magazine facility.

Above: The Spanish A-80 double-action pistol.

Astra Model A-80 Auto Pistol

Manufacturer Astra, Unceta y Cia, Guernica, Spain
Type Locked breech double-action semi-automatic
Caliber 9mm Parabellum
Barrel 3.75in (95mm)
Weight 34.2oz (970gm)
Magazine Capacity 15 rounds

The Astra company has been manufacturing automatic pistols since 1908. It has been providing Spanish military and police pistols since 1913 and has thus gained valuable knowledge of practical requirements as opposed to theoretical desires, and this shows in their latest pistol the A-80.

The A-80 is very much in the modern idiom – a double-action weapon with a large magazine. It is compact, simply built and easy to disassemble, yet it is also of a respectable weight so that it points well and balances nicely in the hand. The breech is locked by the normal Browning swinging link, though, as in most of today's models, the link is actually a shaped cam which withdraws the barrel downwards from engagement with the slide. Safety is attended to by having the firing pin positively locked by a sprung plunger except for the actual moment that the hammer is released by trigger action, at which time a portion of the trigger linkage lifts the plunger out of engagement and frees the firing pin. There is a de-cocking lever on the left side of the frame, its thumb catch just behind the trigger guard. Depressing this drops the hammer to be caught on the rebound notch, after which pulling the trigger will double-action the hammer to full cock and then drop it. An interesting point is that this de-cocking lever can be moved across to the right side for left-handed shooters.

The foresight is a blade with whitened rear face, and the backsight has a white line below the ample notch, so that they can easily be picked up and aligned in poor light. But the rear sight is fixed, except that it could possibly be drifted sideways for zeroing. Even so, the sights appear to be well aligned from the factory and the range performance with a stock model was satisfactory.

The A-80 is also manufactured in .38 Super and .45 ACP chambering; in the latter case the magazine holds nine rounds.

Astra .357 Revolver

Manufacturer Astra, Unceta y Cia, Guernica, Spain
Type Six-shot, solid frame, double-action
Caliber .357 Magnum
Barrel 3, 4, 6 and 8.5in (76, 102, 152 and 216mm)
Weight 40oz (1134gm) (6in barrel)

Astra Unceta have a long history of automatic-pistol manufacture, having made the Spanish Army's service sidearm since World War One, but they did not enter the revolver field until the late 1950s, and then with a relatively cheap line under the name of 'Cadix.' About ten years later, having gained some practical experience, they then produced this .357 Magnum model, an excellent revolver which will stand comparison with anyone's.

Like most Spanish guns, it has a

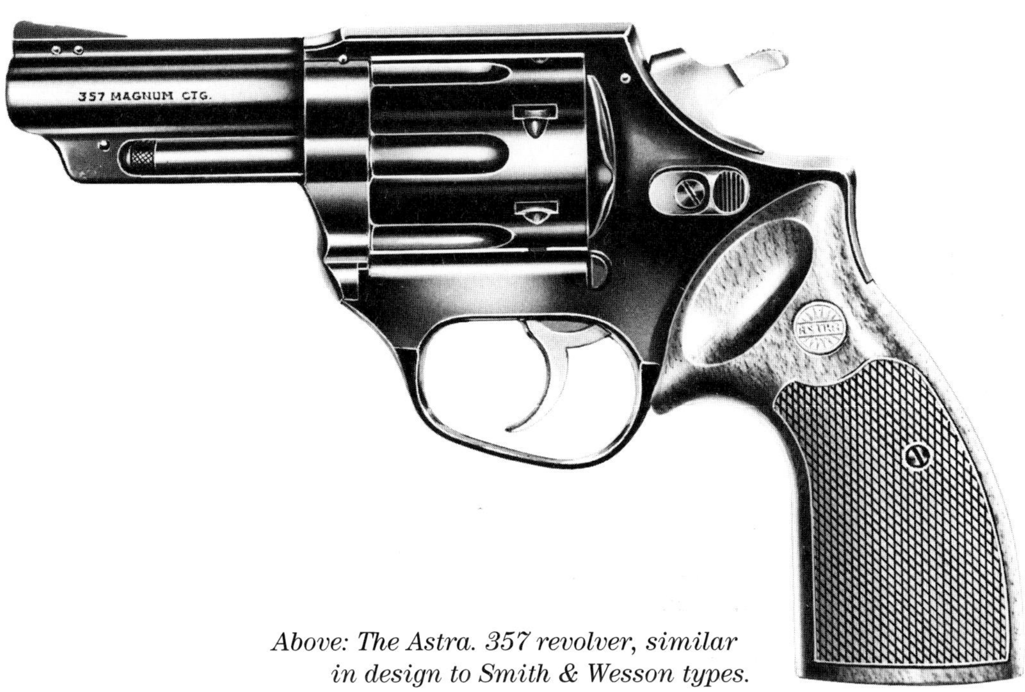

Above: The Astra. 357 revolver, similar in design to Smith & Wesson types.

striking resemblance to the Smith & Wesson family. It is a conventional solid-frame weapon with swing-out cylinder, floating firing pin, and with a safety bar included in the lockwork. An unusual point is that the shorter (3 and 4 inch) barreled models have smaller grips than the longer-barreled models; it seems that their theory is that those who buy the short guns want a handy defensive weapon, while those who buy the longer barrel are looking for target guns and deserve target-style grips. All have fully-adjustable Patridge-style rear sights and ramp foresights.

The fit and finish is first-class; all have fully recessed chambers which enclose the cartridge heads, the walnut grips are neatly checkered, and the metal is well blued and polished to a deep luster. Both hammer spur and trigger are deeply grooved to give them non-slip properties.

The accuracy and reliability of these Astra revolvers is in keeping with their quality of finish. They can be expected to group as tightly as the shooter is capable of holding, and they show no signs of loosening after long wear. Though not inexpensive, they are good value and cost less than many comparable pistols.

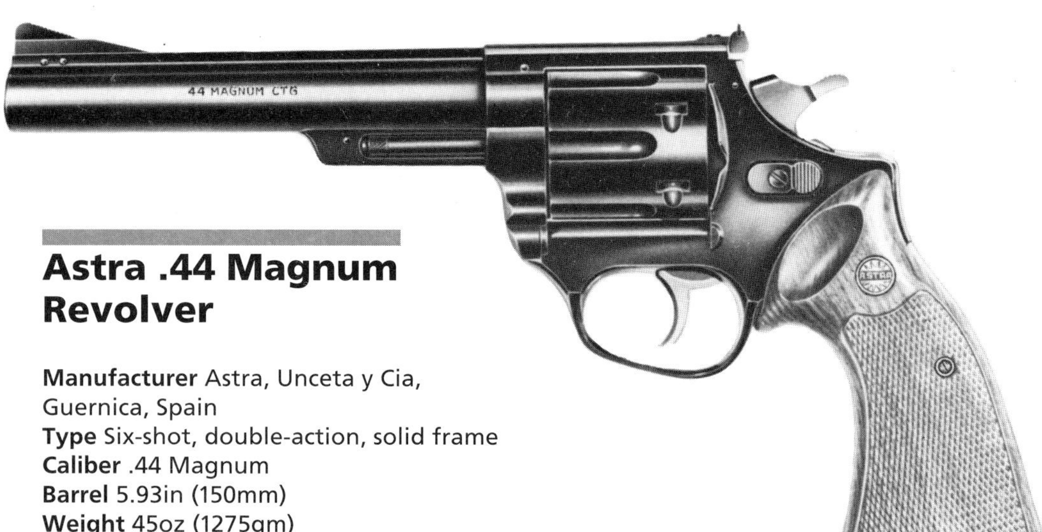

Below: The Astra .44 Magnum revolver.

Astra .44 Magnum Revolver

Manufacturer Astra, Unceta y Cia, Guernica, Spain
Type Six-shot, double-action, solid frame
Caliber .44 Magnum
Barrel 5.93in (150mm)
Weight 45oz (1275gm)

As stated the Astra Unceta company have a long record of manufacturing automatic pistols but they did not go into the revolver business until 1958, and it was several years before they went as far as a .357 Magnum. They have now gone to the limit in revolver calibers in this model, which can also be had in .41 Magnum, .45 Colt and .45 ACP calibers.

The Astra uses a new large frame and, in basic features, follows the Smith & Wesson pattern; a shrouder ejector rod, left side push-forward catch for releasing the cylinder crane and double-action lockwork. The grip is somewhat large, though this may be felt desirable with such powerful cartridges, but it appears not to be everyone's taste as far as the shape goes, being too broad at the foot.

The foresight is a blade set on a ramp, while the rear sight is an open notch adjustable for elevation and windage. With walnut grips and well-blued metal, it is an impressive revolver and is finished to a high standard. It shoots well, has a smooth trigger action, and is capable of making regular two to three inch groups at 25 yards.

Right: The Beretta Model 84 pistol in 9mm Short caliber.

Beretta Models 81 and 84

Manufacturer Armi Beretta SpA, I-25063, Gardone Val Trompia, Italy
Type Blowback double-action semi-automatic
Caliber 7.65mm ACP (Model 81); .380/9mm Short (Model 84)
Barrel 3.81in (97mm)
Weight (empty) 23.5oz (665gm) (Mod 81); 22.5oz (640gm) (Mod 84)
Magazine Capacity 12 rounds (Mod 81); 13 rounds (Mod 84)

These two pistols are members of the double-action family which appeared in 1976. They have met with considerable success both in adoption by many police and security forces and in commercial sales.

In many respects they are updated versions of the well-known Model 1934 Beretta which armed the Italian forces until 1945, robust blowback weapons with fixed barrels and with the unique Beretta configuration of cut-away slide over the barrel. However, bringing them up to date has added double-action lockwork and magazines of much greater capacity, with a better-shaped butt frame and walnut grips. The magazine release is in the forward edge of the butt beneath the trigger guard and can be located on the left or right side, as preferred. The safety catch is at the rear of the slide and can be operated from either side. When the chamber contains a cartridge the extractor protrudes on the right-hand side of the slide and shows a red indication; it can also be checked by feel in the dark.

The two models are identical except for their caliber and magazine capacity; due to changes in the magazine follower, the 9mm Model 84 actually manages to take one more round in the magazine than does the 7.65mm Model 81; the 84 is also slightly lighter, due to the barrel having similar external dimensions but a larger bore.

Beretta Model 92 Auto Pistol

Manufacturer Armi Beretta SpA, I-25063, Gardone Val Trompia, Italy
Type Locked breech, double-action, semi-automatic
Caliber 9mm Parabellum
Barrel 4.92in (125mm)
Weight (empty) 33.5oz (950gm)
Magazine Capacity 15 rounds

This appeared in 1976 as the third member of the new double-action family, and it has since been adopted by the Italian forces and by several other armies as their service pistol.

Breech locking is performed by a dropping block beneath the barrel, very similar in operation to that familiar to most people on the Walther P-38. It is a shaped block which is connected at its front to the underside of the barrel and, by lugs at the rear, to the slide, so locking the two together. A shaped heel rests on a transom in the frame, so that the block cannot unlock from the slide. After firing, recoil forces the slide to pull back, but it is restrained by the fact that the block cannot move down; as the entire barrel and slide unit moves rearward, against the recoil spring, so the locking block moves off the transom and is then free to fall, releasing the slide while the barrel stops. There is ample delay time to permit the bullet to leave the barrel. The return of the slide, reloading the breech, forces the barrel forwards and so lifts the block back on to its transom and also into locking engagement with the slide once more.

The extractor is mounted laterally, on the right side, and when the weapon is loaded it protrudes, revealing a red 'chamber-loaded' indication; this can also be felt in the dark, so that there is always a positive indication available. The safety is on the left side and locks both trigger and slide, and there is a half-cock notch on the hammer. The front sight is a simple blade, integral with the slide, while the rear sight is a square notch unit riding in a dovetail slot so that it can be laterally shifted for zeroing.

The Beretta 92 is a well-made, robust and functional military or police weapon. It is also sold in North and South America as the 'Taurus PT-92' marketed, accordingly, by Taurus S.A. of Sao Paulo, Brazil.

A variant model is the Model 92S which has a slide-mounted safety which, when applied, deflects the firing pin from alignment with the hammer, releases the hammer and breaks the connection between trigger bar and sear. A further variant is the Model 92SB which has the safety lever on both sides of the slide and moves the magazine release from its usual European position at the bottom of the butt to the American position in the front of the butt, just below the trigger-guard; this is normally on the left side, but can be switched to the right if required.

Beretta Model 93R Machine Pistol

Manufacturer Armi Beretta SpA, I-25063, Gardone Val Trompia, Italy
Type Locked breech, double-action, semi-automatic with burst-fire facility.
Caliber 9mm Parabellum
Barrel 6.14in (156mm) including muzzle brake
Weight (empty) 41.2oz (1170gm)
Magazine Capacity 20 rounds

This is an advanced weapon based on the Model 92 but with several additional features which place it in the 'machine pistol' category. It has been adopted by Italian Special Forces and security police, and interest has been expressed in several other countries.

Basically, the pistol is similar to the Model 92 in that it uses a dropping-block locked breech. The principal visible change is the use of a longer barrel which protrudes in front of the slide and has a prominent muzzle brake; there is also a folding front grip, hinged to the frame so that it lies beneath the frame front when not in

Below: The Beretta Model 93R machine pistol.

use or can be folded down to act as a grip for the left (or disengaged) hand. This proves to be more practical than one might think, giving a steadier hold than the more common two-handed butt grip. In addition there is a light metal folding stock unit which can be clipped to the bottom of the butt, and which then converts the pistol into something approaching a light carbine. Finally, the magazine has been lengthened to hold 20 rounds, so that it extends below the bottom of the butt. For those preferring a more elegant shape, the normal Model 92 15-shot magazine can be used.

The reason for all these changes is that under the right butt-plate is a three-round burst controller. The frame-mounted safety catch offers three positions: safe, single shot, and 3-round burst; placing the catch in this last position permits the firing of three rapid shots for one pressure on the trigger, the cyclic rate of fire being about 110 rounds per minute. This is low by machine pistol standards and therefore there is less disturbance of the aim; moreover the forward hand grip and shoulder stock, used either separately or together, and the damping effect of the muzzle brake, allow the firer firm control of the weapon, and high-speed photography shows that there is relatively little 'climb' during the firing of a burst.

Bernardelli P-018 Pistol

Manufacturer Vincenzo Bernardelli SpA, Gardone Val Trompia, Italy
Type Locked breech, double-action, semi-automatic
Caliber 9mm Parabellum
Barrel 4.80in (122mm)
Weight (empty) 35.2oz (998gm)
Magazine Capacity 15 rounds

Originating in 1865 as gun barrel makers, Bernardelli manufactured service revolvers for the Italian Army, 1929-33, and entered the commercial pistol market in 1945. The P-018 was first produced in 1982.

Intended originally as a military and police pistol, the P-018 is most usually found in 9mm caliber, though it has also been produced in 7.65mm Parabellum and 9mm Largo chambering in small numbers. The breech is locked by the familiar Browning dropping barrel, controlled by a shaped cam slot beneath the chamber which engages with the slide stop lever pin. There is an automatic firing pin lock, whereby the hammer cannot drive the pin forward unless the trigger is pulled completely through, the final movement before release of the hammer raising the safety device and freeing the firing pin. The pistol can be fired in either single or double-action modes, but there is no hammer-drop function on the safety catch and lowering the hammer on to the loaded chamber must be done manually.

Right: The Bernardelli P-018 pistol.

Shortly after the introduction of the P-018, requests for something more easily concealed led to the development of the P-018 Compact. This is mechanically the same, but smaller in all dimensions (the barrel is 102mm, the overall length 198mm and the weight 950 grammes) and with a magazine holding 14 rounds.

A third model is the P-020, which is intended for competition shooting. It is chambered for the 7.65mm Parabellum round. It is generally the same as the P-018 but has a somewhat more luxurious standard of finish, with checkered walnut grips instead of plastic, and a micro-adjustable rear sight.

Unlike many of today's weapons, the Bernardelli maintains the tradition of building from steel forgings by machining. As a result they are strong and reliable weapons and are available in a variety of finishes from highly-polished blue to dull black Parkerised.

Browning BDA Auto Pistol

Manufacturer Armi Beretta SpA, I-25063, Gardone Val Trompia, Italy
Marketed by Browning Arms, Rt #1, Morgan, UT 84050, U. S. A.
Type Blowback double-action semi-automatic
Caliber .380/9mm Short
Barrel 3.8in (97mm)
Weight (empty) 23oz (652gm)
Magazine Capacity 13 rounds

This pistol resembles the Beretta Model 84 in most respects, and is actually made by Beretta in Italy, but there have been one or two modifications to bring it to the specification demanded by Browning. Another plus feature is that, in the U.S.A., it costs considerably less than an imported Model 84.

The BDA is a conventional blowback automatic pistol, perhaps unusual in having a larger magazine capacity than is common in American pistols. The principal difference between this and the Beretta 84 is the use of an enveloping slide and the addition of a slide-mounted safety and decocking lever which operates from both sides of the slide. Depressing this lever lowers the hammer from full- to half-cock position and locks it; once the safety is down the pistol cannot be cocked by thumbing the hammer back. Pulling the trigger allows the hammer to fall from the half-cock to the fired position, without touching the firing pin. Releasing the safety allows both thumb-cocking and double-action cock-and-fire action with a single pull on the trigger.

Sights consist of a fixed front sight and a non-adjustable rear sight which is held in a dovetail groove and can be laterally shifted for zeroing. Accuracy is satisfactory, the pistol grouping within a five-inch circle at 50 yards. Finish is excellent, with walnut grips inlaid with the Browning medallion.

Above: The legendary 9mm Browning.

Centrum Free Pistol

Manufacturer Centrum, Germany
Type Competition free pistol, single-shot
Caliber .22 Long RF
Barrel 10in (254mm)

Free pistols are principally a European avocation, being specialized single shot .22 weapons designed solely for national and international competition shooting. It is specifically intended for the UIT .22 free pistol contest in which the 10-ring of the target is two inches in diameter and the range is 50 meters. In short, it is the ultimate test of shooting ability, and the rules permit virtually any sort of pistol in order to evade any mechanical restriction and concentrate entirely on the shooter's skill. Hence the phrase 'free pistol,' which refers to the lack of restriction on style or type. In general these are hand-built and expensive weapons, vehicles for their owners' and designers' pet theories, but there are a few European gunsmithing firms who make 'stock' free pistols which can be the basis for individual modification.

One of the most recent is the Centrum made in Germany. It is a single shot weapon using a falling block breech operated by the trigger guard. The breech is opened and the cartridge loaded until it touches the extractor; the block is then closed and seats the cartridge firmly in the chamber. After firing the block is lowered, which ejects the empty case about one-tenth of an inch, after which a separate extractor, on the left of the chamber, allows the case to be pulled a further quarter of an inch from the chamber; it can be flicked out with the finger-nail. Rapid fire is, obviously, not a requirement in this type of contest.

The pistol has a set trigger which is set by a lever on the left side; the trigger itself can be adjusted for reach, travel, backlash and slack without having to dismantle anything. The foresight is mounted on a large ramp, and the blade is secured in place by a screw so that it can easily be changed. The rearsight is fitted on a dovetail extension over the grip; its location can be altered to suit the individual, and it is capable of adjustment for elevation and windage by click-stopped knobs.

The grip is anatomically shaped so that the barrel is low to the hand and thus there is practically no jump or recoil effect. There is also a wooden fore end, though this is for balance and appearance.

Practical firing shows that this weapon, which is a precision machine, needs to be fed with the best ammunition; it appears sensitive to the ammunition used and does not perform well with cheap cartridges. Each gun is supplied with a test target and a five-year guarantee, the target usually showing four or five shots in the 10-ring. These pistols are capable of doing whatever the shooter is capable of.

Left: The Charter Arms .44 Target Bulldog.

Charter Arms 'Pathfinder' Revolver

Manufacturer Charter Arms Corp,. 430 Sniffens Lane, Stratford, CT 06497, U.S.A.
Type Six-shot, solid-frame, double-action revolver.
Caliber .22 Long Rifle RF, or .22 Winchester Magnum RF.
Barrel 6in (152mm)
Weight 22.5oz (638gm)

This is an enlarged version of the .22 Pathfinder introduced in 1972; the earlier weapon had a 3-inch barrel and proved popular as a pack gun. Now with the adoption of a 6-in barrel the gun becomes even more versatile.

The pistol uses a steel solid frame and an attractive point is that the walnut grips are of a good size to allow a firm grip, a feature frequently overlooked in this caliber. The swing-out cylinder is released by a catch on the left side of the frame or by pulling the ejector rod forward. The six chambers are individually counterbored and the ejector rod is long enough to push the empty cases well clear of the cylinder face. The foresight is a broad blade and the rear a wide slot; the rear sight is fully adjustable for elevation and windage, though demanding a small screwdriver to make the adjustment. The double-action trigger pull is light and smooth, while the single-action release is sharp, requiring 3-4lbs pressure to let off. Firing is by a floating firing pin and transfer bar system, by means of which the hammer cannot possibly contact the firing pin unless the trigger has been correctly pulled.

The pistol is available in either .22LR or .22WMRF chambering, though the cylinders are not interchangeable. The .22RF version will, of course, shoot .22 Long and .22 Short equally well. Either chambering gives perfectly good accuracy: 1½-inch groups at 25 yards.

Charter Arms .44 Target Bulldog

Manufacturer Charter Arms Inc., Stratford, CT06497, U.S. A.
Type Five-shot, solid frame, double-action
Caliber .44 Special
Barrel 4in (102mm)
Weight 20oz (567gm)

Charter Arms started their career by producing robust no-frills revolvers for lawmen and others, and one of their notable innovations was the .44 Bulldog, a short-barreled but powerful pistol which revived the .44 Special cartridge. This is a highly serviceable round which has tended to be overlooked in recent years, being edged out by the .44 Magnum, and it had a good reputation for accuracy. In response to various enquiries and requests, Charter have now redesigned the Bulldog to take maximum advantage of the cartridge's capabilities.

The Target Bulldog differs from the original Bulldog in having a one-inch longer barrel, complete with shroud for the ejector rod, and in having a fully adjustable rear sight. It is also slightly heavier, and the net result of the extra length and weight is a revolver which is rather more controllable than the original and which is sufficiently accurate to shoot two-inch groups at 25 yards all day. Lengthening the barrel has improved the velocity and consistency and has also cut down slightly on the muzzle blast, making the pistol more comfortable to shoot.

For those who consider the .44 Special a little too much, the Target Bulldog is also available in .357 Magnum caliber.

Chinese Type 64 Silenced

Manufacturer Chinese State Arsenals
Type Selective semi-automatic or single shot, blowback, with integral silencer
Caliber 7.65mm (.32, special chambering)
Barrel 4.88in (124mm)
Weight 44.8oz (1270gm)
Magazine Capacity 8 rounds

This remarkable weapon appears to have only one function in life, that of assassination. It is chambered for a special 7.65 × 17mm rimless cartridge with a low-velocity loading; it cannot be used with commercial .32 ACP semi-rimmed ammunition.

The Type 64 can be used either as a manually-loaded single shot pistol or as a blowback semi-automatic. For the utmost silence a selector bar in the upper part of the slide is pushed to the left and this rotates the bolt, locking it into lugs in the breech. When the pistol is fired the breech remains closed and can be opened only by pushing the selector across and manually retracting the slide. If the selector is left in its right-hand position, then the bolt does not rotate, nor does it lock, and when the pistol is fired the slide blows back in the conventional manner.

Silence is achieved partly by the special ammunition, which ensures subsonic velocity of the bullet, and partly by the built-in silencer. The casing which surrounds the barrel extends in front of the muzzle; the gases escaping from the muzzle behind the bullet are expanded into a wire-mesh cylinder surrounded by an expanded metal sleeve, while the bullet passes through a number of rubber discs which prevent the following gas escaping to the outside. When the breech is locked, the pistol is extremely quiet; with the breech unlocked the noise is somewhat greater due to the clatter of the slide moving backwards, but the report is still silenced.

Colt Double Eagle

Manufacturer Colt's Manufacturing Co. Inc., Hartford, CT.
Type Recoil operated semi-automatic, double-action
Caliber .45 ACP, 10mm Auto, .40 S&W, 9mm Parabellum or .38 Super
Barrel 5.0in (127mm)
Weight 39oz (1105gm)
Magazine Capacity 8-round box magazine (9in .38 Super and 9mm calibers)

The Double Eagle is the logical development of the well-known Government Model M1911A1 insofar as it uses the same basic mechanism, but allies it to a double-action trigger mechanism and a choice of modern calibers.

The pistol uses a forged stainless steel receiver and slide, and the traditional Browning method of locking the barrel by means of a link pivoting on the slide locking pin axis. As the slide and barrel recoil, so the link draws the rear end of the barrel down in an arc, withdrawing the lugs on top of the barrel from recesses in the slide top. By the time this withdrawal is complete, the bullet has left the muzzle and the chamber pressure is well within safe limits; the barrel stops and the slide continues to the rear to eject the spent case and then return to load a fresh cartridge.

This, of course, leaves the hammer cocked ready to fire the next shot in single-action mode. But once the pistol is loaded, pressure on a decocking lever beneath the left butt grip allows the hammer to be lowered safely on to the loaded chamber. From that position, simply pulling through on the trigger in double-action mode will raise the hammer to full cock and then release it to fire.

The Double Eagle originally appeared in .45 ACP and 10mm Auto calibers, with a 5-inch barrel. In 1991 these were augmented by 9mm and .38 Super calibers with the same barrel length, and then by new models: the Double Eagle Combat Commander was a .45 ACP pistol with 4.25-inch (108mm) barrel and a weight of 36 ounces (1020 grams); the Double Eagle Officer's ACP was in .45 or .40 S&W chambering with a 3.5-inch (89mm) barrel, weighing 35 ounces (992 grams); and the Double Eagle Officer's Lightweight was in .45 ACP chambering with 3.5-inch barrel and a blued finish, weighing only 25 ounces (708 grams).

All models have a high-profile three-dot sighting system, and an adjustable rearsight may be fitted. Finish is matt stainless steel or, in the case of the Officer's Lightweight, polished blue, while the grips are of impact-resistant synthetic Xenoy material.

Colt 2000

Manufacturer Colt's Manufacturing Co. Inc., Hartford, CT.
Type Locked breech, semi-automatic, self-cocking
Caliber 9mm Parabellum
Barrel 4.49in (114mm)
Weight 29oz (822gm)
Magazine Capacity 15 rounds

Introduced in January 1991, this pistol was originally designed by C. Reed Knight and Eugene Stoner and then adopted by Colt. It is probably the only modern pistol to use barrel rotation to lock and unlock the breech, a system used by comparatively few designs during this century.

The pistol, as originally produced, had a steel slide and polymer frame, though latterly the frame has also been made of steel. The barrel fits

Left: The Colt 2000.

loosely in the slide and is locked to it by lugs on the chamber end which engage into recesses on the inner surface of the slide. The barrel also has a lower lug which engages in a 'cam block' which rests in the frame. The breech is closed by the rear end of the slide, which also carries the self-cocking firing pin mechanism. There is no manual safety catch, and the only external control is the slide stop release; it was the declared intention of the designers to produce an automatic pistol which was as simple and straight-forward to use as a double-action revolver.

Loading is done in the usual manner, by inserting a magazine in the butt and then pulling back and releasing the slide. Thereafter, firing is simply a matter of pulling the trigger; this presses back the striker and then releases it to fly forward and fire the cartridge. Barrel and slide then recoil, locked together, but as they move, so the bottom lug on the barrel is drawn along a curved path in the cam block, turning the barrel through an angle of about 30 degrees so as to free the upper lugs from their engagement with the slide. Once these are free the barrel stops, having come to the end of the cam path, and the slide, continues rearwards to extract the empty case, eject it, and then return under the pressure of its return spring. The next cartridge is loaded and the pistol is again already to fire. The striker is not cocked but is engaged with the trigger set ready for the next shot.

One of the advantages of this design is that a proportion of the recoil force is passed, via the bottom lug, to the cam block and then spread over a much greater area of the frame than is usually the case. This produces a much smaller amount of 'felt recoil' for the firer, and consequently the pistol is more easily brought back to the aim after a shot.

Czech CZ-75 Auto Pistol

Manufacturer Ceskoslovenska Zbrojovka a.s., Uhersky Brod, Czechoslovakia
Type Locked breech, double-action semi-automatic
Caliber 9mm Parabellum
Barrel 4.72in (120mm)
Weight (empty) 34.5oz (980gm)
Magazine Capacity 15 rounds

The CZ-75 is a military-style pistol produced for commercial sale throughout the world. It uses the familiar Browning action of locked breech in which the barrel has lugs above the chamber which engage in recesses in the slide; a shaped cam in a lump beneath the chamber moves across the slide stop pin during recoil, thus pulling the barrel down and withdrawing the lugs from the recesses, so freeing the slide to move to the rear and complete the extraction and reloading cycle. The pistol differs slightly from the usual Browning design by having a deep-waisted frame and the slide guide rails on the inside of this section, so that the shallow rear portion of the slide moves within the frame.

The external hammer is cocked during the recoil stroke in the usual manner, but there is a double-action lock which permits firing the first round from a hammer-down condition. The safety is on the frame and merely locks trigger and hammer; there is no hammer-drop facility. The sights are fixed military pattern, and the foresight is rather small, making deliberate shooting rather difficult. Nevertheless, the CZ-75 is accurate and consistent, and with adjustable sights fitted would make a reasonable competition weapon. The fit and finish are good and the double-action trigger movement is particularly effective. The pistol will accept practically any military or commercial ammunition without malfunction.

Dan Wesson Pistol-Pac

Manufacturer Dan Wesson Arms, Monson, MA 01057, U.S.A.
Type Six-shot, solid frame, double-action
Caliber .357 Magnum
Barrel 2, 4, 6 and 8in (See text) (51, 102, 152 and 203mm)
Weight 36oz (1020gm) (4in barrel)

Dan Wesson revolvers are not new, but the Pistol-Pac concept is so different that it deserves a place in any listing.

The Dan Wesson Company began in 1968 and rapidly made a name for its unique revolvers. The unusual feature was that the barrels were removeable and could be changed for others of different length, so that, for example, one could have an 8-inch barrel for target shooting and a 2-inch barrel for home defense, changing them around as required. The basic action is a solid framed double-action revolver; the barrel screws into the front of the frame in conventional manner, but it is then concealed by a jacket, carrying foresight and ejector rod shroud, which slips over the barrel and is then secured by a retaining nut screwed on to the muzzle of the barrel so as to hold the jacket firmly in place and place the barrel under tension. The jacket is automatically aligned with the foresight upright, and slight placement remains constant when barrels

Right: The Dan Wesson revolver.

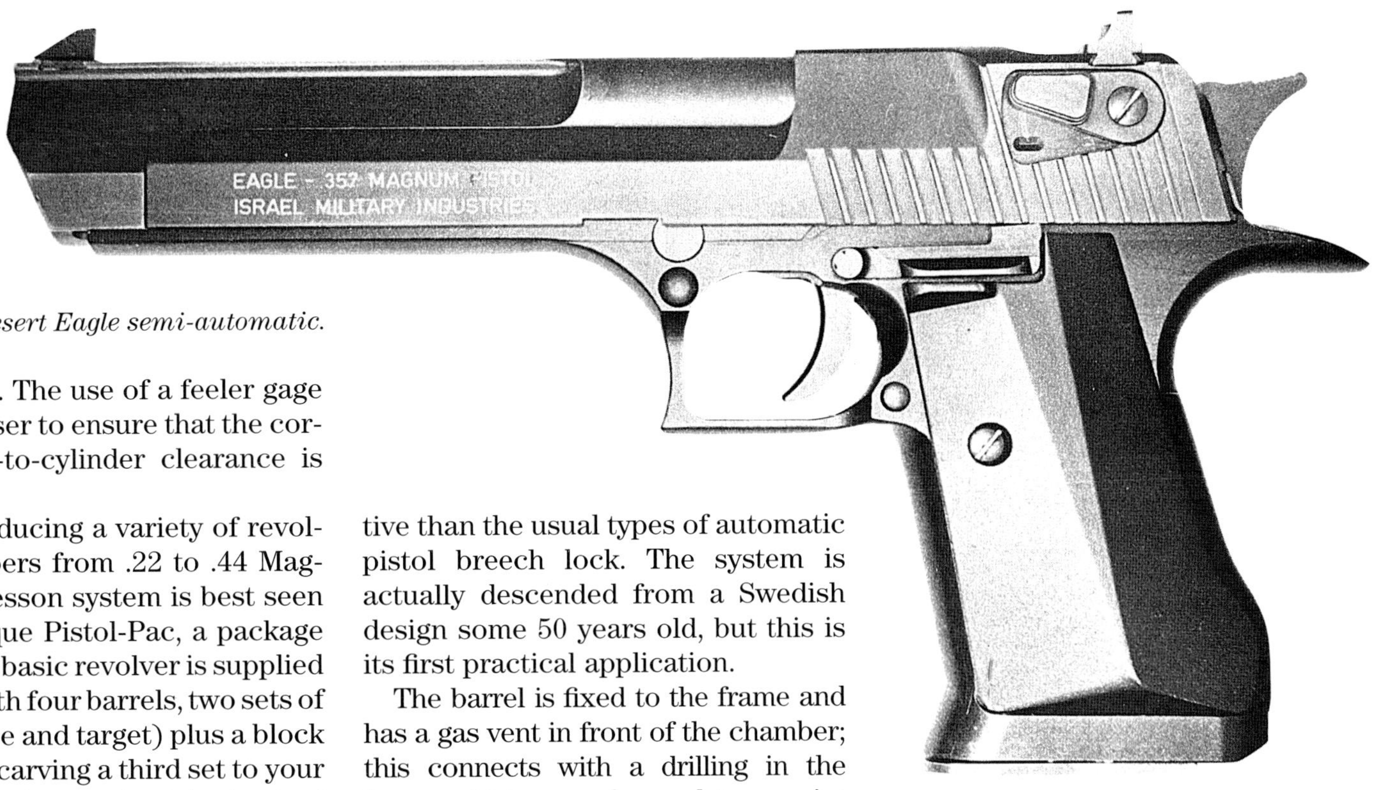

Right: The Desert Eagle semi-automatic.

are changed. The use of a feeler gage allows the user to ensure that the correct breech-to-cylinder clearance is maintained.

While producing a variety of revolvers in calibers from .22 to .44 Magnum, the Wesson system is best seen in their unique Pistol-Pac, a package in which the basic revolver is supplied complete with four barrels, two sets of grips (service and target) plus a block of wood for carving a third set to your own specification, and a stripping tool for removing the jacket and barrel. All this is neatly packed into a hand case lined with sponge rubber. The barrels provided are 2, 4, 6 and 8 inches in length. In .357 Magnum chambering the Model 15-2 is standard and it is supplemented by the 15-2 VH which has heavier barrels and jackets with ventilated ribs.

Dan Wesson revolvers have a high reputation for accuracy and reliability. The Pistol-Pac idea allows the shooter to have the best of several choices at his fingertips at all times.

Desert Eagle

Manufacturer Ta'as Israel Industries, Ramat Hasharon, Israel
Type Gas-operated semi-automatic
Caliber .357 Magnum, .44 Magnum, .41 Action Express or .50 Action Express
Barrel 6.0in (152mm) (A 14-in (355mm) barrel is also available)
Weight 3.88lb (1.76kg) (steel frame)
Magazine Capacity 9 rounds

The Desert Eagle is unusual in being a gas-operated pistol using a rotating bolt breech mechanism, a system more usually expected in rifles than pistols. This is due to the high power of the cartridges selected for use, which demand something more positive than the usual types of automatic pistol breech lock. The system is actually descended from a Swedish design some 50 years old, but this is its first practical application.

The barrel is fixed to the frame and has a gas vent in front of the chamber; this connects with a drilling in the frame which runs forward to a point just beneath the muzzle, then turns down to enter a gas cylinder. Inside this cylinder is a short-stroke piston. The slide has a solid rear section containing the bolt, and two long arms which stretch forward under the barrel.

On firing, gas passes from the barrel, through the drilling, into the gas cylinder and drives the piston backwards. It strikes the front end of the slide and imparts momentum to it, driving it backwards against a spring. As the slide moves, so it first rotates the bolt by means of a cam, unlocking the bolt from the barrel, and then withdrawing the bolt and extracting the spent case. The spring then drives the slide forward, collecting a fresh round and driving it into the chamber, and the final movement of the slide rotates the bolt to lock it to the barrel. The rearward movement also cocks the external hammer.

The pistol was designed to fire the .357 Magnum revolver cartridge, a rimmed round and one not usually found in automatic pistols. This was followed by a larger version to fire the .44 Magnum cartridge, another rimmed round, and a modified version of the original chambered for the .41 Action Express cartridge. In 1992 the ultimate appears to have been reached with a version chambered for the .50 Action Express round, an extremely potent cartridge. It might be added that the original intention for this weapon was long range silhouette shooting, but it has also found favor as a hunting gun. For this purpose the top of the barrel is grooved to accept telescope mounts; the standard sights are fixed, but an adjustable rear sight may be had as an option.

FN BDA9

Manufacturer FN Herstal SA, Liège, Belgium
Type Recoil-operated semi-automatic, double-action
Caliber 9mm Parabellum
Barrel 4.65 inches (118mm)
Weight 32oz (915gm) with empty magazine
Magazine Capacity 14 rounds

The Browning High-Power, or Model 35, became one of the most widely used military pistols in history, being adopted by over 55 armies, and it remains in production to this day, for demand has far from ended. But Fabrique Nationale moved with the times, and responding to more modern specifications they have developed the design into the 'BDA9' (for Browning Double Action 9mm) pistol.

The general appearance shows a definite 'family resemblance' to the older model, and the mechanism is broadly the same, using the FN-designed shaped cam beneath the chamber which, acting against the slide stop pin, causes the rear end of the barrel to be drawn down to disconnect from the slide during recoil. It is interesting to see that FN still adhere to the use of locking lugs machined in the upper surface of the barrel and mating in recesses in the slide, rather than simply forging a square block around the chamber and locking this into the ejection aperture as do many other modern designs. The fitting of the two lugs to their recesses is a precision task, but FN obviously think it worth the effort.

Above and right: The FN BDA9 pistol.

The principal change is the adoption of a double-action trigger mechanism and a de-cocking lever in place of the safety catch; this de-cocking lever is duplicated on both sides of the frame, so that the pistol can be used equally easily in the right or left hand. The magazine release is fitted for right-handed use, but can be easily removed and replaced on the right side of the butt for left-handed users. There is also an automatic firing pin safety system which locks the firing pin except during the final few degrees of trigger movement just before the hammer is released.

As with other pistols of this type, loading is done by inserting a magazine and pulling back and releasing the slide to chamber a round. This leaves the hammer cocked and the pistol can be fired in single-action mode; alternatively the de-cocking lever allows the hammer to be safely lowered on to the loaded chamber. From this position it is only necessary to pull through on the trigger to cock and release the hammer; there is no safety device to be manipulated. After the first shot, subsequent shots are in single-action mode until the hammer is again de-cocked.

FN140DA Auto Pistol

Manufacturer Fabrique Nationale d'Armes de Guerre, Herstal, Belgium
Type Blowback, double-action, semi-automatic
Caliber .380 Auto/9mm Short; .32 ACP/7.65mm
Barrel 3.81in (97mm)
Weight 22.5oz (640gm)
Magazine Capacity 13 rounds (9mm/.380) 12 rounds (7.65mm/.32)

The FN 140DA is intended as a general purpose defense weapon or for use by police and security forces. It uses a steel slide and alloy frame to keep the weight low and has a large magazine capacity, of the sort more commonly found in major-caliber military weapons. An impressive and popular weapon, it is in widespread use, having been adopted by the Belgian and several other European police forces.

The pistol is a simple fixed-barrel blowback in general form, though of extremely high-grade workmanship and reliability. It has a double-action lock and the trigger-guard is particularly large, permitting use in gloved hands. There is a complex safety system; the safety catch is mounted on the slide and has operating levers on both sides. On depressing the catch the firing pin is retracted into a

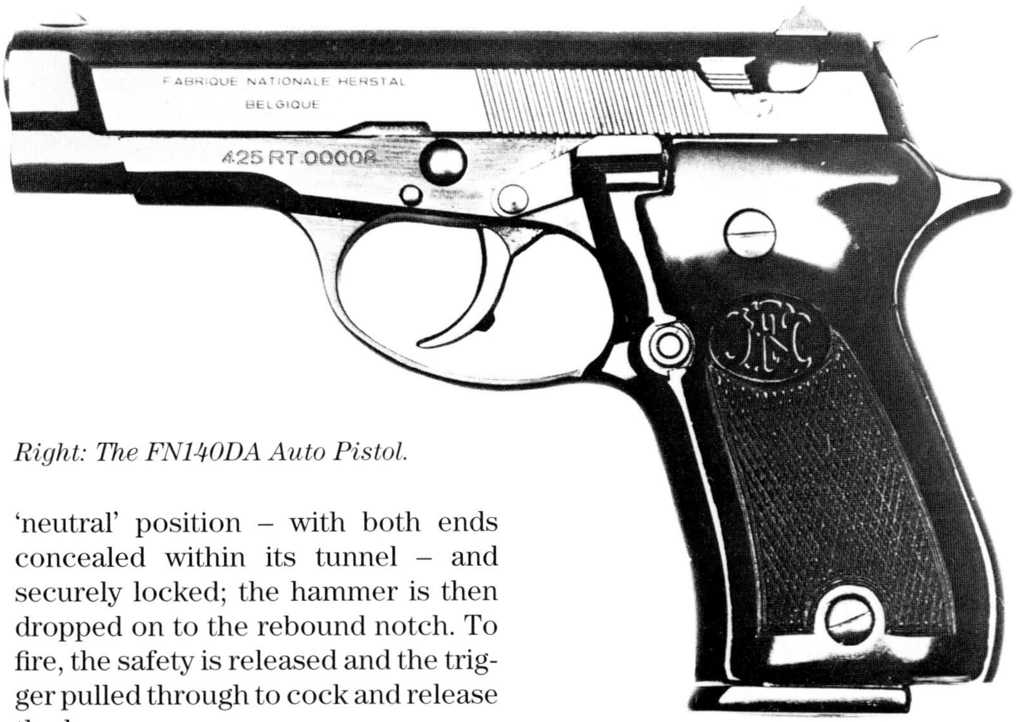

Right: The FN140DA Auto Pistol.

'neutral' position – with both ends concealed within its tunnel – and securely locked; the hammer is then dropped on to the rebound notch. To fire, the safety is released and the trigger pulled through to cock and release the hammer.

Any resemblance between this and the Beretta 84 is far from coincidental, since this is basically the Beretta 84 with some slight changes, notably the use of an all-enveloping slide instead of the open-topped slide which is virtually a Beretta trademark. There are also strong similarities between this and the Browning BDA sold in the U.S.A.

The Glock Pistol

Manufacturer Glock GmbH, Deutsch-Wagram, Austria
Type Recoil-operated semi-automatic, self-cocking
Caliber 9mm Parabellum, 10mm Auto, .40 S&W, .45 ACP
Barrel 4.49 inches (114mm)
Weight 23.8oz (676gm) with empty magazine
Magazine Capacity 17 rounds (19 rounds optional)
(Data refers to Model 17)

In 1980 the Austrian Army needed a new pistol, and for reasons connected with its rather complicated neutrality treaties, found importing one almost impossible. An Austrian manufacturer was therefore necessary, and the Glock company, which had previously been concerned with spades and knives, produced this modern design and obtained the contract. In 1984 the Glock pistol passed all NATO trials and was selected by the Norwegian Army. Now the pistol is in service with armies and police forces worldwide.

The Glock pistol is a product of modern technology, incorporating many innovative design features which provide ease and safety of operation, reliability, simplicity and light weight. The most prominent feature is the use of high-resistant polymer material for the frame; this led to scare stories when the pistol was first introduced, suggesting that it could be smuggled past airport security devices. But steel is still used for the stressed components, and the pistol can be easily detected by any airport security device.

The firing mechanism is also unique to the Glock. There are no safety or decocking levers; the safety devices are internal and consist of a trigger safety lever protruding from the trigger itself; a firing pin safety which prevents forward movement of the pin except when the trigger is pulled, and a drop safety catch which prevents accidental discharge should the pistol be dropped. As the trigger is pulled, these devices disengage in succession and the striker is cocked and released to fire the round. As soon as the shot has been fired the safety devices all revert to their safe condition and remain there until the trigger is pulled for the next shot.

The breech locking system is the familiar Browning dropping barrel, but using a shaped cam beneath the chamber to lower the rear of the barrel and using a squared block formed around the chamber to lock into the ejection opening in the slide instead of the original lugs locking into recesses machined into the slide. The system adopted by Glock is easier to manufacture than the multiple-lug system and gives a very strong lock-up to the breech.

The original Glock design is the

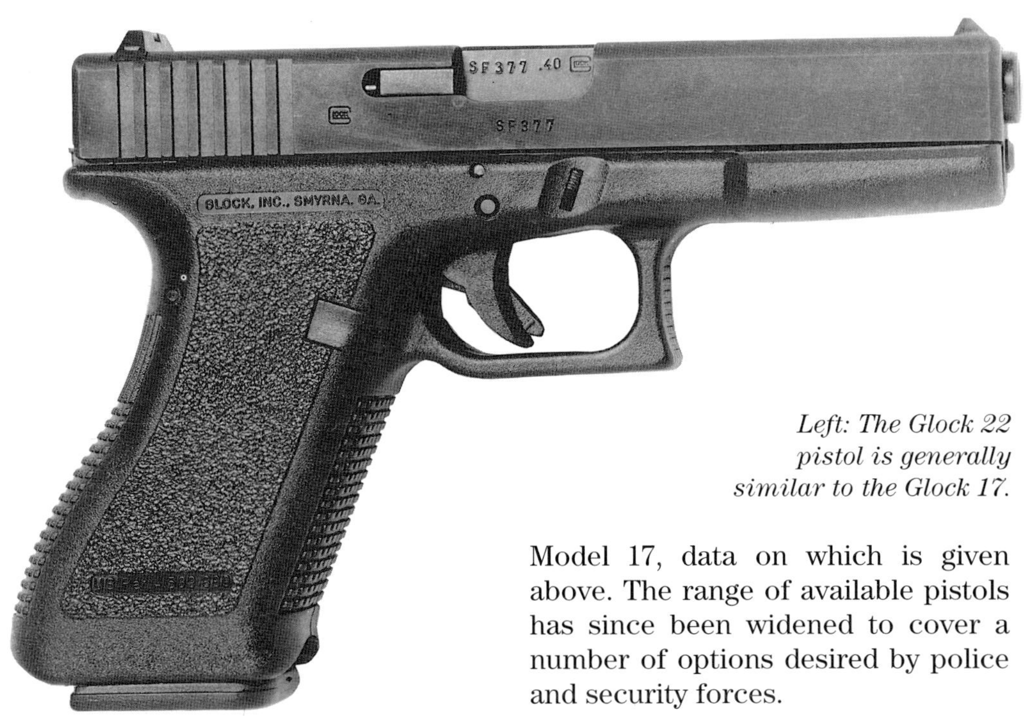

Left: The Glock 22 pistol is generally similar to the Glock 17.

Model 17, data on which is given above. The range of available pistols has since been widened to cover a number of options desired by police and security forces.

Hammerli 215 Target Auto Pistol

Manufacturer Hammerli SA, Lenzberg, Switzerland
Type Blowback semi-automatic target
Caliber .22 Long Rifle RF
Barrel Variable
Weight Variable
Magazine Capacity 8 rounds

Above: The Hammerli target pistol.

The Hammerli company have been in the target pistol business for many years and produce some of the world's finest competition weapons. Unfortunately, due to the strength of the Swiss franc they tend to be very expensive outside Switzerland, which does nothing for Hammerli's sales. As a result they decided to produce a weapon which, while remaining high quality, would be competitive in price.

The Model 215 resembles the older Model 208 in being a chunky semi-automatic using a heavy fixed barrel and a short recoiling slide moving in short frame rails. The trigger guard is a separate component and acts as a slide latch. The rear sight is held on a saddle unit which locks to the outside of the frame and straddles the recoiling slide. Since this would prevent gripping the slide in the normal way, it is made with extended sides which stretch forward, alongside the barrel, and have finger grips for cocking and unloading. The sight saddle unit has to be removed to strip the pistol, but the construction is such that it automatically returns to the pre-set zero when replaced. The pistol is hammer fired. The grips are of hard wood, anatomically shaped and have an adjustable palm rest.

The front sight blade can be easily changed, and blades of various widths are available; the rear sight can also be changed for different widths of slot and is fully adjustable. The trigger pull is smooth, with a consistent pull-off point. A balance weight is fitted beneath the muzzle; it can be adjusted or changed by use of an Allen key.

On the range this pistol performs as Hammerli products are expected to perform, firing with absolute accuracy and reliability. The only concession to price has been in the external finish which is not quite so luxurious as in previous products, but the performance is in no way diminished.

Heckler & Koch Model P7 (PSP)

Manufacturer Heckler & Koch GmbH, D-7238 Oberndorf/Neckar, Germany
Type Delayed blowback, semi-automatic
Caliber 9mm Parabellum
Barrel 4.13in (105mm)
Weight (empty) 27.7oz (785gm)
Magazine Capacity 8 rounds

This unusual pistol can be used rapidly, with neither a safety catch nor a cocking hammer delaying matters, yet it is totally safe while being carried loaded.

The P7 (originally called the PSP for 'Polizei Selbstlader Pistole') is a pocket or holster weapon, relatively small, but firing a powerful cartridge. For this reason it demands some form of breech locking, and this is done by gas pressure. The slide has the usual recoil spring beneath it, with a guide rod inside the spring. But this guide rod is carefully machined and as the slide recoils it moves inside a close-fitting cylinder lying in the frame above the trigger. A port between this cylinder and the barrel allows high-pressure gas to flow in and fill the

Below: The Heckler & Koch 9mm Model P7.

Right: The Heckler & Koch P9S semi-automatic.

cylinder when the pistol is fired; this pressure resists the rearward movement of the recoil spring guide rod, so delaying the rearward movement of the slide. Once the bullet has left the barrel and the gas pressure drops, the rod can move back, forcing the gas out of the cylinder and into the barrel and thence out to atmosphere. Thereafter the action is that of any other blowback automatic pistol.

In order to carry the weapon safely in a loaded condition, the firing pin is not cocked during the recoil stroke as is usual; instead it is controlled by a grip forming the front edge of the butt. When the firer grasps the butt and squeezes this grip, the firing pin is cocked; there is no need for him to keep squeezing, since the grip engages in the cocked position. Once he releases his grip, however, the pistol is de-cocked. It can thus be carried safely with a round in the chamber and brought into action with no delay; if, once uncocked, the shooter drops it, it is uncocked before it hits the floor.

The sights are fixed, but the foresight can be changed and the rear sight moved sideways to zero the weapon. Both sights have inlaid white dots to assist in aligning in poor visibility and it is possible to have 'Beta-light' luminous markers fitted for night firing. Disassembly of this distinctive pistol is easy, though it requires the use of a special stripping tool.

Heckler & Koch P9S Auto Pistol

Manufacturer Heckler & Koch GmbH, D-7238 Oberndorf/Neckar, Germany
Type Locked breech double-action semi-automatic
Caliber 9mm Parabellum
Barrel 4in (102mm)
Weight (empty) 30.8oz (875gm)
Magazine Capacity 9 rounds

The Heckler & Koch P9S is a military and police pistol using an unusual breech locking system derived from the company's highly successful G3 rifle. The P9S has been adopted by German armed forces and police forces and has been widely sold throughout the world. Some have been manufactured in 7.65mm Parabellum chambering and also in .45 ACP chambering for export to the U.S.A., but the 9mm Parabellum version is by far the most common.

The roller locking system for the breech relies on a two-part breech block which is held close by two small rollers which engage in recesses in the barrel extension. The rollers are carried on the forward, lightweight, portion of the block which is actually part of the slide. When the pistol is fired, the light portion, impelled by the pressure on the cartridge case, attempts to move backwards, but the inertia of the slide keeps the rollers forced outwards and the block section locked to the barrel. As the inward pressure on the rollers, due to the pressure on the forward section of the block, gradually overcomes the inertia of the slide, so the bullet speeds up the barrel and leaves, allowing chamber pressure to drop to safe levels before the rollers move in and the slide and breech block assembly is free to move.

The pistol has an internal hammer, with a protruding indicator pin at the rear of the frame which extends when the hammer is cocked. There is a thumb-operated hammer release and re-cocking lever on the left side, allowing the hammer to be lowered under control on to a loaded chamber, or rapidly cocked from the 'down' position. The barrel has a 'polygonal bore' in which the four grooves (6in .45 ACP caliber) are merged into the rest of the bore so that the final result resembles a flattened circle. The manufacturers claim that this reduces friction and bullet deformation and promotes a somewhat higher velocity.

Two variant models exist: the P9, now discontinued, was the same pistol but with conventional single-action lock; the P9S 'Sport' Competition Model has a longer barrel with balance weight, adjustable trigger stop, fine-adjustment rear sight and an anatomical wooden grip. The barrel is 5.5in (140mm) long, leading to a slight increase in muzzle velocity; with barrel counterweight fitted and a full magazine it weighs 45.2oz (1290gm).

Jericho

Manufacturer Ta'as Israel Industries, Ramat Hasharon, Israel
Type Recoil-operated, semi-automatic, double-action
Caliber 9mm Parabellum or .41 Action Express
Barrel 4.40in (112mm)
Weight 39oz (1103gm)
Magazine Capacity 16 rounds (9mm) or 11 rounds (.41AE)

The Jericho's family resemblance to the Desert Eagle is entirely cosmetic; under the skin the operation is entirely different. The Jericho is a conventional recoil-operated pistol using the Browning tilting barrel controlled by a cam beneath the chamber. Indeed, much of it is bought from Tanfoglio of Italy, Ta'as Israel Industries being responsible for clothing the barrel and trigger mechanism in a body designed to resemble the Desert Eagle. One result of this cosmetic change is that the slide is designed to ride inside the frame, instead of the more usual method of riding outside the frame. Though somewhat more difficult and expensive to make, this system gives the slide better support and is generally agreed to provide better inherent accuracy.

There is a slide-mounted safety catch which also functions as a hammer de-cocking lever, and this is duplicated on both sides of the slide for the benefit of left-handed users. A conversion kit is available, to alter the pistol from 9mm to .41 calibers or vice versa; the components (barrel, return spring and magazine) are supplied with the pistol and are color-coded so that it is difficult to assemble the pistol wrongly.

Korth .357 Magnum

Manufacturer Willi Korth Sportwaffen-Herst, D-2418 Ratzeburg, Germany
Type Six-shot, double-action, solid-frame
Caliber .357 Magnum
Barrel 3in (76mm); 6in (152mm)
Weight 35oz (992gm) with 3in barrel

Above and left: Exterior and interior views of the Korth .357 Magnum.

Right: A stripped-down Jericho semi-automatic.

The firm of Willi Korth is little known outside Germany; it is a subsidiary of the Dynamit-Nobel group and has produced limited numbers of sporting weapons in the past. It is now exporting a revolver which, at well over $1000, must qualify as the most expensive handgun in existence.

The Korth .357 Magnum is a conventional solid frame pistol with swing-out cylinder with some likeness to the Colt Python. Under the skin, however, there are some interesting differences. The barrel, for example, is a separate component shrouded within a steel jacket which also forms the extractor rod shroud. The barrel screws into the frame, the jacket passes over it, and the whole assembly is then secured by a barrel nut on the muzzle.

The cylinder crane is released by pushing a serrated catch on the right side of the hammer, which presses forward the ejector rod and allows the crane to move. Once open, the cylinder can be slipped from the crane by depressing a spring latch. The clearance between the face of the cylinder and the rear of the barrel is minimal, so that gas leak is negligible, but this does mean the interface must be cleaned regularly.

The firing pin is a separate component, mounted in the frame, and there is a safety system linked to the trigger which prevents the pin being struck by the hammer unless the trigger is pulled. The trigger action is smooth, if a trifle heavy at double-action, but the let-off point is clean and crisp. The trigger is adjustable for travel.

The foresight is a conventional ramp blade, while the rear sight is a notch, adjustable for windage and elevation. The grip fills the hand well and gives good control of the pistol when firing. Finish is excellent, the metal being well blued and the grips being high-grade walnut, while hammer, trigger and barrel lock nut are chromium-plated.

In use the Korth is pleasant to shoot and as accurate as might be expected, capable of delivering tight groups in single-action mode, slightly larger in double-action. So far as performance goes, I would say that it is on a par with other high-quality revolvers; the finish, inside and out is excellent, the design good; but I cannot honestly see where the high price is justified in any concrete manner. But then again, one could perhaps make the same sort of observation about some breeds of cameras and automobiles which carry a high price tag but still sell all they can make.

Left: The Llama 'Comanche' revolver.

Llama 'Comanche' Revolver

Manufacturer Gabilondo y Cia, Vitoria, Spain
Type Six-shot, solid frame, double-action
Caliber .357 Magnum
Barrel 4in (102mm) or 6in (152mm)
Weight 31oz (880gm)

The Gabilondo company began business in 1904 making cheap pocket revolvers; during World War One it moved to cheap automatic pistols, and then in the early 1930s began making a line of good quality autos under the 'Llama' trade name. Revolvers were added after World War Two, using the Llama name for the best models and the name 'Ruby' for the cheaper ones.

The 'Comanche' has been on sale for some time, but deserves mention as the top pistol in the line-up. It is a conventional solid frame double-action revolver bearing more than a passing resemblance to the Smith & Wesson pattern. The finish is excellent, a smooth and lustrous blue with well-checkered walnut grips of good hand-filling shape. Both single- and double-action trigger pulls are smooth, with crisp let-off. There is a ramp front sight with a square-notch rear sight which is adjustable for both elevation and windage.

The interior of the pistol is to the same standard as the exterior, and the double-action trigger is smooth and not of excessive tension, while the single-action let-off is crisp and consistent. Accuracy is good, and in practical use will group as closely as the skill of the owner allows.

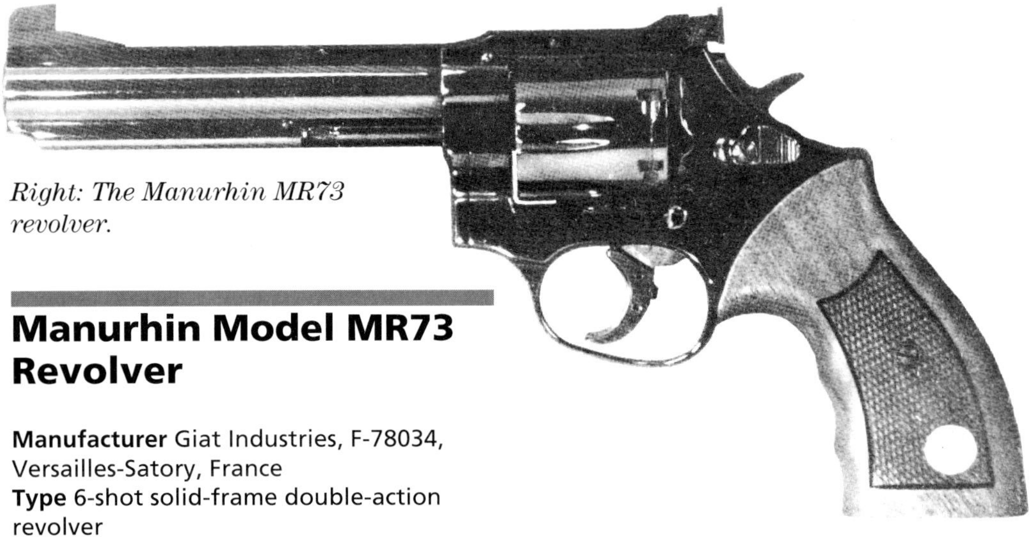

Right: The Manurhin MR73 revolver.

Manurhin Model MR73 Revolver

Manufacturer Giat Industries, F-78034, Versailles-Satory, France
Type 6-shot solid-frame double-action revolver
Caliber .357 Magnum or 9mm Parabellum
Barrel 2.5in (63.5mm); 3in (76.2mm); 4in (102mm); 5.25in (134mm); 6in (152mm) and 8in (203mm)
Weight (empty) 31.4oz (890gm) (3in barrel)

This is a compact revolver basically intended for police use, though the longer-barreled versions can also be bought in competition form. They are currently used by French police and security agencies and are commercially sold.

The MR73 is a conventional solid-frame revolver with swing-out cylinder. In 'combat' form (ie with 2.5, 3 or 4in barrels) it has the usual fixed blade and notch sights. In competition form (ie with 4, 5.25, 6 and 8in barrels) an adjustable rear sight is provided. The cylinder is removeable and can be replaced by a special cylinder which chambers the 9mm Parabellum rimless cartridge; in this case the cartridges must be loaded with a special spring clip in order to position them correctly and also to ensure that the empty cases are ejected properly. The standard cylinder is designed for use with rimmed .357 Magnum or .38 Special cartridges.

The lockwork is fairly conventional and there is a safety bar which prevents the firing pin striking a cartridge unless the trigger is pulled. The linkage between trigger and hammer spring, via the rebound slide, is engineered so that the load felt by the trigger finger remains almost constant throughout the double-action pull.

Merrill Single Shot Pistol

Manufacturer Merrill Co., Fullerton, CA 92631, U.S.A.
Type Single shot
Caliber Various
Barrel 9in (228mm) or 12in (305mm)
Weight ca. 68oz (1920gm)

Single shot pistols are less common today than in years gone by, when 'saloon' and 'parlor' pistols firing low-power ammunition were a popular source of amusement. Today the single shot survives for two principle purposes; specialized target shooting and hunting, and the Merrill will perform either of these very well indeed.

The Merrill uses a stainless steel frame and standing breech, to which is hinged the barrel, fixed so that it drops down to expose the chamber for loading. As the barrel is opened, so it automatically cocks the striker, and as it is closed so an automatic safety comes into play, locking the trigger and firing pin. This safety can only be released by pressing the safety lever at the top of the left hand grip plate with the thumb. To cater for left-handed shooters, a left-handed model is available which has the safety on the other side.

The barrel unit can be in carbon or stainless steel, and is easily interchanged since the hinge-bolt is an Allen-type socket screw. Barrels in over a dozen calibers, from .22RF upwards, can be obtained, and they can be in either smooth 'bull' contour or with ventilated ribs. Two standard lengths are used, nine or 12 inches.

The front sight is a blade, the rear a Patridge-type notch, fully adjustable. The sight normally provided is of Micro manufacture, but other makes can be supplied to order. Trigger pull is adjustable by a set-screw at the rear of the frame.

The accuracy of the Merrill is beyond reproach; in virtually any caliber it should be possible to make one-inch groups at 25 yards and in the larger calibers this makes an excellent hunting or silhouette-shooting weapon.

The Resolver

Manufacturer SITES SpA, Turin, Italy
Type Blowback or short recoil (see below)
Caliber .380 Auto, 9mm Parabellum or .40 S&W
Barrel 5.9-6.3in (150-160mm)
Weight 19-23oz (550-650gm)
Magazine Capacity 8 or 9 rounds

Some people have to carry pistols for self-protection all day but are usually given something heavy which, eventually, they get tired of carrying. So one day they leave it behind, and that's the day they need it. Moreover, many of these people are not weapons experts; in an emergency they do not want to have to remember to take off the safety, cock the weapon, take up the correct grip . . . they want to pull out the pistol, point it at the enemy and start shooting. The Resolver has been designed for these people. Finally, the designer of the Resolver considered that there was no good reason for a large magazine capacity; if you haven't disposed of the criminal in eight shots, you are unlikely to do so with 15, should you live that long.

There are two models. The basic .380 Resolver fires the .380 Auto cartridge (also called 9mm Short in Europe) and is a simple blowback automatic. There is no manual safety device, and the trigger mechanism is self-cocking. It is light and slim (only 0.65 inch thick) and can be carried all day without inconvenience, and when required, all that is necessary is to

Left: The Resolver M380.

draw it and pull the trigger. For those countries where the law demands a safety catch, one can be provided; but there is, of course, no need to use it.

Generally speaking, the 9mm Short bullet is enough to deter the casual robber; but for those people who feel that a more powerful cartridge may be needed, the M9/M40 Resolver is available. This is a locked-breech pistol which can be had in 9mm Parabellum or .40 S&W calibers. Breech locking is by the usual Browning tilting barrel system, but the dimensions have still been kept to the minimum and this weapon is very little larger than the .380 blowback, being only 19.8mm (less than three-quarters of an inch) wide. On request it can be chambered for other cartridges, including the .38 Super Auto, 7.62mm Tokarev and .32 Auto.

Left: The Ruger Mark II Auto Pistol.

Ruger Mark II Auto Pistol

Manufacturer Sturm, Ruger & Co., Southport, CT 06490, U.S.A.
Type Blowback semi-automatic
Caliber .22 Long Rifle RF
Barrel 4.75in (120mm)
Weight (empty) 36oz (1019gm)
Magazine Capacity 10 rounds

The Sturm Ruger company virtually made its name with its 'Standard' .22 automatic pistol which was first introduced in 1949 and has been the firm's anchor ever since. At the end of 1981, with over one million of this and its target version the 'Mark One' sold, it was announced that an improved version, the 'Mark II', would be marketed during 1982.

The Mark II maintains the same basic form and appearance as its predecessor, a blowback pistol using a fixed barrel and a bolt which reciprocates within a tubular receiver; several component parts are, in fact, interchangeable between old and new models. The changes are minor in form but add up to significant improvements; the trigger has been changed in material and shape, and its pivot system has been redesigned so that it is now possible to retract the bolt to unload or examine the chamber while the safety is applied and with the sear firmly locked; the magazine has been reworked and now accepts 10 rounds instead of the former nine; the rear of the receiver has been cut away on each side so that it is now easier to grasp the bolt retraction ears; and a new bolt hold-open device has been adopted. The old model used the safety catch as a hold-open device, but the Mark II has a small catch above the left grip which, when depressed, allows the bolt to close after it has been held open by the magazine follower after the last shot has gone.

An impressive weapon, the Mark II Ruger Auto Pistol is available in Standard models with fixed sights and with 4.75in or 6in barrel lengths, a Target model with fully adjustable sights and a 6in barrel, and a 'Bull Barrel' model with adjustable sights and a heavy 5in barrel.

Right: The Ruger P-89.

Ruger P-89

Manufacturer Sturm, Ruger & Co. Inc., Southport, CT 06490, U.S.A.
Type Recoil-operated semi-automatic, double-action
Caliber 9mm Parabellum
Barrel 4.49in (114mm)
Weight 32oz (907gm)
Magazine Capacity 15 rounds

Sturm, Ruger & Co. began with a .22 automatic pistol and then built up a high reputation for excellent revolvers. In 1987 they announced a military-style automatic pistol, the P-85, and since then it has been steadily improved and is now the P-89. Mechanically, it used the familiar Browning link swivel to draw down the rear end of the barrel as the slide and barrel recoil after firing, but instead of using lugs above the barrel to lock to the slide, the Ruger design uses a squared section around the chamber which locks into the ejection slot in the slide. The barrel is of stainless steel, as are the hammer, trigger and most internal components. The frame is of lightweight aluminum alloy, hardened to withstand wear and finished in matt black. The slide is of chrome-moly steel, also finished in matt black. A safety catch is on the rear of the slide; this can be used by either hand and, when applied, locks the firing pin, blocks the hammer and disconnects the trigger.

The firing mechanism is double-action, the trigger guard being large enough to allow firing in a gloved hand and reverse-curved so as to provide a grip for the non-firing hand. The magazine release is in the forward edge of the butt and can be operated by either hand.

A number of variations have been developed in response to demand:
KP89 This model is the same as the basic Model P-89 but with a stainless steel slide.
De-Cocker P89 This has a de-cocking lever on the slide in place of the usual safety catch. When pressed, this blocks the firing pin and lowers the hammer. Thereafter the pistol can be fired by a double-action pull on the trigger or by thumb-cocking the hammer and firing single-action.
Double-Action-Only P-89 This mechanism can only be fired by pulling through on the trigger; after each shot the hammer follows the slide back and comes to rest in the down position.
KP90DAC Similar to the De-Cocker P-89, this is chambered for the .45 ACP cartridge.
KP91DAC Like the KP90DAC, but chambered for the 10mm Auto cartridge.

Ruger Redhawk Revolver

Manufacturer Sturm, Ruger & Co., Southport, CT 06490, U.S.A.
Type Solid frame double-action 6-shot revolver
Caliber .44 Magnum
Barrel 7.5in (190mm)
Weight 52oz (1474gm)

Sturm Ruger have acquired a fine reputation for their heavy revolvers, and this is one of their masterpieces.

The Redhawk is a conventional double-action solid frame revolver made of stainless steel, with the cylinder swinging out on a crane for loading and ejection. The cylinder has ample metal on the outside of the chambers and is securely locked by an additional lug in the crane which engages into the frame, as well as the usual ejector rod locking points. A small but important detail is that the cylinder locking notches are located off the axis of the chambers so that they are not liable to weaken the chamber walls. The barrel is ribbed and both the rib and the ejector rod shroud are forged in one piece with the barrel. The foresight is of blued steel with a red insert, and the backsight, also of blued steel, is a Patridge type notch with a white line around it and is capable of adjustment for both windage and elevation.

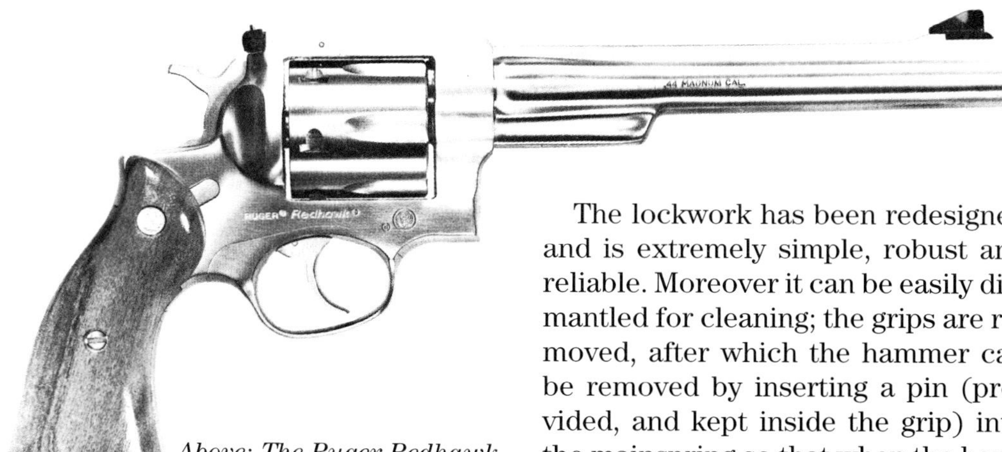
Above: The Ruger Redhawk.

The lockwork has been redesigned and is extremely simple, robust and reliable. Moreover it can be easily dismantled for cleaning; the grips are removed, after which the hammer can be removed by inserting a pin (provided, and kept inside the grip) into the mainspring so that when the ham-

Left: The Armi Renato Gamba .38Sp.

Below: The SAB G90 semi-automatic.

mer is cocked, tension is taken off it and the pivot can be removed and the hammer slipped free. The mainspring can now be removed, and by pulling on a stud behind the trigger guard the entire trigger guard and trigger mechanism can be taken from the frame. There is a rising transfer bar which acts as an intermediary between the hammer and the firing pin only when the trigger is correctly pressed, so that the pistol cannot be accidentally discharged.

On the range, this elegant pistol performs well; like any .44 Magnum it is a handful, but the weight and size allow good control and it is capable of close groups at all ranges. For day-to-day practise the .44 Special can be used, although the sights require altering; with this loading one can shoot all day without discomfort.

SAB Trident Super Revolver

Manufacturer Sociéte Armi Bresciane Srl, Gardone Val Trompia, Italy
Type 6-shot double-action solid frame revolver
Caliber .38 Special
Barrel 4in (102mm)
Weight (empty) 25.4oz (720gm)

This is a conventional design of solid frame revolver with swing out cylinder and rod ejection. The grip is well-proportioned to fill the hand and the barrel is slab-sided to lighten it, which results in a particularly well-balanced weapon. The foresight is mounted on a ventilated rib and the back-sight is fully adjustable for elevation and windage. The finish is in bright blueing, with well-checkered walnut grips, and the workmanship is good.

SAB HSc80 Auto Pistol

Manufacturer Sociéte Armi Bresciane Srl, Gardone Val Trompia, Italy
Type Blowback, double-action, semi-automatic
Caliber 7.65mm ACP, 9mm Short or 9mm Police
Barrel 3.34in (85mm)
Weight (unloaded) 24.7oz (700gm)
Magazine Capacity 13 rounds

The Sociéte Armi Bresciane of Gardone Val Trompia, Italy is a relatively new company in the firearms field. They obtained a license from Mauser to manufacture the Mauser HSc automatic pistol, a prewar design, and have done this for some time. They have now made some improvements to the design. The butt has been lengthened, allowing the magazine capacity to be increased to 13 rounds, and the frame has been altered to give the trigger guard a recessed curve on its forward edge so as to make it suitable for a two-handed grip. The pistol can be obtained chambered for 7.65mm ACP, 9mm Short or 9mm Police cartridges. It retains the

double-action feature of the original HSc, is a simple blowback, and in 9mm Police caliber would appear to be a sound pistol for use by police or security forces or for home defense.

Semmerling LM-4 Pistol

Manufacturer Semmerling Corp., Newton, MA 02160, U.S.A.
Type Manual repeating pistol
Caliber .45 ACP
Barrel 3.656in (92.8mm)
Weight (empty) 26.5oz (751gm)
Magazine Capacity 4 rounds

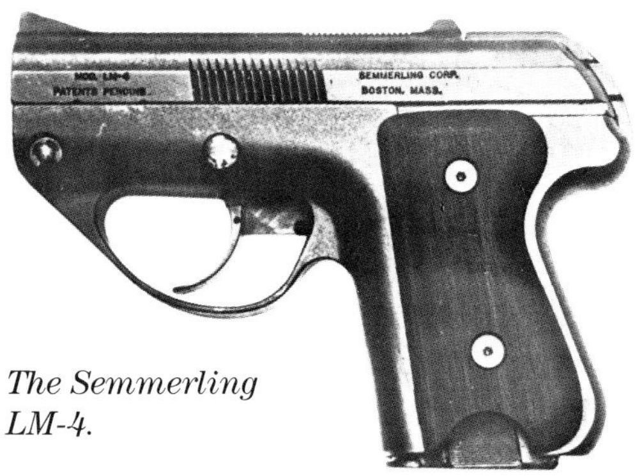

The Semmerling LM-4.

This is one of the most unusual pistols in existence, a pistol designed solely as a defensive weapon and using a unique mechanical action. It is also one of the strongest and probably the most expensive .45 – the last quoted price was $748. Manufacture ceased in the late 1980s, but the unusual features of the pistol make it a desirable addition to any collection.

The Semmerling looks like an an automatic but is actually hand-operated. The frame carries a heavy standing breech and the four-round magazine and trigger mechanism; on the forward section of the frame is the barrel unit which can slide forward, exposing the chamber. When it is manually pushed forward and pulled back, the chamber slides over the top round in the magazine and the breech is closed. Pulling the trigger now brings up a lock to hold the barrel in place during firing and then cocks and releases the hammer to fire the cartridge. The firer then pushes and pulls once more on the barrel, first ejecting the fired case and then reloading the fresh round.

This all sounds very difficult, but with practice it all works very well; the light weight and small size of the LM-4 demand a two-handed grip, and thus the free hand is ready to perform the reloading movement. This can be done by thumb pressure on the serrated area on top of the barrel, or by grasping the side serrations. The firer must remember to release the trigger, however, since as long as the trigger is pressed, the barrel is securely locked to the breech; conversely, if the breech is not properly closed, then the trigger cannot move and the pistol cannot be fired.

There is no manual safety; however, there is a slight possibility that in drawing the pistol from a holster the barrel could be pulled forward, and to guard against this there is a 'holster lock' lever on the right side which can be set to hold the barrel firmly closed. It is automatically disengaged as the trigger is pulled to fire the first shot. The sights compromise a fixed blade front and square notch rear.

The recoil is quite violent, but accurate shooting in combat is no problem. It should only be used with standard military or jacketed commercial .45 ACP ammunition, and handloading should be done carefully so as not to exceed standard pressure levels.

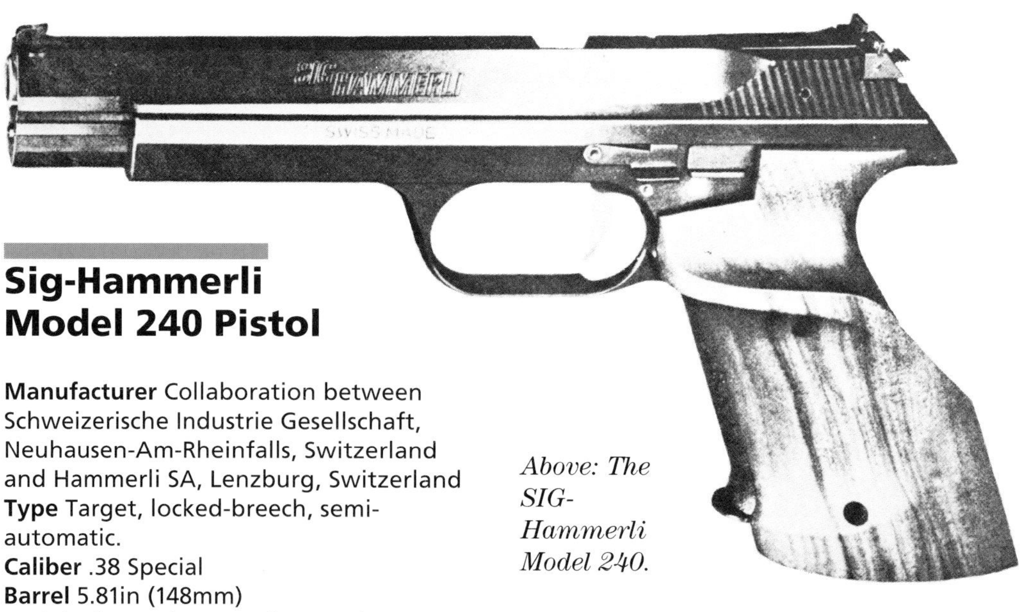

Above: The SIG-Hammerli Model 240.

Sig-Hammerli Model 240 Pistol

Manufacturer Collaboration between Schweizerische Industrie Gesellschaft, Neuhausen-Am-Rheinfalls, Switzerland and Hammerli SA, Lenzburg, Switzerland
Type Target, locked-breech, semi-automatic.
Caliber .38 Special
Barrel 5.81in (148mm)
Weight (empty) 43.5oz (1233gm)
Magazine Capacity 5 rounds

This is a highly-specialized pistol intended for one purpose only, making holes in targets with supreme accuracy, and that only in international-class formal contests. It is not intended for combat shooting, either real or simulated, or casual plinking at vermin.

The P-240 might be said to be a SIG P-210 which has been worked over by the Hammerli people to give it the accuracy desired. SIG are without peers for producing well-built and fitted automatic pistols, while Hammerli, as we have pointed out elsewhere, have a long history of producing prize-winning match pistols, and the combination is unbeatable.

The 240 uses the now-standard Browning cam breech lock system in which the barrel is withdrawn from engagement with the slide by a shaped cam beneath the breech. Having said that, one has to add that in this case the machining and fit is to the finest tolerances and the muzzle is shaped to fit closely into the slide. The slide itself, in SIG fashion, rides inside the frame, a method which gives good support to the moving parts. The barrel is rifled to very close tolerances, which is part of the secret of its accuracy, and the loading ramp is particularly carefully contoured since this pistol fires only one type of ammunition, the .38 Special Wadcutter, a most unusual cartridge to find in an automatic but one with enormous potential for accuracy.

The grip is large, plain wood, and with a palm rest, giving an excellent grip, and the whole pistol is large and muzzle-heavy, promoting a firm and steady aim. The wide trigger is fully adjustable for tension, slack and overtravel, with a clean and consistent let-off. The foresight is a blade, the rear sight a square notch adjustable for elevation and windage.

The accuracy of this gun is beyond question; to put it plainly, it is capable of whatever accuracy the shooter can bring to it, and quoting figures would be meaningless.

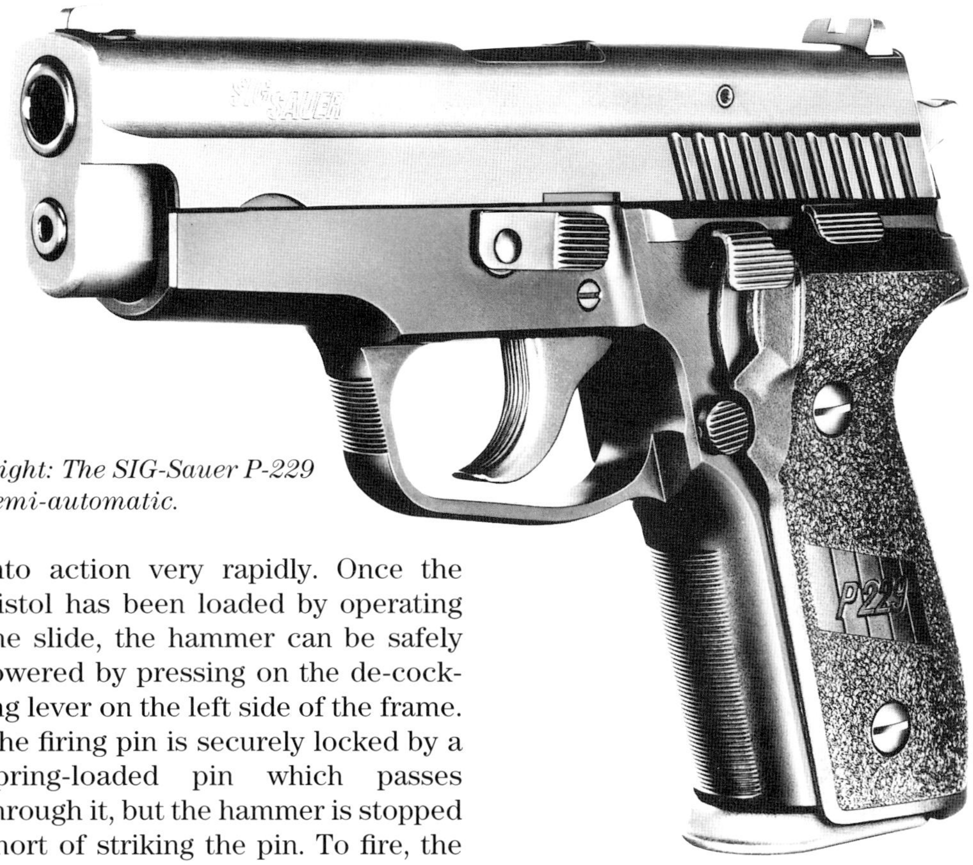

Right: The SIG-Sauer P-229 semi-automatic.

Sig-Sauer Model P225 Auto Pistol

Manufacturer J. P. Sauer & Son, Eckernforde, Germany; Schweizerische Industriegesellschaft Neuhausen-Am-Rheinfalls, Switzerland
Type Locked breech, double-action, semi-automatic
Caliber 9mm Parabellum
Barrel 3.85in (98mm)
Weight (empty) 26.1oz (740gm)
Magazine Capacity 8 rounds

This pistol was designed by SIG (Schweizer Industrie Gesellschaft) of Neuhausen-Rheinfalls, Switzerland and was first announced in 1978. Due to the restrictions placed on arms sales by the Swiss Government, SIG have entered into agreements with J. P. Sauer & Son of Germany so that the SIG designs can be manufactured by Sauer, this giving them an export market since the German government's regulations are much less restrictive. The Swiss-manufactured pistols have been adopted by the Swiss police, while those made in Germany, the 'Pistoles 6', have been adopted by the German Border Police, Customs Administration, and six regional police forces.

The P225 is a slightly smaller and slightly modified version of the earlier P220. It uses the well-known Browning link method of breech locking, using a shaped cam to withdraw the barrel from engagement with the slide. Its principal feature is the incorporation of improved safety devices, and there is no applied safety, so that the weapon can be brought into action very rapidly. Once the pistol has been loaded by operating the slide, the hammer can be safely lowered by pressing on the de-cocking lever on the left side of the frame. The firing pin is securely locked by a spring-loaded pin which passes through it, but the hammer is stopped short of striking the pin. To fire, the trigger is pulled through to raise the hammer and then release it; as the hammer reaches the full-cocked position, a safety lever is rotated by the trigger bar. This rises beneath the firing pin and pushes the locking pin up and clear of the hole, so that as the hammer drops the firing pin is free to move when struck. As soon as the slide moves on recoil, the disconnector allows the firing pin safety pin to drop back into place and the pin is again securely locked.

The design is well balanced and the P225 performs well on the range. Like all SIG products the finish is immaculate, and quality control is such that parts from Swiss or German pistols are freely interchangeable.

Sig-Sauer P-229

Manufacturer Schweizerische Industriegesellschaft, Neuhausen-Am-Rheinfalls, Switzerland
J.P. Sauer & Son, Eckernforde, Germany
Type Recoil-operated semi-automatic, double-action
Caliber .40 S&W or 9mm Parabellum
Barrel 3.85in (98mm)
Weight 30.5oz (865gm)
Magazine Capacity 12 rounds (13 rounds in 9mm)

The Swiss Industrial Company (SIG) have produced some of the best pistols in the world, but the Swiss neutrality laws make the export of weapons very difficult; as one Swiss said, "We are only allowed to sell guns to people who don't want them." As a result, SIG set up a combined operation with the German company of J. P. Sauer & Son, an old-established and well-respected company, so that Sauer can make SIG pistols and sell them into countries where the Swiss cannot.

The P-229 developed from earlier designs; this series began with the P-220 which more or less set the general pattern: a recoil-operated pistol using a shaped cam beneath the breech to pull down the rear of the barrel, thus disengaging a squared-off section around the chamber from its lock in the ejection port of the slide, SIG were the pioneers of this system, which is gradually replacing the original Browning system of machined lugs on the barrel mating with slots in the slide. The P-220 was a full-sized pistol adopted by the Swiss Army as their Model 75.

Next came the P-225, which was slightly smaller and lighter than the P-220 and which had improved safety features including an automatic firing pin safety, decocking lever, drop safety device, but no applied safety catch, so that it can be brought into action very quickly indeed. In late 1980, when the U.S. Army advertised for a new pistol, SIG modified the P-225 to meet the American requirements, resulting in the P-226; the principal change was the addition of an ambidextrous magazine catch and a 15-round magazine capacity. Although not adopted by the U.S. armed forces, the P-226 was widely purchased by police and security agencies.

The P-228 came next, a compact pistol, smaller than the other members of the family but with a 13-round magazine capacity. And finally came the P-229, which is virtually the same as the P-228 but chambered for the .40 Smith & Wesson cartridge. Developed primarily for police use, it has high-contrast sights and the usual automatic firing pin safety, drop safety and de-cocking lever. The basic P-229 has a steel slide and aluminum alloy frame; the P-229SL is similar but with the slide in stainless steel; and this version is also available in 9mm Parabellum caliber. (In effect, this latter model is a P-228 with stainless steel slide.)

SIG-Sauer P230 Auto Pistol

Manufacturer J. P. Sauer & Son, Eckernforde, Germany
Type Blowback semi-automatic
Caliber 7.65mm/.32 ACP; 9mm Short/.380; 9mm Police
Barrel 3.62in (92mm)
Weight (empty) 16.2oz (460gm) in 9mm Short
Magazine Capacity 8 rounds (7.65mm); 9 rounds (9mm caliber)

This is another Swiss-designed, German-manufactured fruit of the cooperation between SIG and J. P. Sauer & Son. It is used by a number of European police forces and enjoys a wide commercial sale.

The P230 is a simple blowback weapon with double-action lockwork and is provided with a de-cocking lever on the left side, by means of which the hammer can be lowered on a loaded chamber. As with the P225 the firing pin is securely locked at all times except for the instant that the hammer is released by the trigger. There is no manual safety catch.

The various caliber types are identical in appearance and major dimensions but there are differences in weight; the 7.65mm and 9mm Short versions have an alloy frame and there is only 5 gm difference between them. But the 9mm Police version, firing a more powerful cartridge, uses a steel frame which adds 170gm, and also has a heavier slide so as to reduce the recoil force, adding another 70gm to make the total weight 690gm or 24.3oz.

The 9mm Police (9 × 18mm) cartridge is a special round developed in Germany in order to obtain the maximum possible performance from an unlocked-breech weapon. It is not yet commercially manufactured in the U.S.A.

Smith & Wesson Distinguished Combat Magnum

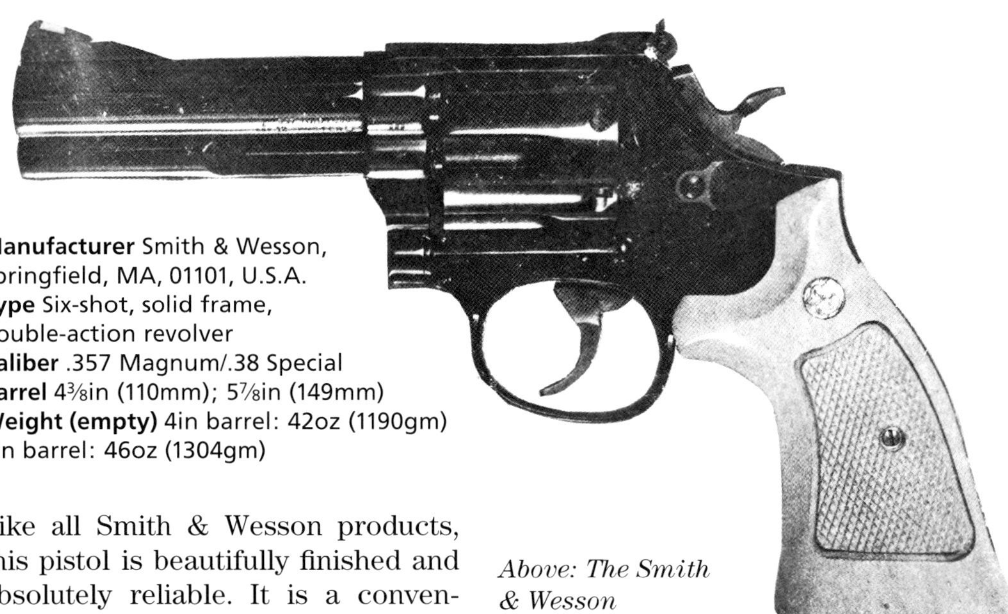

Above: The Smith & Wesson Distinguished Combat Magnum.

Manufacturer Smith & Wesson, Springfield, MA, 01101, U.S.A.
Type Six-shot, solid frame, double-action revolver
Caliber .357 Magnum/.38 Special
Barrel $4\frac{3}{8}$in (110mm); $5\frac{7}{8}$in (149mm)
Weight (empty) 4in barrel: 42oz (1190gm) 6in barrel: 46oz (1304gm)

Like all Smith & Wesson products, this pistol is beautifully finished and absolutely reliable. It is a conventional enough double-action revolver of the type they have been producing since before the start of the century, but it incorporates one new feature, their 'L' frame. Smith & Wesson have long categorized their pistols according to the size of the frame, the smaller and lighter weapons using the 'K' and the very large revolvers the 'N'; the 'L' falls between these, giving additional strength and size to cope with today's magnum ammunition but not increasing the size by an inordinate amount.

There are, in fact, four distinct models in this range; the Model 586 comes in steel with a blued finish and has 4in or 6in (nominal – the actual lengths are as quoted above) barrel lengths. The Model 686 is similar but in stainless steel with a satin finish. Both models have adjustable rear sights. Model 581 is steel, blued, with a 4in barrel and fixed frame notch rear sight, while the Model 581 is the same but in stainless steel with satin finish.

There are certain refinements; revolvers with 4in barrels and 'target accessories', and all revolvers with 6in barrels are furnished with a trigger stop; the 'standard' 4in barrel models – ie the 581 and 681 – will not have a trigger stop. The 586 and 686 are fitted with Goncalo Alves checkered target grips cut away for use with a speed loader, while the 581 and 681 have straightforward checkered walnut grips.

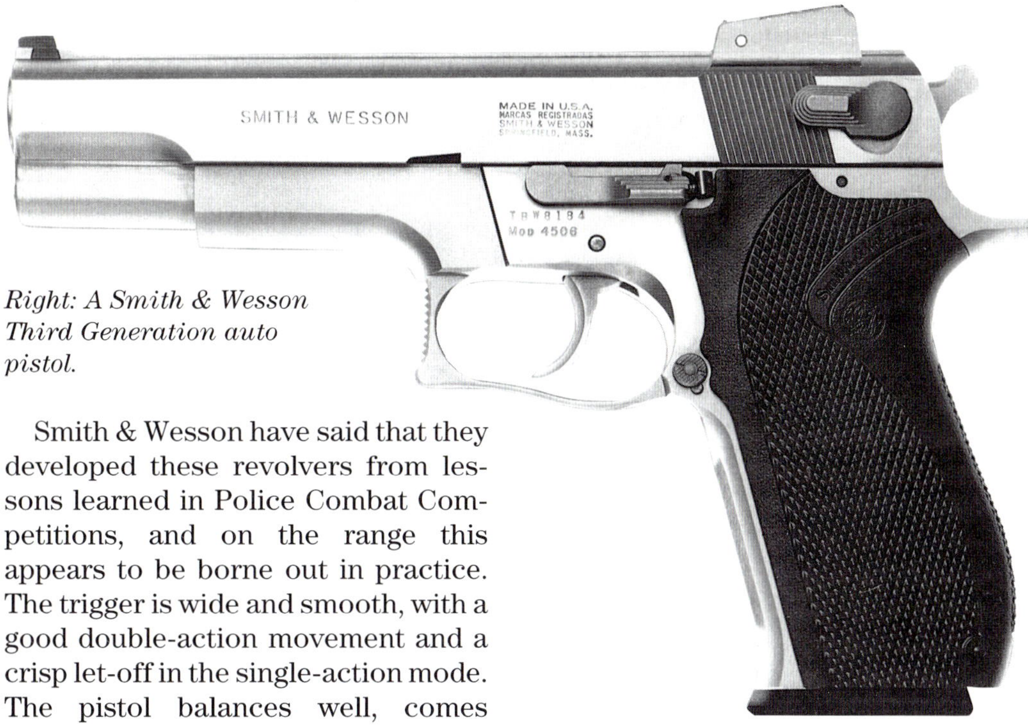

Right: A Smith & Wesson Third Generation auto pistol.

Smith & Wesson have said that they developed these revolvers from lessons learned in Police Combat Competitions, and on the range this appears to be borne out in practice. The trigger is wide and smooth, with a good double-action movement and a crisp let-off in the single-action mode. The pistol balances well, comes quickly to the aim and is as accurate as anyone could wish. There is sufficient weight and good balance to prevent excessive throw-off after firing, so that the shooter can quickly regain his point of aim. For practical shooting contests, or for service, it would be hard to fault this weapon.

Smith & Wesson Third Generation Auto Pistols

Manufacturer Smith & Wesson Inc., Springfield, MA, 01101, U.S.A.
Type Recoil-operated, semi-automatic, double-action
Caliber 9mm Parabellum
Barrel 4.0in (101.6mm)
Weight 28.5oz (808gm)
Magazine Capacity 14 rounds
(Data for Model 5903)

This series of pistols has completely replaced earlier models and has been designed with the assistance of many U.S. law enforcement agencies, who were encouraged to make suggestions and criticisms. Features incorporated in these new pistols include fixed barrel bushes for better accuracy and simpler stripping, an improved trigger pull, three-dot sights, wrap-around grips, a bevelled magazine aperture for quicker reloading, and a triple safety system incorporating an automatic firing pin safety, an ambidextrous manual safety catch and a magazine safety.

The 9mm **5900 Series** can be considered as the baseline series. There are three models, the 5903, 5904 and 5906; the '03 has an alloy frame and stainless steel slide, the '04 an aluminum frame, carbon steel slide and stainless steel barrel and is finished in blue, and the '06 is entirely of stainless steel and is satin-finished. All are fitted with wrap-around grips, adjustable sights are optional, and all have the same 4-inch barrel.

The 9mm **3900 Series** generally resembles the 5900 series but is slimmer, lighter and with a smaller magazine capacity.

The 9mm **6900 Series** has a reverse-curved trigger-guard. It is larger and uses the same length of barrel but has a 12-round magazine.

The **Model 4006** generally resembles the 5906 but is chambered for the .40 Smith & Wesson cartridge and has a magazine capacity of 11 rounds.

The **4500 Series** is chambered for the .45 ACP cartridge and adds the power of a well-proven cartridge to the other advantages of the Third Generation system.

The **Model 1000 Series** resembles the 5900 series but is chambered for the 10mm Auto cartridge. The Model 1076 is specially made for the FBI and does not have a safety catch on the slide but instead, a frame-mounted de-cocking lever.

All models have fixed sights as standard, and most are available with adjustable rear sights as an option.

Sphinx AT-2000

Manufacturer Sphinx Engineering, Porrentruy, Switzerland
Type Recoil-operated, semi-automatic, double-action
Caliber 9mm Parabellum or .41 Action Express
Barrel 4.53in (115mm)
Weight 35.2oz (1000gm)
Magazine Capacity 15 rounds (9mm) or 11 rounds (.41 AE)

Below: The Sphinx AT-2000.

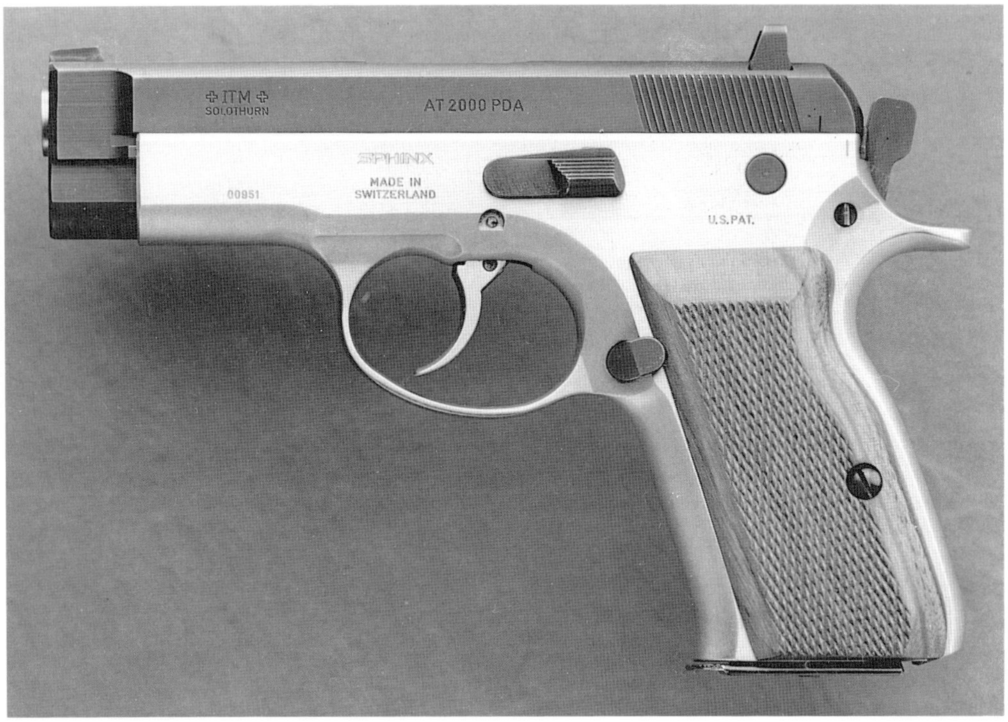

Above: The Sphinx AT-2000PDA.

This was originally the ITM 2000 pistol, announced in 1984, but ITM was bought by Sphinx Engineering and the pistol re-named accordingly. In fact, it originated as a licensed copy of the Czechoslovakian CZ-75 pistol, but over the years there have been a number of small changes in detail and various improvements, to the point that the AT-2000 can now be considered as a completely independent design. Assembly tolerances and finish have been greatly improved, and the dimensions of the barrel have been slightly changed so that it is no longer possible to interchange a Czech CZ-75 barrel. Barrels are now made in Germany by Peters Stahl and have exceptional accuracy and resistance to wear.

The AT-2000 series are therefore recoil-operated pistols using the usual type of Browning dropping barrel for their breech lock. The safety catch can be applied whether the pistol is cocked or uncocked, and in 1987 an automatic firing pin safety system was introduced, preventing any movement of the firing pin except during the final few degrees of trigger movement prior to releasing the hammer. Recent designs have an ambidextrous safety catch and, if desired, the slide stop pin can be fitted to the right of the frame, a refinement seen on no other pistol.

The pistol was originally designed for the 9mm Parabellum cartridge but was one of the first to accept the .41 Action Express round and a conversion kit was supplied to permit a change of caliber. Since the .41 AE uses the same rim diameter as the 9mm Parabellum, only the barrel, return spring and magazine need be changed.

The basic model of the range is the **AT-2000S**, a full-sized holster pistol by police and military use. The **AT-2000P** is a shorter and lighter version designed by Sphinx; except for the dimensions (93mm barrel, 910 grams weight) it is the same as the 2000S and a similar 9mm/.41 conversion kit is available.

The **AT-2000H** is the 'hideaway' version, mechanically similar to the other members of the family but even smaller than the 2000P, weighing only 740 grams, with an 87mm barrel and a 10-shot magazine. Normally supplied in 9mm Parabellum caliber, it can be converted to either .41 Action Express or the new 9mm Action Express, and a patented design of magazine has been developed which will accept and feed all three calibers without the need for change.

The **AT-2000SDA, 2000PDA** and **2000HDA** are the same as the three pistols described above, but, as the 'DA' suffix indicates, are arranged so as to fire in the 'double-action only' or self-cocking mode. The pistols are automatically de-cocked and made safe after each shot, but pulling the trigger will raise the hammer, disconnect the automatic firing pin safety and drop the hammer to fire the weapon. These pistols have the same ability to interchange between 9mm Parabellum and .41 AE calibers as the original versions.

The **AT-2000R** is similar to the double-action-only DA models but has the additional ability to be thumb-cocked to allow single-action firing when required. In normal use the hammer always falls to the safe position, but stands sufficiently clear of the slide to be pulled back by the thumb for a more deliberate shot. This 'R' variation can be applied to any of the three standard 2000 models, thus producing the 'PR', 'SR' or 'HR' varieties.

Spitfire Mark II

Manufacturer JSL Ltd, Hereford, England
Type Recoil-operated semi-automatic, double-action
Caliber 9mm Parabellum or 9 × 21mm IMI
Barrel 3.7in (94mm)
Weight 35.2oz (1000gm)
Magazine Capacity 15 rounds

The Spitfire is another derivative of the Czechoslovakian CZ-75, but, like the Sphinx 2000, has undergone a number of modifications in the course of its development, so that it can now be considered a completely different weapon.

The Spitfire is a conventional recoil-operated pistol using the Browning tilting barrel, controlled by a cam beneath the chamber and locked by lugs above the chamber engaging in recesses in the slide. The entire pistol, except for the grip surfaces and springs, is made from investment-cast and machined stainless steel, and machining is done on computer-controlled machines to a tolerance of 5

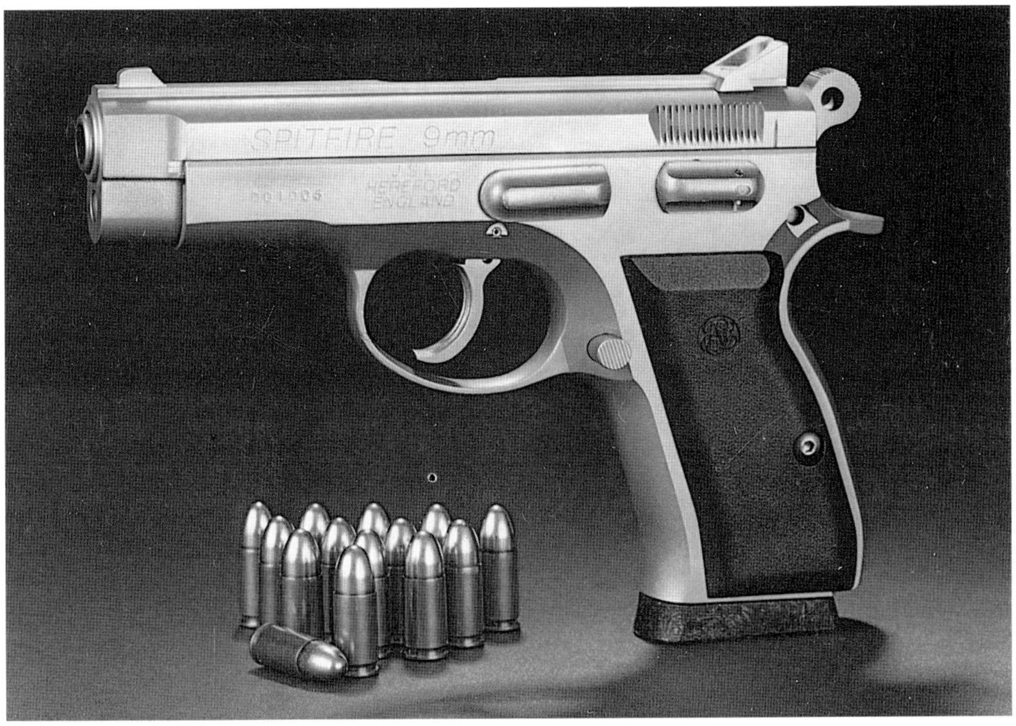

Two types of the Spitfire Mark II, including the Competition Model (below).

microns. This produces a pistol which is tight throughout, with no looseness in the fit of components and a very crisp trigger pull.

The sights are fully adjustable for elevation and windage and produce a clear picture. Three models are currently produced: the **Standard** with fixed sights; the **Stirling** with adjustable rear sight, and the **Competition Model** with fully adjustable sights and a muzzle compensator. All models are available in either 9mm Parabellum or 9 × 21mm chambering, the latter being particularly recommended for competition shooting, since it appears to be somewhat more accurate than the Parabellum round.

The Standard model has been tested by various military and police authorities and is in wide use as a police pistol in Europe.

Star Model BKM Auto Pistol

Manufacturer 'Star', B. Echeverria, Eibar, Spain
Type Locked breech, semi-automatic
Caliber 9mm Parabellum
Barrel 3.9in (100mm)
Weight 26oz (737gm)
Magazine Capacity 8 rounds

The Star line of 9mm automatic pistols has generally been developed along military lines, but in the late 1970s, with the 9mm Parabellum cartridge beginning to become popular in the U.S.A., they were prevailed upon to produce a smaller weapon, one more suited to concealment for personal defense. Their answer was the BKM.

With an overall length of just over seven inches and weighing less than two pounds when loaded, this meets the specification, but the result is something of a handful. A light alloy frame helps to keep the weight down, but the combination of short-barrel, light weight and the 9mm Parabellum cartridge means recoil and muzzle blast both heavier than average; this is particularly noticeable when firing some types of European military 9mm ammunition. It is rather more acceptable when using commercial 'Luger' loadings.

The finish is excellent, with blued slide, anodized black frame, and well-checkered walnut grips. The foresight is the usual blade and the rear a square notch which is rather too narrow for easy alinement in a hurry. The rear sight may be drifted sideways in its notch for zeroing but there is no other adjustment. The breech locking is by the traditional Browning-Colt swinging link, though there is only one locking lug on top of the barrel to engage with the slide. It is worth noting that the firing pin is not an inertia type, and this pistol should never have the hammer lowered on to a loaded chamber.

In practical use the BKM delivers good accuracy for such a short barrel, giving two to three inch groups at 25 yards quite regularly. Like many autos it tends to be fussy over its ammunition, and several brands should be checked for their compatability before deciding which to use. Once the recoil and noise are mastered, the BKM becomes an extension of the hand, and is well-suited to the defensive role.

Star Model FR Target Pistol

Manufacturer 'Star', B. Echeverria, Eibar, Spain
Type Blowback, semi-automatic
Caliber .22 Long Rifle RF
Barrel 7in (178mm)
Weight (empty) 29oz (820gm)
Magazine Capacity 10 rounds

The number of target shooters who cut their teeth on the Star Model F target pistol in years gone by must be astronomical; it was cheap, reliable and sufficiently accurate to satisfy the beginner at target work and it also made a very satisfactory 'fun gun'. Unfortunately Echeverria found more lucrative things to do in the early 1960s and stopped making it. They have now returned to this field with the new 'Model FR' which is simply the old Model F revived and somewhat better made.

This is a basic blowback pistol, having a heavy barrel fixed into the frame and a slide which has a front arms frame which traps the recoil spring beneath the barrel. It is simple to dismantle; one merely pulls the slide slightly back, presses the dismantling button above the left grip, lifts the slide and slips it off forward, over the barrel. End of dismantling; nothing further is needed.

There is an external hammer and a safety catch which locks the slide while disconnecting the trigger. A hold-open catch ensures that the slide stays to the rear after firing the last shot in the magazine; with a new magazine in, the slide can be closed by pressing this catch or by simply pulling it back and releasing it. The foresight is on a ramp and is adjustable for elevation; the rear sight, a square notch, is adjustable for windage. Balance weights are available, which can be attached to the barrel to adjust the point of balance for the individual shooter.

Altogether the FR is a good beginner's pistol which will provide accuracy enough to satisfy many shooters for their entire career.

Below: The Star Model FR Target Pistol.

Above: The Spanish Star Model BKM.

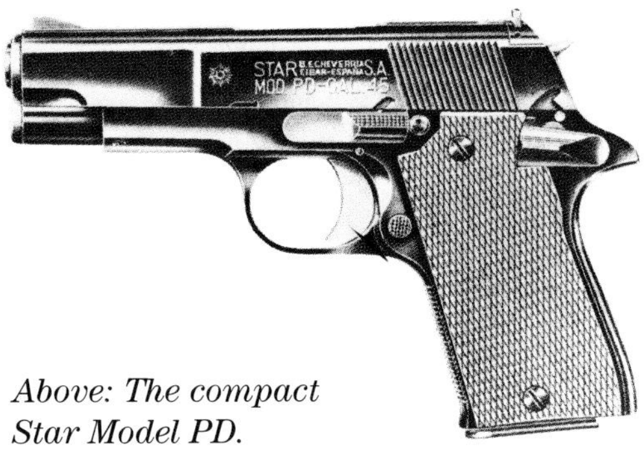

Above: The compact Star Model PD.

Star Model PD

Manufacturer 'Star', B. Echeverria, Eibar, Spain
Type Locked breech semi-automatic
Caliber .45 ACP
Barrel 3.94in (100mm)
Weight 25oz (710gm)
Magazine Capacity 6 rounds

The venerable U. S. Government Colt M1911A1 pistol is a splendid weapon for stopping malefactors, but it is rather bulky and heavy; as a result there has long been a tendency to develop lighter and smaller pistols firing the .45 ACP cartridge. Many have been short-lived hack-and-chop jobs done on the basic Colt, but some have been designed from the ground up, as it were, and have been considerably more successful.

The Star PD is one of the earliest of this group and probably the most long-lived. In order to bring the size down there have been some changes from the basic Colt-Browning swinging link breech locking system; there is only one interlocking lug and notch holding slide and barrel together, and the recoil spring and guide rod are an assembled unit instead of separate components. The frame is of alloy, and there is no grip safety. The foresight is a blade and the rear sight a fully adjustable leaf with open notch.

The PD is much lighter than the Colt M1911A1 and, consequently, rather more difficult to control, though it is not uncomfortable to shoot. Due to the short barrel the velocity and muzzle energy is less than in full-sized pistols but there is still ample stopping power, and the PD is a sensible gun for those who need a potent but concealable pistol.

Sterling Mark II Auto

Manufacturer Sterling Arms Corp., Lockport, NY 14094, U.S.A.
Type Blowback, double-action, semi-automatic
Caliber .380 Auto/9mm Short
Barrel 3.56in (90.5mm)
Weight 25.5oz (723gm)
Magazine Capacity 8 rounds

The .380 Auto, or 9mm Short as it is known in Europe, is a somewhat under-rated cartridge. It has served as a police cartridge throughout Europe for several decades and as a military cartridge too. The bullet will deliver something in the order of 165 foot-pounds of energy at the muzzle, which is sufficient to make most people stop and think, and it is also less likely to ricochet than higher powered cartridges such as the 9mm Parabellum. For many years it was just about the most powerful cartridge which could be managed in a blowback action without going to extremes, another point which counted in its favor.

The Sterling is one of the few .380 automatic pistols made in the U.S.A.; it is an inexpensive pistol and the standard of finish reflects its price, but there is nothing wrong with its quality of construction and it is surprisingly accurate. The action is a straightforward blowback with an external hammer, and with double-action trigger. There is a slide-mounted safety which, when operated, moves a steel barrier behind the firing pin, so that should the hammer fall it cannot discharge a cartridge. Once the safety is on, the hammer may be lowered by controlling it with the thumb while pressing the trigger; thereafter the pistol can be fired by releasing the safety and pulling the trigger to cock and drop the hammer. Once the first shot has been fired, subsequent shots are in single-action mode, the recoiling slide cocking the hammer.

The foresight is a fixed blade, the rear-sight, a square notch adjustable for elevation and windage. The Sterling is comfortable to fire and can deliver consistent three- to four-inch groups at 25 yards range.

TA 382

Manufacturer Fratelli Tanfoglio SpA, Gardone Val Trompia, Italy
Type Blowback, semi-automatic
Caliber .380/9mm Short: .32 ACP/7.65mm
Barrel 3.75in (95mm)
Weight 28oz (794gm)
Magazine Capacity 11 rounds (.380); 12 rounds (.32)

Under the name Tanfoglio & Sabotti this company exported large numbers of inexpensive auto pistols to the U.S.A. in the 1950s, one of them being a .25 auto called the 'Titan'. The 1968 Gun Control Act stopped this trade and shortly afterwards there was news of an American company being set up to import component parts and assemble them in the U.S. This does not seem to have prospered particularly well, and now Tanfoglio (Sabotti having left the concern) have completely rebuilt the Titan into the TA 382 and are marketing it in the U.S.A.

The new pistol follows the current fashion in having a magazine larger than was previously considered normal during its first production run, but apart from that it is of conventional design, somewhat resembling Beretta from its use of an open-topped slide. The safety catch on the left side of the frame, above the trigger, locks the trigger. In addition to this there is a magazine safety and a half-cock notch on the hammer. The frame safety catch also doubles as a stripping catch; when turned to the 'safe' position the slide can be pulled back and lifted off the frame at its rear end, then slid forward to clear the barrel. With the catch in the 'fire' position dismantling is impossible.

Above: The TA 382 by Tanfoglio.

The sights are roughly what one might expect in this sort of pistol; a blade at the front and a fixed notch at the rear, mounted in a block which can be knocked sideways for windage correction when zeroing. Accuracy is likewise average for the class, about four-inch groups at 25 yards. On the whole the TA 382 is a reliable and robust workaday pistol.

Tanfoglio TA90

Manufacturer Fratelli Tanfoglio SpA, Gardone Val Trompia, Italy
Type Recoil-operated semi-automatic, double-action
Caliber 9mm Parabellum, 9 × 21mm IMI, .40 S&W, .41 Action Express, 10mm Auto, .45ACP
Barrel 4.7in (120mm)
Weight 35.8oz (1015gm)
Magazine Capacity 15 rounds (9mm)

The Tanfoglio company have manufactured pocket pistols for some years, but in the 1980s decided to market a military-style heavy-caliber pistol; like many others, they chose the Czech CZ-75 as their model, though since then several variants have been developed.

The basic pistol of the Tanfoglio range is the TA-90, a conventional 9mm pistol using the Browning tipping barrel system of breech locking, controlled by a fixed cam beneath the breech and locking into the slide by two lugs above the chamber. The frame is of cast steel, while the slide and barrel are machined from forged steel. All models are supplied in black finish or hard chromed and are also available with frame and slide in stainless steel.

On the standard models there is a manual safety catch on the slide which locks the firing pin and also disconnects the hammer and trigger. On the 'Combat' models there is a frame-mounted safety catch which allows the weapon to be carried cocked and locked. All models are double-action, but there is no provision for de-cocking the hammer on any of them.

The TA90 is paralleled by the TA40, TA41, TA10 and TA45, and the only difference lies in the caliber, which can be deduced from the model numbers. There are also 'Combat' versions of all these models, differing only in the safety arrangement, as described above.

The 'Baby Standard' models are compact versions of the standard, differing only in dimensions; they have a 90mm barrel and weigh about 30oz (850 gm) empty.

The 'Baby Combat' models resemble the Baby Standard but have the Combat safety arrangement. All the Baby models are available in the same range of calibers as the full-sized Standard and Combat models.

Below: The Tanfoglio TA90.

The Taurus PT-92 (top) and PT-99 pistols.

Taurus PT-92 and PT-99 Auto Pistols

Manufacturer Forjas Taurus SA, Estrada do Forte 511, CP44, Porto Alegre RS, Brazil
Type Locked breech, double-action semi-automatic
Caliber 9mm Parabellum
Barrel 4.9in (125mm)
Weight (empty) 34oz (964gm)
Magazine Capacity 15 rounds

These two pistols bear a considerable resemblance to two Beretta designs, and it would appear that they are based on Beretta models but with slight modifications, and made under license in Brazil. They are currently being offered on the commercial market in the Americas and they have been adopted by Brazilian military and security forces.

The PT-92 and PT-99 are virtually identical, the difference being that the 92 uses fixed sights and is intended as a service or combat weapon, while the

99 has wooden grips and adjustable rear sights and is intended for target shooting. The general form is that of the Beretta Model 92, a locked breech pistol using a variation of the Walther P-38 dropping block to lock barrel and receiver together during firing. The principal change is in the trigger guard, the front edge of which has a reverse curve which is serrated to provide a good grip for the popular two-handed grasp. The magazine is slightly different from the Beretta design, having a number of small holes in the rear face through which the cartridge contents can be counted.

The workmanship and finish of the Taurus pistols is very good, and they are of above-average accuracy for basic military pistols. The adjustable-sight model, once zeroed, is very good, being capable of off-hand two-inch groups at 25 yards in the hands of moderately-practised shooters.

Thompson-Center Super 14 Contender

Manufacturer Thompson-Center Arms Ltd., Rochester, NH 03867, U.S.A.
Type Single shot pistol
Caliber Various
Barrel 14in (355mm)
Weight ca 46oz (1315gm)

The Thompson-Center single shot pistol has been in existence since the late 1960s and has proved a very successful design. It has been made available in almost every possible caliber at various times; the company is a small one and staffed by practical men who, if they see a trend, can rapidly produce barrels to suit. Thus in the days when .17 caliber was all the rage, they produced several .17 chamberings, and when the fashion died away they abandoned them. It would profit us little to tabulate all the variations that have existed. The latest model, the Super 14, is intended principally for silhouette shooting, though it is likely to appeal also to hunters who prefer to use handguns.

The Super 14 would appear to have gained its name from the combination of several powerful chamberings and a 14in barrel; it is available in .22LR, .222 Rem, 7mm TCU, .30-30 win, .35 Rem Maximum, .44 Magnum, 10mm Auto and .445 Magnum.

The basic design has changed little over the years. The Contender is still an elegant single-shot with a standing breech and a barrel which hinges down for loading. The Super 14 has a new grip, designed to provide a more firm anchorage when firing heavy loads, and a nicely-shaped fore end which is designed for a two-handed hold.

The foresight is a blade, while the rear sight can be had in two forms, open notch or aperture, both fully adjustable for elevation and windage. The long and heavy barrel gives good balance and a long sight base, so that the pistol is certainly capable of as much accuracy as the shooter is likely to bring to it. Fired from a rest at 50 yards, groups between three and four inches are easily obtainable, though some care should be taken in selecting the ammunition.

Uberti Single Action Revolver

Manufacturer Aldo Uberti, SpA, Brescia, Italy
Type Six shot, solid frame, single-action
Caliber .45 Colt
Barrel 7.5in (190mm)
Weight 40oz (1134gm)

This is not exactly new, though it reappears under a new name every few months. In the 1960s the 'spaghetti western' movies and the quick-draw craze appear to have hit Italy and several companies began making cheap and cheerful copies of the Colt 1873 'Frontier' to meet the demand.

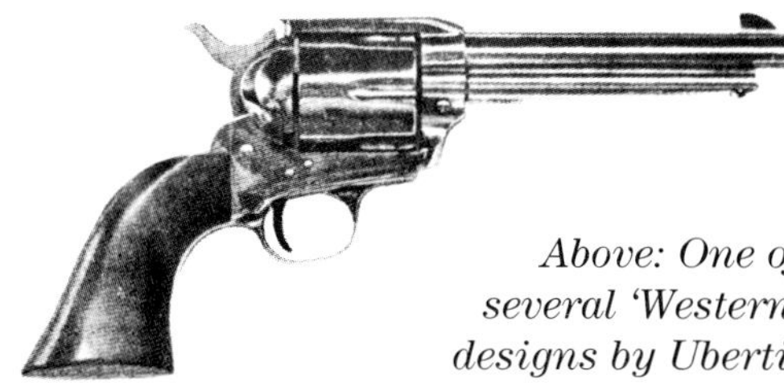

Above: One of several 'Western' designs by Uberti.

One or two of them realized that there could be something better in this, and seeing that there was a large demand for good single-action revolvers (since Colt had stopped making theirs) began making good quality pistols and exporting them. Uberti are one of the best, and their products have appeared under their own name, under the names of various importers in the U.S. (eg Mitchell Arms Corp, Costa Mesa, CA.; Western Arms, Santa Fe, NM; Iver Johnson, Middlesex, NJ; and many more), and under various brand names – Cattleman, Buckhorn, Trailblazer and so forth.

The Uberti standard .45 uses a 7.5in barrel on a nicely color-hardened frame with brass trigger guard and solid walnut grip. The foresight is a serrated blade on a ramp, the backsight a square notch with adjustment for elevation and windage. The finish, both in appearance and in fit of the cylinder, is excellent, and the single-action trigger 'breaks' very cleanly with a consistent feel. It is capable of very good accuracy, provided some care is taken over selecting compatible ammunition; groups of under two inches at 25 yards are possible when rest-fired.

The Uberti design can be had in a wide variety of caliber and barrel length options; .44 Magnum and .357 Magnum chamberings are offered, and barrel lengths of 4.75, 5.5, 7.5, 10, 12 and 18 inches are possible; with the latter a shoulder stock is available.

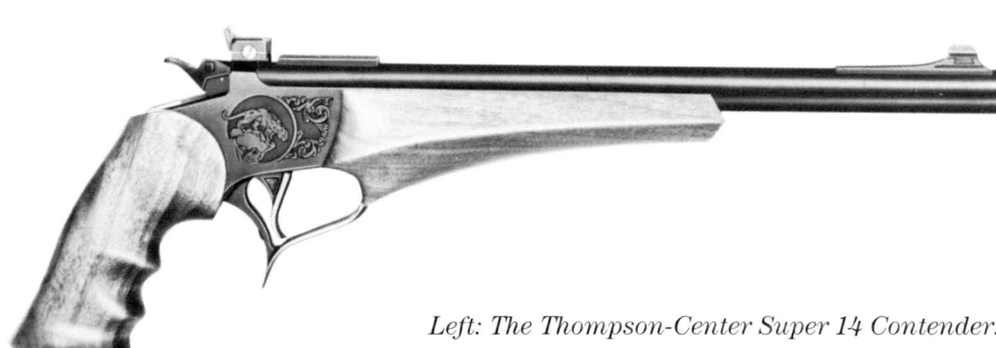

Left: The Thompson-Center Super 14 Contender.

4.5mm Underwater Pistol

Manufacturer Russian state arsenals
Type Multi-barrel repeater
Caliber 4.5mm special
Barrel About 8.25in (210mm)
Weight 33.5oz (995gm)
Magazine Capacity 4 rounds

Weapons designed for underwater use by frogmen have been in the inventories of major armies for some years, but are not publicized, and the first such weapon to be seen at an international arms exhibition was this Russian pistol, first shown in 1992. Conventional firearms do not perform well under water, for various technical reasons, and thus the design of this pistol is quite unlike any weapon used on land.

There are four barrels, arranged in a block so that they can be tipped down to expose the breech end for loading. The round of ammunition is a drag-stabilized dart 115mm long, the rear end being secured inside a cartridge case of fairly conventional shape. Four rounds are held together by a clip, so that the whole clip can be handled as one unit and the four rounds slipped into the four barrels. The barrels are then folded down and locked to the breech, which contains a self-cocking firing mechanism which fires each round in succession for four pulls of the trigger. The cartridge contains a piston which, when the powder explodes, is driven forward and launches the dart from the barrel; the piston is stopped by the bottle-neck of the cartridge so that no gas escapes into the water.

The darts are sufficiently accurate to strike within a 150mm (6in) circle at 100 meters range when fired in air, and the short-range under water accuracy is said to be comparable. The effective underwater range varies according to the depth and water pressure; at five meters depth the dart has lethal effect at 17 meters range, while at 40 meters depth the effective range is only six meters. At these ranges the darts are capable of penetrating all types of wet or dry suit, face-masks and helmets. And, of course, they can be used as self-protection weapons against the more dangerous types of fish and mammals liable to be encountered during underwater activities.

The Russians have also developed a 5.66m underwater rifle using a dart cartridge. With approximately double the range of the pistol, it is a semi-automatic weapon which uses a similar mechanism to the Kalashnikov rifle.

Unique DES-69U Target Auto Pistol

Manufacturer Unique SA, France
Type Blowback, semi-automatic
Caliber .22 Long Rifle RF
Barrel 6in (152mm)
Weight 37oz (1050gm) (without weights)
Magazine Capacity 5 rounds

This is another specialized weapon, specially tailored to suit the requirements of the European 'Standard Pistol' match, which is based on the U.S. National Match rules. The dimensions of the weapon and such parameters as sight radius, trigger pull and weight are all closely regulated, so that the manufacturer's job is to produce the most accurate machine within those tolerances that he can.

The Unique DES-69 is one of the best known stock European pistols for this type of contest and it is made by a company who have been in the pistol business since 1923. It has a long record of successes and will be seen on almost every pistol range.

The DES-69 is a simple blowback using a heavy fixed barrel and a short breech-block/slide with long 'wings' which run alongside the barrel and are serrated to provide finger grips for retracting the slide. The wooden grip is anatomically shaped, with palm rest, and frame and grip run back, over the web of the thumb, to form a support for the rear sight, so as to take advantage of the maximum limits for sight radius of 8.6 inches (220mm). The construction is such that the barrel 'sits' low in the hand, and since all mechanical movement is confined to a short space above the grip, there is minimal disturbance of aim with each shot. Balance weights of 150, 260 or 350gm are provided and can be secured to the barrel, forward of the slide.

The pistol is hammer fired, the hammer operating in a well between the breech and the sight unit, though it is possible to reach it for thumb-cocking. The five-round magazines are loaded through the bottom of the butt in the usual way, and there is a magazine release button low on the grip. The trigger is fully adjustable for reach, pull weight, slack and backlash, and the sear spring is also capable of adjustment, so that the shooter can tune the pull-off.

On the range the DES-69 is capable of ultimate accuracy, but most shooters agree that it should be tested with various brands of ammunition in order to find one which is ballistically suited. Once this is determined, half-inch groups at 25 yards should be possible.

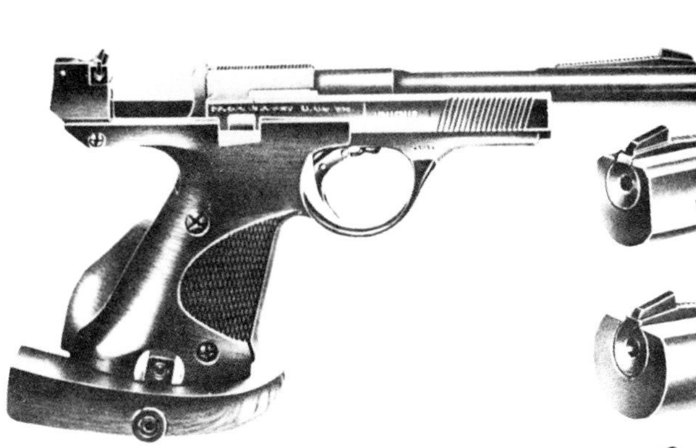

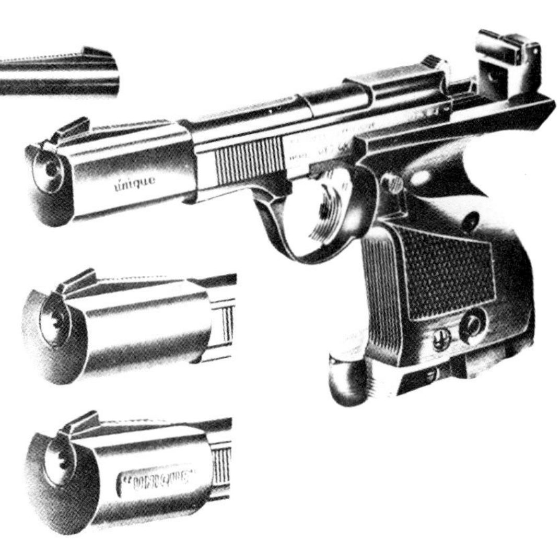

Above: The Unique DES-69 target pistol, with the various balance weights.

Walther Model GSP-C Target Pistol

Manufacturer Carl Walther GmbH Sportwaffenfabrik, Ulm, West Germany
Type Blowback, semi-automatic
Caliber .32 S&W Long
Barrel 4.2in (107mm)
Weight 2.875lbs (1305gm)
Magazine Capacity 5 rounds

This is the latest of a series of pistols developed by Walther for various types of pistol competition. The International Shooting Union (UIT) standard pistol contest has .32 as the minimum caliber, and since it is obviously advantageous to use the lowest caliber so as to have the least recoil and disturbance of aim, the .32 Smith & Wesson long cartridge became popular in Europe as a competition round. Walther had developed their GSP pistol for .22 Long Rifle rimfire, and seeing the rise of interest in .32 S&W, they modified the design to centrefire and produced the GSP-C.

The pistol has a fixed barrel and a reciprocating bolt which works inside the square receiver. A box magazine fits ahead of the trigger guard, which helps, with the heavy barrel block, to keep the weight forward and thus arrive at the balance preferred by contestants. The rimmed cartridge might be expected to give problems in feeding from the magazine, but this has been overcome by raking the magazine rather sharply so that the rounds are loaded with the rims ahead of each other; feeding is thus smooth and feed jams are unknown.

The wooden grips are angular in appearance but fit the hand well and there is a palm rest on the right side. The foresight is a blade, interchangeable for others of different height and thickness, while the rear sight is a leaf with square notch, fully adjustable for elevation and windage. The trigger assembly is an interchangeable unit; there are adjustments for slack, trigger position, travel and weight of pull within certain limits; if these limits do not suit the firer he can change the unit for one with a different range of pull tension and begin adjusting again. The trigger unit can also be replaced by a special training unit which has a ratchet device and gives five 'dry shots' for every winding.

Accuracy is what one would expect from a pistol of this type and quality; groups fractionally over one inch at 25 yards when fired from a rest. Certainly the pistol will be capable of as much accuracy as the firer will be able to put into it.

Above: The Walther GSP-C target pistol.

Walther Model P5 Auto Pistol

Manufacturer Carl Walther GmbH, Post Box 4325, D-7900 Ulm, Germany
Type Locked breech double-action semi-automatic
Caliber 9mm Parabellum
Barrel 3.5in (90mm)
Weight (empty) 28oz (795gm)
Magazine Capacity 8 rounds

This is virtually an updated version of the well-known Walther P-38, used by the German Army from 1938 to 1945 and afterwards, as the P-1, adopted by the Bundeswehr. Like the Heckler & Koch P7 it was designed in response to demands from the West German police for a pistol which combined rapid response with total safety. Walther took the well-proven locking system of the P-38 and wrapped a completely new configuration of pistol round it, incorporating several new safety features.

The P5 has an enveloping slide, but the barrel is semi-fixed and breech locking uses the familiar dropping block of the P-38, in which a locking plate holds slide and barrel together during a short recoil, after which the plate descends and the slide is free to move backwards. An external hammer is cocked during this movement. However, the double-action now incorporates a large thumb-lever which in one movement activates all the safety devices and drops the hammer safely on a loaded chamber. From this position the firer needs only to pull the trigger to fire the pistol; there is no manual safety catch to be operated.

Safety relies on the fact that until the very moment of firing the firing pin is held aligned with a recess on the face of the hammer; thus if the hammer should accidentally fall it will surround the firing pin head without touching it. In addition, the firing pin is never aligned with the solid part of the hammer except at the instant the hammer is released by the action of the trigger. There is also a disconnector which ensures that the trigger cannot affect the hammer unless the slide is closed and the breech securely locked.

When the trigger is pulled it begins to cock the hammer, and as the hammer reaches full cock so a trip lever is extended upwards and forces the firing pin into alignment with the hammer's solid face just as the hammer is released. If the hammer is thumb-cocked, or cocked by the action of the slide, then the releasing action of the trigger will still cause the trip lever to rise and align the firing pin.

The P5 has been adopted by the Netherlands Police and by the police forces of Baden-Wurttemburg and Rheinland-Pfalz in Germany.

Walther P-88

Manufacturer Carl Walther Waffenfabrik, Ulm, Germany
Type Recoil-operated semi-automatic, double-action
Caliber 9mm Parabellum or 9 × 21mm IMI
Barrel 4in (102mm)
Weight 31.7oz (900gm)
Magazine Capacity 15 rounds

Walther pistols have been well-known since the 1920s, and they were the first to make a success of the double-action trigger system using a de-cocking device. Their first major caliber locked-breech pistol was the Pistole 38, designed for the German Army and

Above: The Walther P-88 compact.

first issued in 1939, and this used a block locking system which has been used by all Walther heavy-caliber pistols ever since, as well as being adopted by Beretta and other manufacturers. The P-38 is still manufactured, having been re-adopted by the reconstituted German Army in 1955 as the Pistole 1.

In the middle 1980s, however, with competition from newer manufacturers eroding their markets, Walther decided on a totally new pistol and developed the P-99; in doing so they broke with tradition and abandoned the locking block system and the familiar open barrel and short slide which was almost their trademark.

The P-88 is a conventional design, using an enveloping slide and locking the breech by means of the familiar Browning tilting barrel, controlled by a cam beneath the chamber and locking to the slide by a squared section around the chamber engaging with the ejection slot in the slide. The trigger mechanism is double-action, with an ambidextrous de-cocking lever mounted on both sides of the frame. There is also an ambidextrous magazine catch in the front edge of the butt.

Safety is achieved by a complicated firing pin arrangement: the firing pin normally rests at an angle, and the face of the hammer is recessed so that should it accidentally fall, the end of the firing pin enters the recess and there is thus no pressure on the pin and no danger of firing. When the trigger is pulled the rear end of the firing pin is moved upwards until it is lined up with the solid portion of the hammer face and is held there while the trigger releases the hammer and the hammer falls, striking the firing pin and firing the shot. As soon as the slide begins to move backwards after the shot, the trigger connection is broken and the firing pin drops back to its safe position, to remain there until the trigger is pressed once more. There is thus no way by which the firing pin can be driven forward except when the trigger is being correctly pulled with the intention of firing a shot.

The P-88 is normally supplied in 9mm Parabellum chambering; it can, though, be supplied in 9 × 21mm IMI chambering should this be required.

Walther PP Super Auto Pistol

Manufacturer Carl Walther Sportwaffenfabrik, Ulm, Germany
Type Blowback, double-action, semi-automatic
Caliber 9mm Police
Barrel 3.62in (92mm)
Weight (empty) 30oz (850gm)
Magazine Capacity 7 rounds

The Walther PP (Polizei Pistole) is well-known around the world and has been the source of inspiration for a number of copyists for many years; in spite of its age it still sets the standard for the rest and sells as fast as Walther can make it. It is an elegant design, reliable and accurate, and it pioneered a double-action lock which has rarely been surpassed for smoothness of operation. In the mid-1970s Walther decided to give it a face-lift and a new caliber in order to keep up with the changing demands of police authorities in Europe; though not exactly new, this pistol is so little-known outside Germany that we feel it is worth bringing into sharper focus.

The PP Super uses the same basic mechanism as the older PP but has an entirely new frame and slide assembly and is chambered for the 9mm Police (or 9mm × 18mm) cartridge, a round devised in Germany in order to obtain the maximum power from a blowback pistol, combined with good stopping power and a low risk of ricochet for use by police in urban areas. The frame is slightly longer, the slide longer and more 'squared-off' at its front end. The grips are carefully molded to a hand-filling shape and provided with a thumb-rest; wooden grips of similar contour can be had as an alternative. The trigger guard has been made slightly larger and with a vertical front edge to facilitate a two-handed grip of the pistol. The front sight blade has a night-aiming luminous spot in its rear face, while the rear sight is a square notch adjustable for windage and with a central luminous patch which can be aligned with the front spot in poor light.

The most significant change has been in the safety arrangements. In the old PP the safety catch on the slide dropped the hammer, locked the firing pin, and locked the trigger. With the pistol loaded, pressing the safety dropped the hammer and left everything locked; to fire, it was necessary to push the safety up and then pull the trigger to double-action the hammer to cock and drop. In the PP Super the safety locking function has been omitted; the safety catch is now only a decocking lever, and once the pistol is loaded this lever is pressed down; this rotates a block in front of a shoulder on the firing pin and releases the hammer. The firing pin is capable of vertical movement, and at this time is forced down in its housing by a spring, so that its end is aligned with a recess on the face of the hammer. Thus when the hammer falls, the face strikes the rear of the slide while the recess surrounds the firing pin but does not touch it. If the trigger is now pulled, the hammer begins to rise to the cocked position, while a linkage forces the firing pin upwards in its housing, against the spring. This lifts it clear of the safety block and lines the end of the pin up with the solid face of the hammer, so that when the hammer falls, the pin goes forward to fire the cartridge. It is thus unnecessary to move the safety catch when firing in a hurry. This arrangement may sound somewhat unsafe, but it should be remembered that this is a weapon intended for use by police and similar well-trained people, so that some degree of short-cutting is acceptable.

Right: The Walther PP Super.

Wichita Mark 40 Target Pistol

Manufacturer Wichita Arms, 333 Lulu, PO Box 11371, Wichita, KS 67211, U.S.A.
Type Bolt-action single shot target pistol
Caliber .308 Winchester (7.62mm NATO)
Barrel 13in (330mm)
Weight (empty) 4.5lbs (2.04kg)

This is a highly-specialized pistol known more specifically as a 'Silhouette Pistol' since it is primarily designed for the competitions organized under the rules of the International Handgun Metallic Silhouette Association. Briefly, these involve shooting high velocity ammunition against life-like animal silhouettes at long ranges; there is, though, no reason why this pistol should not make a good hunting weapon, fitted with suitable sights.

The Mark 40 pistol uses an aluminum receiver which has a steel insert for attachment of the barrel; within the receiver slides a breech bolt using three lugs to lock into the breech, giving an extremely secure lock. The bolt handle is on the left side of the pistol, and has a flattened and turned-down handle which can be operated by the shooter's left hand while he retains his hold on the pistol with his

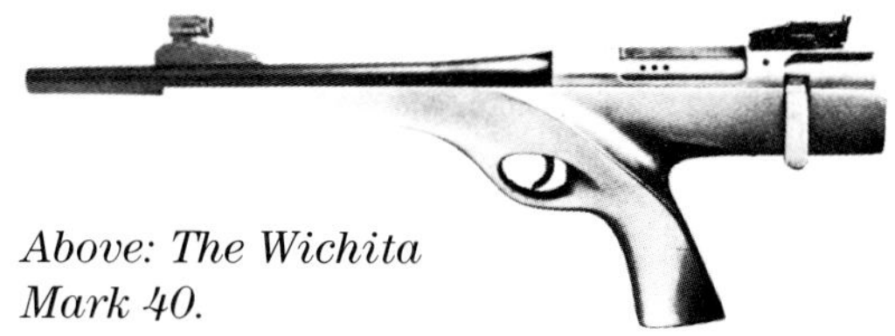

Above: The Wichita Mark 40.

right. There are three holes in the bolt which will allow a safe venting of gas should a primer be punctured.

The stock of the pistol is of glass fiber-reinforced plastic and is shaped into a comfortable pistol grip with a thumb rest. The trigger is fully adjustable for travel and weight of pull and is smooth in action with a crisp let-off point.

The sights consist of a tubular front with post insert and an open rear with arcuate notch; the two combine to form the 'Wichita Multi-Quick' system in which the front sight can be adjusted in elevation and the rear sight for both elevation and windage. The rear sight has a knurled adjusting knob which can be used to set pre-determined values once these have been established by zeroing and the sight settings recorded by tightening specified screws in the rear sight unit. The front sight can be used for making corrections on the day to compensate for minor meteorological and other changes.

In practical use the pistol is heavy, but necessarily so when one considers that this is firing a full-sized rifle cartridge. The sights are clear and the pistol is extremely accurate; indeed, some observers have said that it really needs a telescope sight to bring out its full potential, though this, of course, is going beyond what the designer set out to do. For its specified purpose the Mark 40 sets a very high standard and reaches it admirably. Like most target weapons it needs to be fired with various types of ammunition to decide which suits it (and the shooter) best, but with this question settled, two-inch groups at 100 yards are well within its capability. It can be obtained chambered for a specialized 'wildcat' cartridge, the 7mm IHMSA, a round developed for silhouette shooting and based on the .308 Winchester case.

RIFLES

AAI Advanced Combat Rifle

Manufacturer AAI Corporation, Baltimore, MD., U.S.A.
Type Gas-operated, semi-automatic and three-round bursts
Caliber 5.56mm special
Barrel 20.6in (525mm)
Weight 7.78lbs (3.53kg)
Magazine Capacity 30 rounds

The American search for an Advanced Combat Rifle (ACR) began in the early 1980s with the decision to seek a new rifle design for adoption in about 1995. Multi-million-dollar contracts were awarded to a number of companies to develop caseless rifles, and, later, further contracts to other companies to examine non-caseless solutions. The designers were given a free hand within broad limits of weight and size, the primary stipulation being that the rifle had to give 100 percent improvement in first round hit probability over the current M16A1 rifle.

Eventually, in 1989, four candidate weapons were tested, from Heckler & Koch of Germany, Colt and the AAI Corporation of the U.S.A., and Steyr-Mannlicher of Austria. Testing was prolonged and expensive, and at the end of it the U.S. Army decided that while all the candidate rifles showed merit, none provided the quantum leap in performance that was desired. The program was placed on hold in 1990, and that was that. However, the various designs are worth study, because they suggest the way that the next generation of rifles might go, as and when the armies of the world show sufficient interest.

The AAI rifle, compared to some of the others, looks quite conventional; but it actually fires fin-stabilized fléchettes, dart-like projectiles, at the high velocity of 4600 feet per second (1400 m/sec) and cannot fire conventional ammunition. The rifle is driven by a gas piston, and although full details of the breech mechanism have not been revealed, it is said to be derived from an earlier AAI design which, in its most efficient form, used a three-chambered breech unit which moved very quickly in and out of engagement with the barrel to allow very fast cycling of a three-round burst. There is no provision for full automatic fire.

A four-power optical sight is fitted, with iron sights as backup, and the muzzle carries a rather unusual compensator/muzzle brake which has been specially designed to work with fléchettes.

The barrel is rifled with a very slow twist – one turn in 85 inches – which gives the fléchette a degree of roll stabilization and helps accuracy. The fléchette idea is not new; several makers, including AAI, experimented with fléchettes as rifle projectiles in the 1960s, but at that time the materials and construction of the fléchette cartridge was not particularly good. By now new materials and improved technology has made the fléchette concept more acceptable, and the AAI rifle was considered a good design, although not sufficiently accurate for the purpose intended.

Anschutz Model 54 Silhouette Rifle

Manufacturer J. G. Anschutz GmbH, Ulm, West Germany
Type Bolt-action, single shot
Caliber .22 Long Rifle RF
Barrel 21.63in (550mm)
Weight 7.92lb (3.59kg)

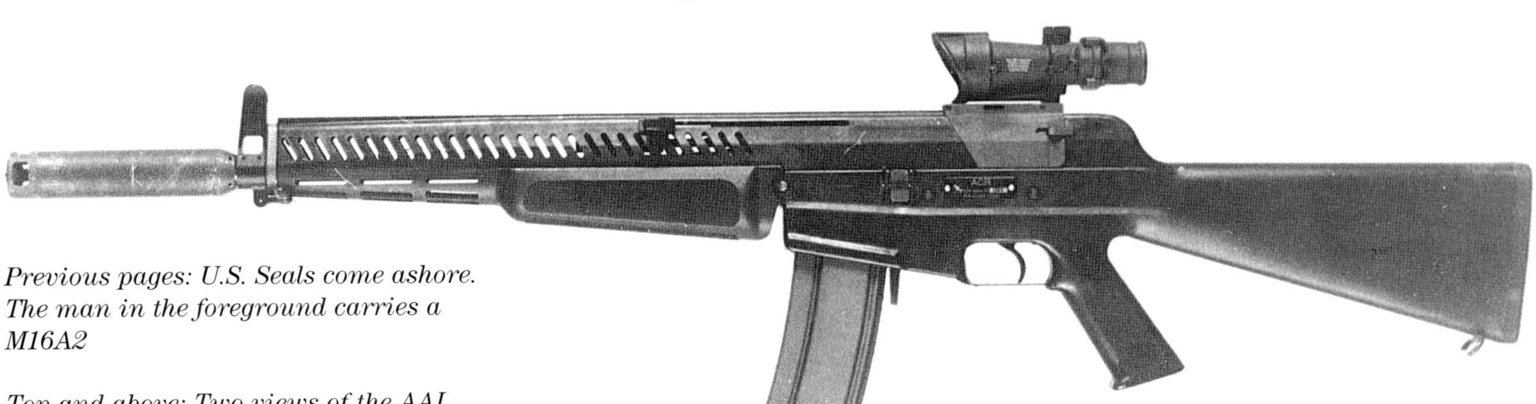

Previous pages: U.S. Seals come ashore. The man in the foreground carries a M16A2

Top and above: Two views of the AAI Advanced Combat Rifle.

The Anschutz Model 54 rimfire target rifle has been in production for some time, but this is a specially developed model intended to suit the growing sport of 'silhouette shooting' in which metal silhouettes of various animals are engaged at long range from the standing position, the idea being to approximate to hunting conditions. In smallbore silhouette shooting the targets are scaled down and the ranges are shorter than those used in full-bore contests, but the basic features remain the same.

The principal difference between this and 'prone' target rifles lies in the shape of the stock, which has a deep pistol grip and a high Monte Carlo comb so that the sights fall to the eye with minimum neck-twisting and the shooter can get a really firm grip on the rifle. The stock material is walnut, well finished and liberally stippled wherever the hand is likely to need to grip.

The bolt is substantial, and the trigger can be adjusted for first pressure and tension. The muzzle is counter-bored to protect the edges of the rifling, and no sights are provided. The receiver is grooved to accept telescope mounts, which are the standard means of sighting in this type of shooting and the reason for the high comb of the stock.

The barrel is almost an inch in external diameter and heavy, and as might be expected the accuracy of this rifle is beyond reproach. Fired from a rest at 50 yards it should give groups well under an inch in diameter with almost any brand of ammunition, and if care is taken to match ammunition to rifle, then successive shots will practically go through the same hole.

Barrett Light Fifty M82A1

Manufacturer Barrett Firearms Manufacturing Inc., Murfreesboro, Tennessee, U.S.A.
Type Recoil-operated, semi-automatic
Caliber .50in
Barrel 29in (737mm)
Weight 28.4lbs (12.9kg)

The Barrett rifle was one of the first successful designs in an entirely new field which appeared in the 1980s. Generally referred to as a 'long range sniping rifle', its purpose is not sniping at enemy personnel but at vulnerable high-technology equipment. The scenario envisaged for this type of weapon is a two or three-man infiltration party which can slip through enemy lines, set up on a hill perhaps a mile away from a forward radar station or a fighter airstrip or a communications center, and then, by a few well-aimed and powerful shots, wreck the equipment. The rifle can then be abandoned and the men make their escape; the loss of a few thousand dollars' worth of rifle is trifling against the destruction of half-a-dozen fighter aircraft or a vital air defense radar.

The Light Fifty is a semi-automatic rifle firing the .50in Browning heavy machine gun cartridge and is capable of making accurate hits on ranges up to 1800 yards, depending upon the type of target. The barrel and locked bolt recoil about 25mm in the frame on firing, which absorbs a good deal of the recoil force, making the rifle about as comfortable to fire as a normal big-game rifle. An accelerator arm un-

Above: The Anschutz Model 54 target rifle.

Left: The Barrett Light Fifty M82A1.

locks the bolt, though the recoil continues for another 20mm or so. The barrel then stops and the bolt continues rearwards to extract and eject the empty case. The barrel is returned to its forward position by a spring, after which another spring drives the bolt forward, stripping a fresh cartridge from the magazine and chambering it; finally, the bolt rotates and locks into the chamber.

The barrel is fitted with a high-efficiency muzzle brake, which reduces the recoil by some 65 percent, and an adjustable bipod is fitted. A 10x telescope sight is fitted as standard, and this has a special sighting reticle which is calibrated to the particular ammunition. The manufacturers recommend using the armor-piercing explosive/incendiary bullet for maximum target effect, but the rifle will fire any type of standard Browning ammunition.

The Barrett Light Fifty has been used by the U.S. Army, Navy and Marine Corps and it is also in use by several agencies as a device for dealing with explosive ordnance – terrorist bombs and unexploded bombs – which can be destroyed from a safe range by one shot.

Barrett Model 90

Manufacturer Barrett Firearms Manufacturing Inc., Murfreesboro, Tennessee, U.S.A.
Type Bolt-action repeating rifle
Caliber .50in
Barrel 29in (736mm)
Weight 22lbs (9.98kg)

The Model 90 is a simpler weapon than the Barrett Light Fifty, being a bolt-action magazine rifle. This change in mechanism has been accompanied by other modifications, resulting in a weapon which is shorter and lighter than the semi-automatic Light Fifty. It is in 'bullpup' form, with the action well back in the stock; the chamber is under the firer's cheek, so as to accommodate the maximum length of barrel within the minimum overall length. A very efficient muzzle brake is fitted, together with a special absorbent butt pad, reducing the felt recoil to a manageable level.

There are no iron sights on the Model 90, nor is any sight provided as standard, but the top of the receiver is dovetailed to accept most types of sighting telescope or night vision sight. In general terms, the Model 90 will do anything the Light Fifty will do, but is a more convenient load to carry for long distances.

Beretta 70/90

Manufacturer Pietro Beretta SpA, Gardone Val Trompia, Italy
Type Gas-operated, selective fire
Caliber 5.56mm (.223)
Barrel 17.7in (450mm)
Weight 8.4lbs (3.8kg)

The Beretta 70/90 system was developed to meet the Italian Army's requirements for a modern assault rifle, and was taken into service in 1990. The system consists of four weapons: the assault rifle AR70/90 for infantry, the carbine SC70/90 for Special Forces, the special carbine (short) SCS70/90 for mechanized troops, and the light machine gun AS70/90 for use as the infantry squad automatic weapon.

The AR70/90 is an improved version of an earlier 5.56mm design, the 70/223, and its design was influenced by experience with that weapon. Certain weaknesses in the earlier design were corrected, and a number of new features introduced. The method of operation is the usual modern system of a bolt carrier with a rotating bolt driven by a gas piston mounted in a cylinder above the barrel. As the gas follows the bullet up the barrel, a small amount is tapped off to drive the piston backwards. This pushes the bolt carrier, and a cam path in the carrier rotates the bolt to unlock it, after which carrier and bolt run back, extracting the empty case and ejecting it. A spring then drives the carrier and piston forward again, collecting a cartridge from the magazine and chambering it, and as the carrier comes to rest, so the cam rotates the bolt to lock it into the chamber. A hammer mechanism, controlled by the trigger is left cocked ready to fire.

The trigger mechanism has a selector lever which allows single shots, three-round bursts for a single pressure of the trigger, or sustained automatic fire. Optionally, fire can be restricted to single shots and three-round bursts.

The rifle feeds from a 30-round magazine, and the magazine housing is NATO-standard so that it will accept magazines from other NATO-standard rifles such as the M16 or the British L85.

A carrying handle is fitted above the receiver, clipped in place and holding a luminous source for illuminating the sights at night. The handle can be removed, leaving a dovetailed receiver cover which will accept most types of night vision or telescopic sight.

The carbine SC70/90 differs from the rifle only in having a folding butt, while the short carbine SCS70/90 also has a shorter barrel and is thus slightly lighter. The machine gun version AR70/90 has a heavier barrel, surrounded by a perforated handguard, fixing points for vehicle or tripod mounting, a bipod folded beneath the handguard and a different butt with a shoulder rest and facilities for gripping it more firmly. As with the rifle and carbines, it is possible to launch grenades from the muzzle of the machine gun.

Calico M-900S Carbine

Manufacturer Calico Inc., Bakersfield, CA, U.S.A.
Type Delayed blowback, semi-automatic
Caliber 9mm Parabellum
Barrel 16.1in (409mm)
Weight 7.06lbs (2.87kg), loaded, with 50-round magazine
Magazine Capacity: 50 or 100 rounds

The Calico carbine is part of a complete weapon system which contains pistols, sub-machine guns and carbines, all of which operate upon the same principles. They are unusual weapons, principally because of their magazine system, which allows a very large capacity magazine to fit into a compact space.

The company began by developing a helical-feed magazine for a .22 rifle in 1985. They then produced improved versions to accept 9mm parabellum cartridges, and from this went on to develop a number of different weapons in this caliber which have

Below: The Calico M-900S Carbine.

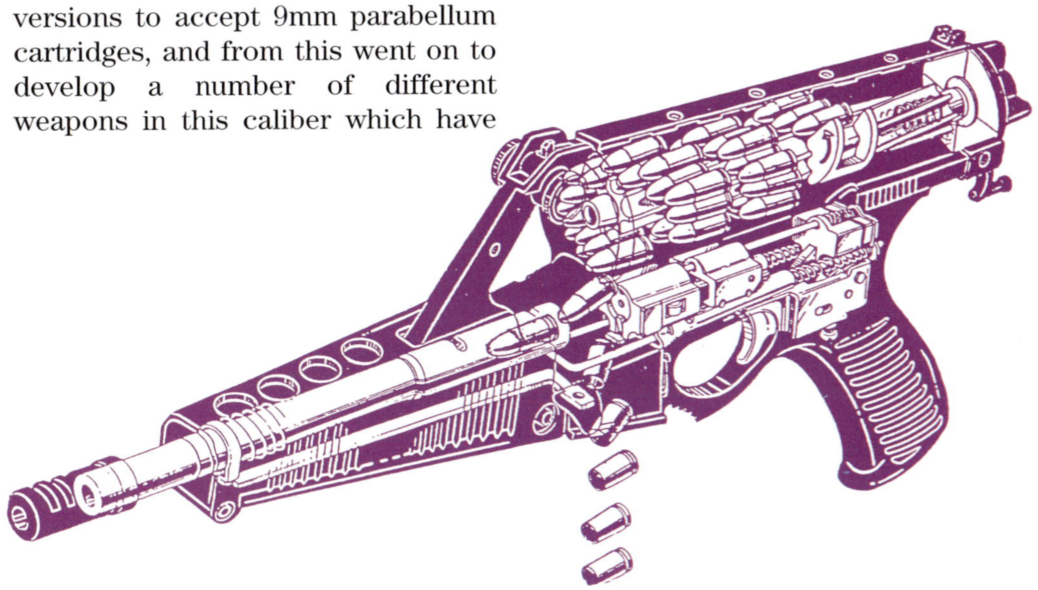

Left: The Beretta SCS70/90.

Left: The standard Beretta AR70/90.

Above: The Carl Custav AK5 assault rifle.

Above: The Calico M-900S Carbine.

been adopted by several military and security forces round the world.

The helical magazine is a plastic moulding only 57mm in diameter. Using a staggered helix principle, the rounds are driven forward along a fluted cartridge carrier as they press against the helical walls of the magazine. The driving pressure is provided by a torsion spring. The cartridges are fed one by one to a feed port, from where they are guided into the top-loading chamber of the weapon. Loading the magazine is easily done, and a 50-round magazine can be loaded in 22 seconds.

The receiver is of cast aluminum, with steel inserts in areas subject to wear. The breech is closed by a roller-locked bolt of similar design to that used in the Heckler & Koch and CETME assault rifles and submachine guns, which allows the weapon to fire from a closed bolt and delays bolt opening long enough for the bullet to leave the muzzle, and the chamber pressure to drop to a safe level. Ejection of the spent case is downward, in front of the trigger guard, and it is possible to fit a cloth 'brass catcher' to collect the fired cases.

In spite of the long barrel, the 178mm sight base is relatively short, the rear sight forms part of the magazine and the foresight is mounted on an elevated base at the front end of the magazine. The rear sight flips between a notch and an aperture, and the front sight is adjustable for elevation and windage.

The 100-round magazine fits in exactly the same place as the 50-round,but extends backwards over the stock; it also adds 1.69 lbs (0.77kg) to the weight of the loaded weapon.

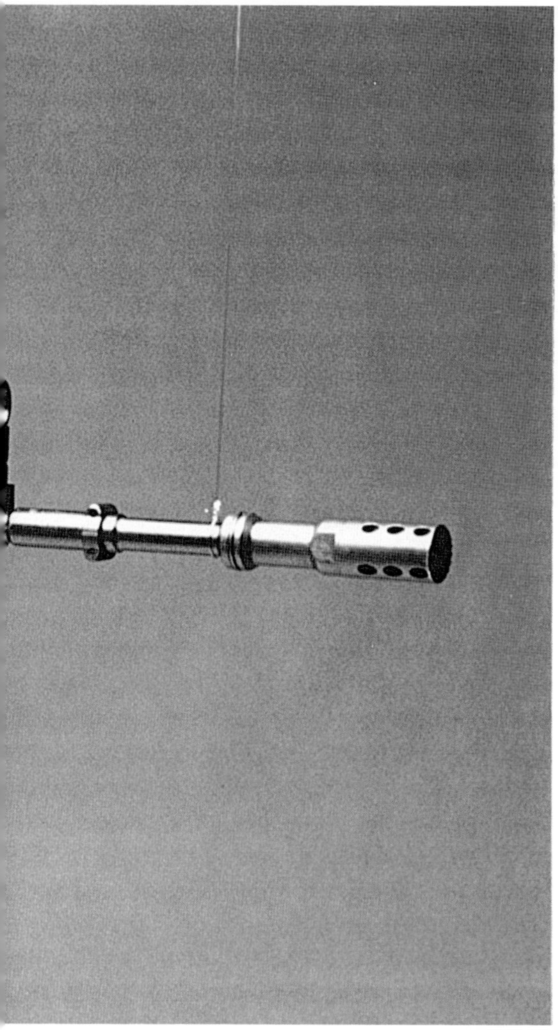

Carl Gustav AK5

Manufacturer Bofors Ordnance, Eskilstuna, Sweden
Type Gas-operated, selective fire
Caliber 5.56mm (.223)
Barrel 17.7in (450mm)
Weight 8.6lbs (3.90kg)
Magazine Capacity 30 rounds

The Carl Gustav AK5 assault rifle is a good example of how a stock weapon can be modified to suit the requirements of a particular purchaser, provided, of course, that he purchases enough of them.

In the mid-1970s the Swedish Army began looking for a new assault rifle to replace its existing 7.62mm weapons. All the available designs were studied, and the choice reduced to either the Israeli Galil or the Belgian FN-FNC. A quantity of each was bought and subjected to long technical and troop trials in 1979/80, and as a result of this the Galil was dropped and the FNC selected as being capable of further development to what the Swedes required. Their principal concern was to have a rifle which would withstand the severe northern climate; extreme cold places unusual stresses on a firearm, and handling weapons in cold conditions often demands modifications.

More trials took place, with changes being made to prototype FNC designs, until finally the Army was satisfied, and in 1985 the AK5 was finally approved for adoption.

The changes from the original FNC did not affect the basic mechanism; that remained the same gas-operated rotating bolt type. But the three-round burst mechanism was removed, leaving only the choice of single shots or automatic fire at 650 rounds per minute. The greatest changes were strengthening parts such as the butt, bolt, extractor, handguard, gas block, cocking handle, selector switch and sling swivels. The cocking handle and trigger guard were enlarged so that they could be operated easily by a man wearing heavy gloves, and the handguard was increased in size for the same reason.

The sights are a simple two-position flip with apertures for 250 and 400 meter ranges, and the front sight is hooded to reduce reflection. Optical and electro-optical sights can, of course, be fitted. The surface finish is for a gun of this type; the metal is first sand-blasted, then Parkerised, and finally has a coat of dark green enamel baked on.

CETME Model L Assault Rifle

Manufacturer Centro de Estudios Tecnicas de Materiales Especiale (CETME), Madrid 46, Spain
Type Delayed blowback, selective fire
Caliber 5.56mm (.223)
Barrel 15.75in (400mm)
Weight 7.49lbs (3.4kg)
Magazine Capacity 20 rounds
Cyclic rate of fire 750 rounds/minute

CETME is the Spanish government research and development establishment, and in the early 1950s a Herr Vorgrimmler went to work there. Vorgrimmler worked for Mauser during World War Two, particularly on their Sturmgewehr 45 project which was never completed, and he adapted the Mauser design to produce the first CETME rifle. Several countries showed interest in this, and eventually the Germans obtained a license; with some working over by Heckler & Koch it became the G3. Meanwhile CETME continued development and their 7.62mm 'Model C' was adopted by the Spanish Army. In conformity with the general move to smaller calibers they have now developed a 5.56mm rifle, the Model L, and this was evaluated by the Spanish Army and became their new service rifle.

As might have been inferred from the reference to the G3 above, the

Below: The CETME Model L assault rifle.

Above: The CETME L's structure is mainly plastic.

CETME relies upon the same divided bolt and roller locking system as the Heckler & Koch rifles. CETME have made one important addition, though, in the form of a spring-loaded locking lever in the bolt assembly which adds resistance to the initial opening movement of the bolt. No reason has been given for this, but it is likely that the increased unit pressure on the smaller base of the 5.56mm case led to too-fast initial opening and stretched or blown cases.

The structure of the rifle is largely plastic, with a sheet metal receiver. There is a selector on the left side which gives single shots, three-round burst fire or full automatic fire. The standard magazine is a 20-round model, but 10- and 30-round alternatives are available. The foresight is an adjustable post, between protective wings, and the rear sight is a rotating disc with a notch for 100m and apertures for 200, 300 and 400 meters. A mount base is incorporated and may be used for optical or electro-optical sights.

In addition to the standard rifle there is a short model which has a 12.6in (320mm) barrel and a telescoping metal butt.

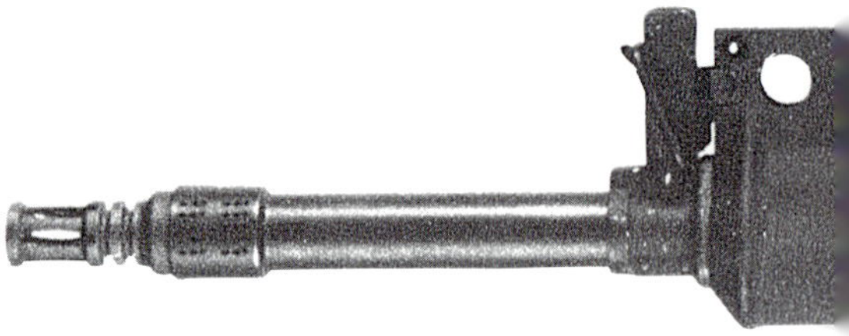

Colt Advanced Combat Rifle

Manufacturer Colt's Manufacturing Co. Inc., Hartford, CT, U.S.A.
Type Gas-operated, selective fire
Caliber 5.56mm (.223)
Barrel not known
Weight 7.28lbs (3.306kg)
Magazine Capacity 30 rounds

The Colt entrant for the Advanced Combat Rifle program was, quite simply, a progressive improvement upon their existing M16A2 service rifle, but designed to fire a new 'duplex' cartridge carrying two bullets instead of the usual one; it can also fire the standard 5.56mm cartridge, and this is recommended for long-range shooting. For ranges up to 325 meters the Duplex round gives a higher chance of a hit; the theory is that the leading bullet goes where it is aimed, but the second bullet has a slightly random dispersion about the point of aim which is intended to compensate for any human error. Or, in plain words, if you miss with the aimed shot, you might get lucky with the random one. This idea was tested in the 1960s, and Duplex ammunition was used in Vietnam with some success. As with fléchette ammunition, the past 30 years have seen some design improvements so that one can now expect better performance.

The Colt ACR is gas-operated and uses exactly the same rotating bolt system as the M16A2. The handguard, pistol grip and buttstock have all been redesigned to improve handling, and the handguard incorporates a top rib which allows instinctive shooting in a manner similar to handling a shotgun. The barrel is fitted with a very advanced muzzle brake/compensator which, together with a new oil-spring buffer in the receiver, reduces recoil to about 40 percent of that of a standard M16A2 rifle. The firing mechanism permits single shots and full automatic fire, but there is no three-round burst facility.

A 3.5-power optical sight is provided, and two-range flip iron sights are fitted. The U.S. Army tests showed that the Colt ACR improved upon the M16A2, but not sufficiently to make it worthwhile contemplating a complete change of equipment.

Colt M16A2 Assault Rifle

Manufacturer Colt's Manufacturing Co., Inc. Hartford, CT, U.S.A.
Type Gas-operated, selective fire
Caliber 5.56mm NATO
Barrel 20.07in (510mm)
Weight 7.5lbs (3.40kg)
Magazine Capacity 20 or 30 rounds
Rate of fire 700 to 900 rounds per minute

The M16A2 is the current service rifle of the U.S. Armed Forces and of some 55 other countries. It is the latest version of a weapon which has been the U.S. standard since 1967 and it has a well-earned combat reputation.

Like the original M16A1, the M16A2 is a gas-operated automatic rifle using a direct gas blast to drive back the bolt carrier; this causes the bolt to be rotated and unlocked, then drawn back to eject the spent case and cock the firing hammer, after which a spring returns the bolt, loading a fresh round and leaving the hammer cocked. The rifle is built in 'straight line' form, the butt lying on the axis of the barrel, so that there is little lever action to lift the muzzle onto the air on recoil, as happens with rifles having conventional sloped butts. This, together with the relatively low recoil energy of the 5.56mm cartridge means that the rifle does not deviate far from its point of aim and can be quickly brought back for a second shot. On automatic fire the muzzle climb is minimal, putting the maximum number of rounds into the target area.

The firing mechanism can provide single shots, automatic fire or three-round bursts, according to the user's requirement. The U.S. Army's M16A2s can fire single shots and automatic fire; the version adopted by the Canadian Army as their C7 rifle is adjusted to give single shots and three-round bursts, without the automatic facility. The rifle can be fitted with the M203 grenade launcher, and the muzzle is to NATO standard dimensions so that any NATO-approved rifle grenade may be fired.

Left: The Colt Advanced Combat Rifle.

Czech CZ58 Assault Rifle

Manufacturer Czeskoslovenska Zbrojovka, Uhersky Brod, Czechoslovakia
Type Gas-operated, selective fire
Caliber 7.62 × 39mm Soviet
Barrel 15.78in (401mm)
Weight 6.92lbs (3.14kg)
Magazine Capacity 30 rounds
Cyclic rate of fire 800 rounds/minute

Although there is a superficial resemblance to the Kalashnikov AK47, the CZ58 is a totally different weapon, designed and built in Czechoslovakia and owing nothing to Russian design. With low production costs in comparison with rifles of a similar specification, the CZ58 was standard issue for the Czech army for many years. In its original form it was even of a different caliber to the rest of the Warsaw Pact countries, but this was thought too much of a deviationist measure, and it was re-chambered to fire the standard Communist 7.62mm short cartridge.

The rifle is gas-operated, using a chrome-plated short-stroke piston; this strikes the bolt carrier a sharp blow, sufficient to send it backwards. After a short free travel the breech lock is freed from engagement with the receiver and the bolt is withdrawn from the chamber by the movement of the carrier. The locking of the breech is done by a hinged plate beneath the carrier which closely resembles the locking system used on the Walther P-38 automatic pistol. Firing is done by a hollow hammer tube which lies in the bolt and is propelled by a spring; when released by the sear, the hammer flies forward and strikes a floating firing pin. It is cocked by being caught by the sear during the recoil movement; indeed, if the firing pin was attached, the whole assembly would be called a striker.

The stock and fore end of the rifle are of wood-powder-reinforced plastic material, with a polished finish, and the metal work is blued or phosphated. The receiver is machined from the solid, and has a sheet steel cover. The rear sight is a tangent V-notch mounted on a steel block welded to the receiver and acting as a gas piston rod guide. The foresight is a post with protective ears, set well above the muzzle.

The CZ58 is light and robust, with a degree of internal finish which is sufficient for the job in hand, but without excessive frills. It is a highly satisfactory military rifle, and the folding-butt variation appears to be used in place of submachine guns in the Czech Army.

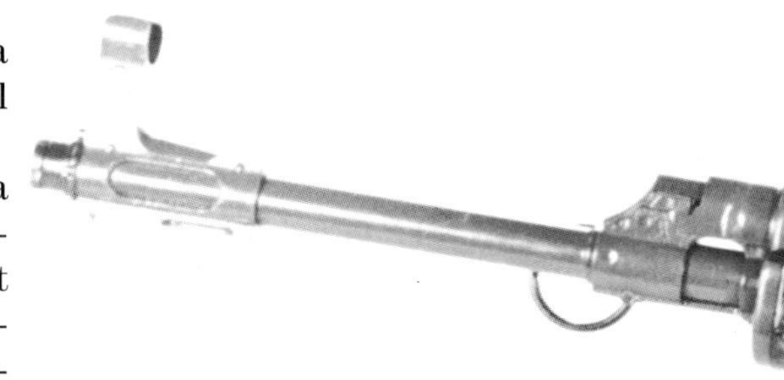

Above: The Daewoo 5.56mm K2 rifle.

Daewoo K2

Manufacturer Daewoo Precision Industries Ltd, Pusan, South Korea
Type Gas-operated, selective fire
Caliber 5.56mm (.223)
Barrel 18.3in (465mm)
Weight 7.18lbs (3.26kg)
Magazine Capacity 30 rounds

The Daewoo company gained experience in manufacturing rifles by making the U.S. M16 under license for the South Korean Army. Once the initial requirements had been met, the company set about developing their own design. After a series of prototypes and limited-production models, the K2 has become the standard South Korean Army rifle.
The mechanism is the usual gas piston driving a bolt carrier holding a rotating bolt. A selector lever permits firing single shots, three-round bursts or automatic fire. The receiver is made from two aluminum alloy forgings, and the plastic butt is hinged so as to fold round to the right of the receiver, making the weapon more compact for carrying inside a vehicle.

There are two unique features about this rifle. The three-round burst mechanism does not re-set itself when the trigger is released. When the trigger is pressed for a second time, the burst picks up from where the last one stopped. This could be a trifle off-putting if you expect three rounds and only get one. The sights are also unusual; the rear sight is a two-position flip unit, but instead of two apertures for two ranges it has one aperture for daylight shooting, and the other flip has a notch and two white spots for night firing. Range adjustment is performed by turning a cam beneath the sight mount, so lifting the entire unit; the maximum range setting is 600 metres.

The barrel is rifled with one turn of the rifling in nine inches; this allows good shooting from either the older U.S. M193 ammunition (which normally uses one turn in 12 inches) or from the newer NATO-standard SS109 ammunition (which normally uses one turn in seven inches).

Left: The Czech CZ58 assault rifle.

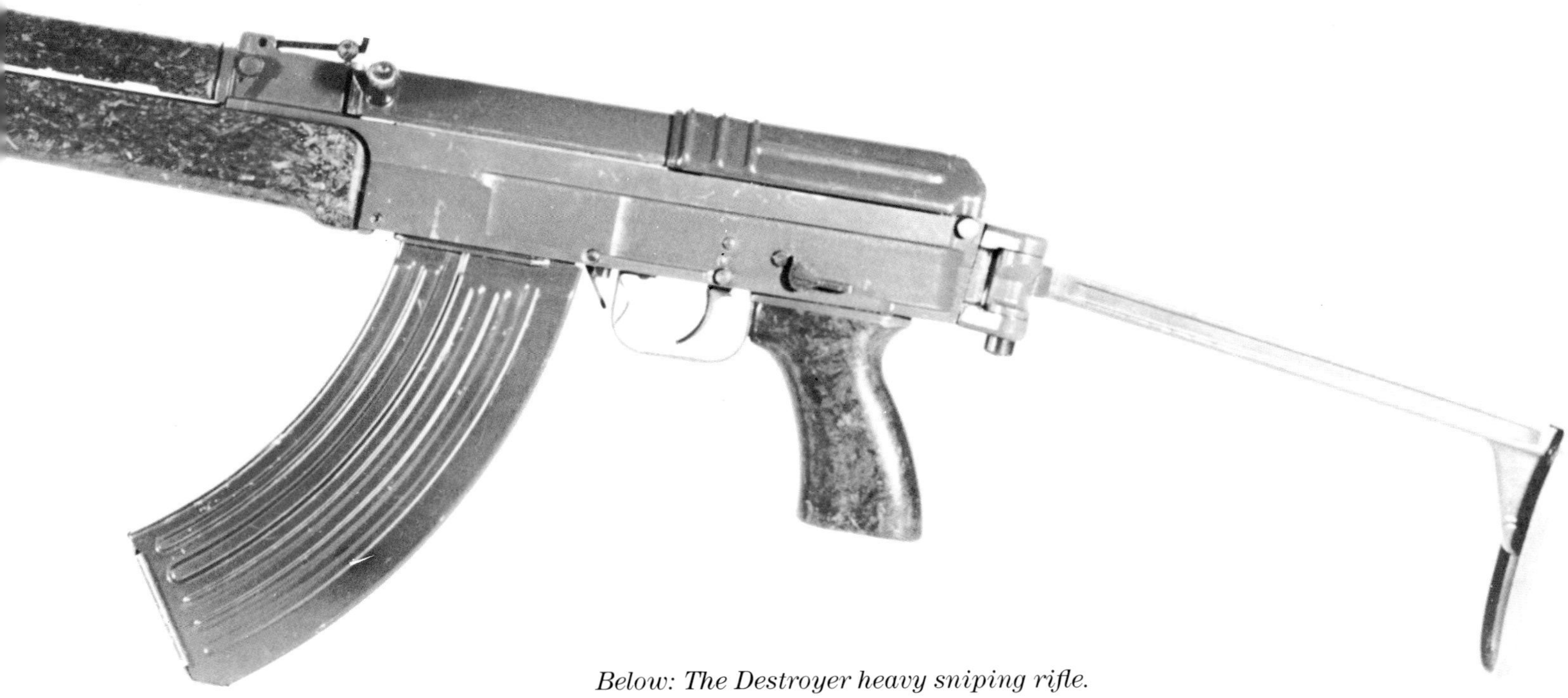

Below: The Destroyer heavy sniping rifle.

Destroyer Heavy Sniping Rifle

Manufacturer Istvan Fellegi, Miskolo, Hungary
Type Recoil-operated semi-authomatic
Caliber 0.57mm (14.5mm)
Barrel 53.15in (1358mm)
Weight 37.5lbs (17kg)
Magazine Capacity 5 rounds

When the .50 heavy sniping rifles began to appear in the U.S.A., one or two people wondered what sort of performance these might have if they were given a really potent cartridge. The same question arose in Hungary, and when Istvan Fellegi completed the development of the Destroyer rifle in 12.7mm caliber, he set about developing an improved model firing the powerful ex-Soviet 14.5mm cartridge.

This cartridge was devised during World War Two for an anti-tank rifle, and it was so effective that it remained in use against light German armor throughout the war, long after every other country had abandoned anti-tank rifles as being useless. The 994 grain (64.4 grams) bullet has a core of tungsten carbide, a muzzle velocity of 1000 meters per second, and is capable of penetrating 16mm of armor steel at 1000 meters range.

Such a cartridge will, of course, produce a tremendous recoil, and the Destroyer has been built to minimize this as much as possible. There is a large muzzle brake, and the entire receiver and barrel can recoil inside the supporting frame of the rifle, damped down by a hydraulic record buffer. The butt is heavily padded, and while the effect on the firer is a good deal more severe than any ordinary rifle, it is tolerable to a trained soldier.

The rifle is semi-automatic, reloading automatically after every shot. The barrel and receiver recoil within the support frame for a short distance, after which the unit comes to a stop and the bolt is then unlocked and free to move backwards due to the momentum of the recoil. It loads a heavy return spring, then goes forward again, collecting a cartridge from the magazine and loading it into the chamber. The bolt then locks and the entire unit then runs back to the firing position. The rifle is automatically cocked during the recoil stroke and the next shot can be fired as soon as the firer has taken aim once more.

Dragunov SVD

Manufacturer Soviet State Arsenal, Izhevsk, CIS
Type Gas-operated, semi-automatic
Caliber 7.62mm Russian M1891
Barrel 24.5in (622mm)
Weight 9.5lbs (4.3kg) with sight
Magazine Capacity 10 rounds

The Dragunov SVD rifle has been the standard Soviet Army sniping rifle since 1965, and it was also adopted by the other armies of the Warsaw Pact, as well as being copied by Chinese, Egyptian, Iraqi and Yugoslavian makers. The Soviets were the first to adopt a semi-automatic rifle for sniping purposes, at a time when all other armies considered that semi-automatics were not sufficiently accurate for this role.

The operation of the Dragunov is, in principle, the same as that of the Kalashnikov rifle, using a gas piston and rotating bolt. But there are two very significant differences. Firstly there is no provision for automatic fire, since this is unnecessary on a sniping rifle. And secondly, the gas piston action is different. The Kalashnikov, like most gas-operated military rifles, uses a long stroke piston which gives a great reserve of power for dealing with dirt and sticky cartridge cases, but which shifts the balance of the rifle as it moves. This is not conducive to accuracy, and so the Dragunov uses a short-stroke piston which only moves a fraction of an inch and gives the bolt carrier a sharp blow, imparting enough momentum to drive it back and initiate the reloading cycle. One is entitled to assume that a sniper will keep his rifle clean and lubricated and be fussy about his ammunition, so the reserve of power is not necessary.

The cartridge is virtually an antique – the rimmed 7.62mm full-power round introduced with the Mosin-Nagant bolt-action rifle in 1891 – but it is an accurate and powerful round, which is what counts in this role. As with all rimmed cartridges there is a danger of jamming if the rims override each other, but the magazine is carefully made with guide ribs to control the cartridges and jams are extremely rare. (One report says that the design of the magazine took more time than any other part of the rifle, an indication of the importance of reliable feed.)

The standard sight is the four-power PSO-1, a somewhat clumsy but robust design with adequate optics. It also incorporates a 'Metascope', a small electronic device capable of detecting infra-red light at night and thus warning the sniper of being under observation. Unfortunately modern infra-red sights do not need IR illumination, and thus this device is no longer of much use.

With the recent change in the political climate, it can be expected that numbers of Dragunov rifles, not necessarily of Russian manufacture, will appear on the commercial market around the world.

Below: The Dragunov SVD rifle.

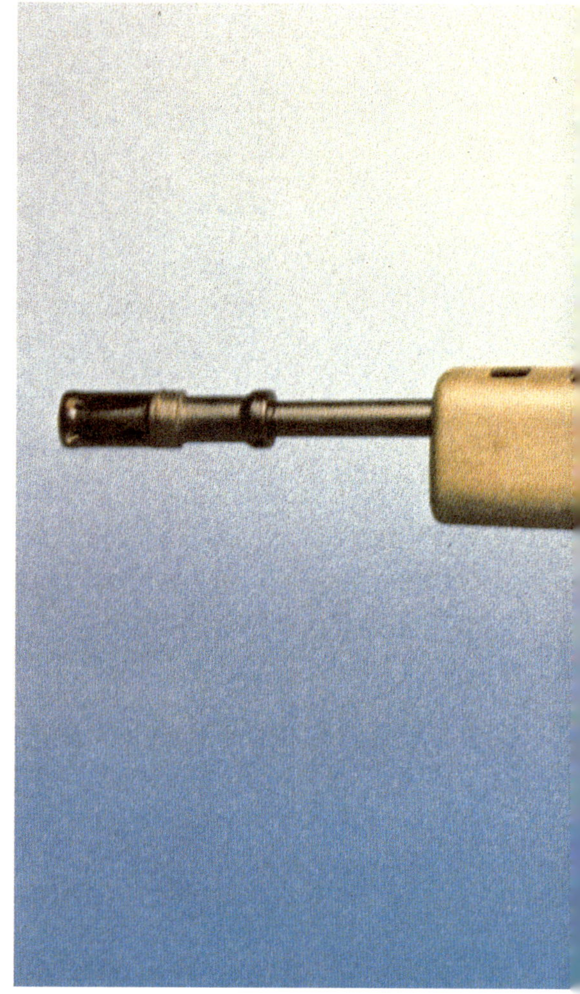

Enfield L85A1 Individual Weapon

Manufacturer Royal Small Arms Factory, Nottingham, England
Type Gas-operated, selective fire
Caliber 5.56mm (.223)
Barrel 20.4in (518mm)
Weight 8.20lbs (3.72kg)
Magazine Capacity 20 rounds
Cyclic rate of fire 800 rounds/minute

The British Army began looking for an automatic rifle in about 1910, but the research program was interrupted several times and it was not until 1950 that a design was finally approved. Just as it was about to go into production, though, the politicians got into the act and the design was dropped in favour of the Belgian FN-FAL and the 7.62mm NATO cartridge. When this rifle began to be outdated, Enfield began designing once more, this time with a new cartridge of 4.85mm caliber, ready for the 1978 NATO small arms trials. Their 1950 model,

Above and below: The Enfield SA-80 Individual Weapon.

Left and below: The Light Support Weapon variant of the SA-80, L73.

Right: A stripped down view of the SA-80.

the EM1, had been dropped because it could not be reworked into 7.62mm caliber (from 2.80) when the need arose, so the designers of the new rifle were wise enough to build it so that it could be recalibered if necessary. When the NATO trial decided on 5.56mm as the next standard caliber their foresight paid off; the Enfield design was rejigged to 5.56mm and has now been approved for service. It is believed that a number of pre-production models were evaluated in combat during the 1982 Falkland Islands campaign. The rifle was adopted for use by the British Army in the mid-1980s.

The Enfield 'Individual Weapon' is a conventional gas-piston-operated design, using a rotating bolt in a carrier which rides on two guide rods. It is of 'bullpup' layout, the magazine being well behind the trigger and the action lying under the firer's cheek. The receiver is a pressed-steel component which requires little machining since the guide rods control the bolt's movement. The furniture is of sturdy plastic, and the gas system has a three-position regulator giving normal use, extra power for fouled actions, and in closed position for grenade launching.

The standard sight is the 'SUIT' or

'Sight Unit, Infantry, Trilux,' a short optical telescope containing an illuminating source for shooting in bad light. This is a sealed unit and adjustments for elevation and windage are carried out on its supporting bracket. On top of the SUIT unit there are emergency iron sights; there are no sights on the body of the rifle, though a foresight blade and a two-aperture backsight can be fitted if desired.

The Enfield rifle is extremely easy to shoot, popular with soldiers and very accurate; in spite of its compactness, the bullpup layout ensures a good barrel length, and the latest models will be rifled to suit the new SS109 NATO standard 5.56mm bullet. There is also a heavy-barrelled version with a bipod which is intended as the squad automatic weapon; this rejoices in the name 'L86 Light Support Weapon'.

Erma EM1 and EGM1 Carbines

Manufacturer Ermawerke GmbH, Dachau, D-8080 Germany
Type Blowback, semi-automatic
Caliber .22 Long Rifle RF
Barrel 18in (457mm)
Weight 5.5lbs (2.49kg)
Magazine Capacity 10 rounds

The U.S. Army's M1 Carbine of World War Two had a mysterious charisma which made people lust after it, even though it was a pretty dismal combat weapon at anything over 50 yards range. As a result there have been numerous lookalikes over the years, and the German Erma company, renowned for military weapons in days gone by, have now produced a pair of

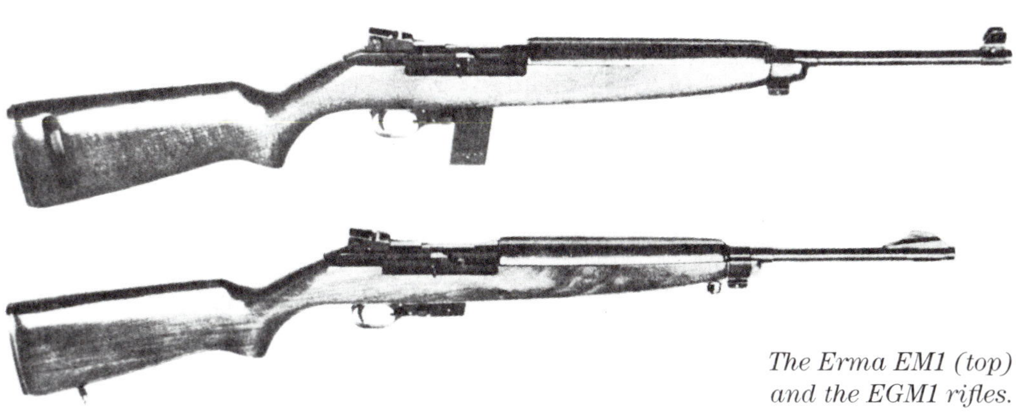

The Erma EM1 (top) and the EGM1 rifles.

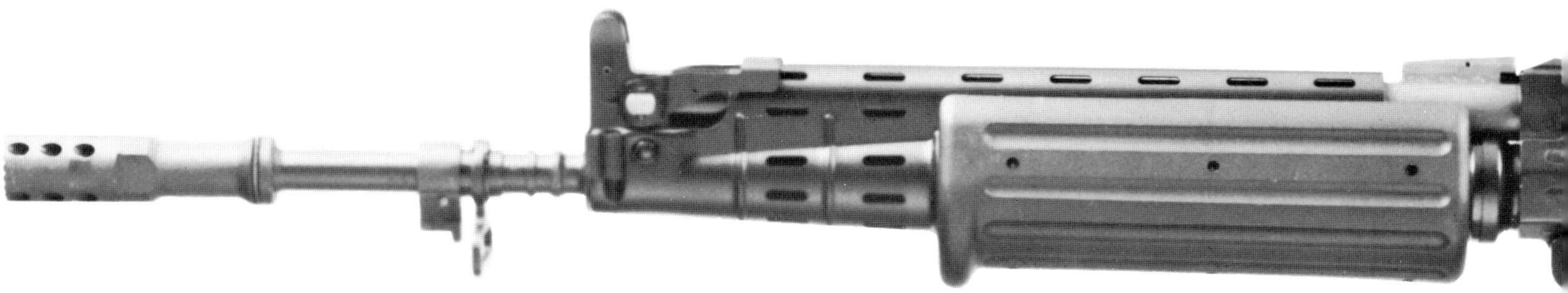

.22 rimfire carbines which look almost like carbon copies of the 'real thing'.

There are two models which are mechanically identical; the EM1 is the 'standard' and is almost indistinguishable from an M1; the EGM1 is the 'de luxe' version fitted with a sporterized walnut stock. The receiver is of alloy, blackened to match the finish of the steel barrel, and the cocking handle operating rod vanishes forward into the woodwork just as did that of the M1, but has nothing on the forward end except the return spring and its guide rod; the bolt is a straightforward blowback action. Since there is thus no need to revolve the bolt, the connection between cocking handle and bolt is not so complex as that of the M1. Firing is performed by a spring-driven firing pin which has a bent protruding below the bolt to be caught by the sear on the reloading stroke.

The carbines are equipped with replicas of the original sights; a front blade between protective ears, and a rear aperture 'battle' sight. They are efficient within their capabilities, and on the range the carbine showed itself to be capable of sufficient accuracy for its purpose in life, which is eminently that of a 'fun gun' for casual plinking or vermin shooting at moderate ranges. It is light, handy, reliable if cleaned regularly of the grease and fouling which 'shooting' .22 ammunition generates, and good value for money.

Erma EG73 Carbine

Manufacturer Ermawerke GmbH, D-8080 Dachau, Germany
Type Lever-action, rimfire, magazine
Caliber .22 Winchester Magnum RF
Barrel 19.5in (495mm)
Weight 5.5lbs (2.49kg)
Magazine Capacity 12 rounds

Although the experts are fond of telling us that lever-action carbines are inherently inaccurate, up until now nobody has told the carbines anything of the sort and they still go on shooting straight. There is no doubt that there is a great visual appeal in the classic saddle-gun lines of straight stock and short fore-end, with the barrel and tubular magazine in front, and as long as this appeal remains, gunmakers are going to produce them and sell them.

The Ermawerke of Germany have had considerable experience in weapon design and construction, and one of their latest offerings is this Magnum carbine. Its lines follow the classic Winchester, though the action is entirely their own, with a solid-topped receiver. The bolt is unlocked and retracted by full 90° swing of the under-lever, and in doing so it cocks the external hammer and lifts a fresh cartridge from the magazine. Pulling the lever back chambers the round and locks the bolt, ready to fire. The action is exceptionally smooth, being made to fine tolerances and well fitted, and the quietness will be appreciated by hunters.

The magazine is of steel, unlikely to be accidentally dented, and holds 12 cartridges, after which a 13th can be loaded into the breech. The foresight is a post concealed in a hood, while the rear sight is a notch on a step-adjustable leaf. There is no windage adjustment as such, though the sight can be moved sideways in its mounting for zeroing. The only safety device is the usual half-cock notch on the hammer.

The stock is of walnut and well finished, the steel of the barrel, magazine and action, is blued and polished, and the whole weapon makes an attractive and functional package.

Fabrique Nationale FNC Rifle

Manufacturer Fabrique Nationale d'Armes de Guerre, Herstal, Belgium
Type Gas-operated, selective fire
Caliber 5.56mm (.223)
Barrel 17.7in (450mm)
Weight 8.37lbs (3.80kg)
Magazine Capacity 30 rounds
Cyclic rate of fire 650 rounds/minute

Some years ago the FN company developed a 5.56mm rifle which they called the 'CAL' (Carabine Automatique Legère), anticipating that 5.56mm would become popular as a

Above: The Erma EG73 carbine.

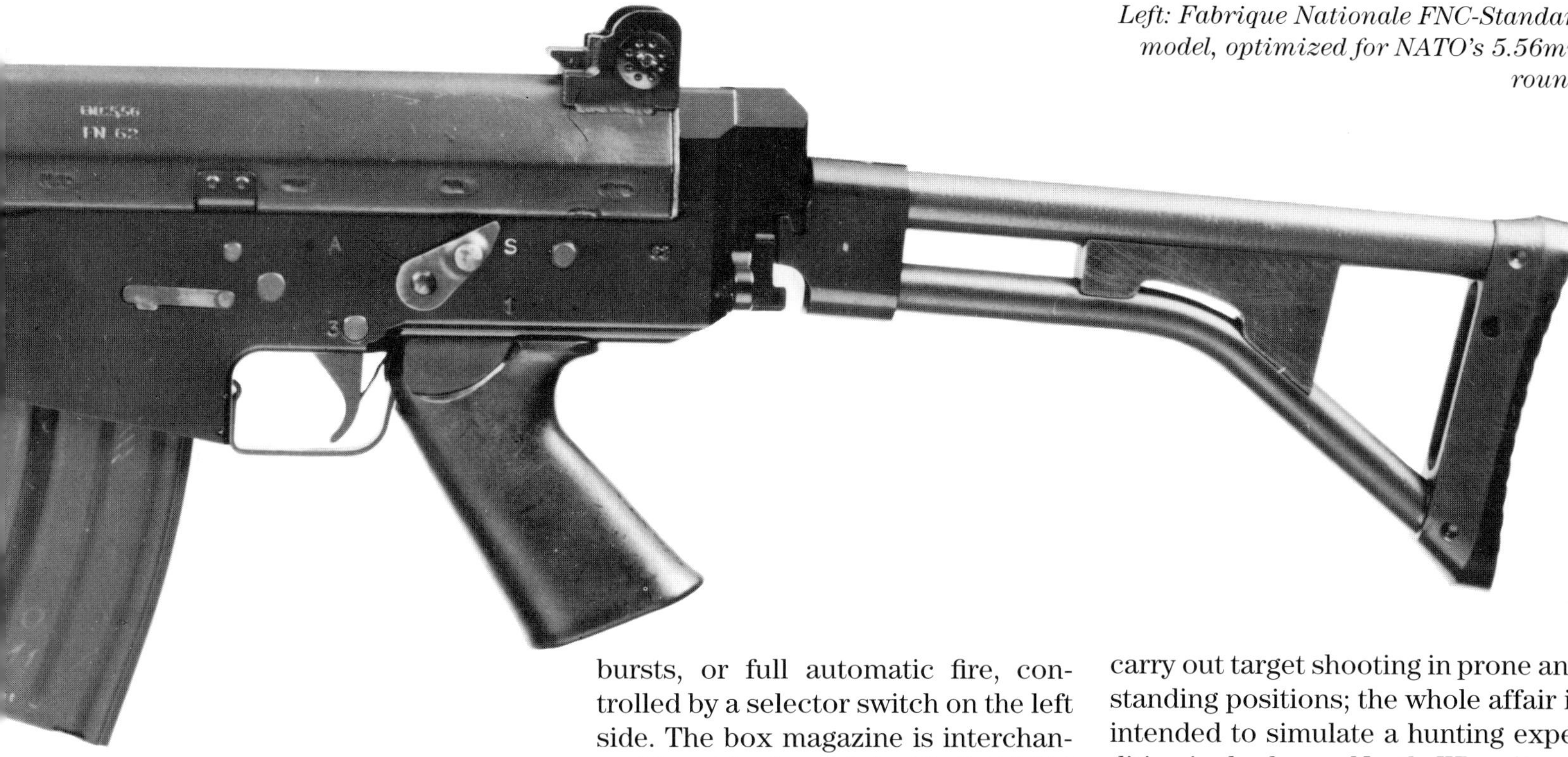

Left: Fabrique Nationale FNC-Standard model, optimized for NATO's 5.56mm round.

military caliber; they were right, but it took longer than they thought and the CAL was rather in advance of its time. Several armies bought small quantities for evaluation, and their reports, together with FN's own expertise, suggested that it should be possible to develop a cheaper and better design; this FN did, the result being the FNC. It has undergone extensive military trials in Sweden and in some NATO armies, and the Indonesian Army has adopted it for service.

The FNC makes extensive use of pressed steel and plastic components; it follows the general pattern of FN automatic rifles and the body opens on a front hinge pin to allow the working parts to be withdrawn to the rear. Operation is by gas tapped from the barrel and fed to a conventional gas cylinder above the barrel. The gas piston is driven back to strike a bolt carrier which contains the usual type of two-lug rotating bolt. The bolt and carrier are among the few components in the FNC which demand precision machining. The gas cylinder has a two-port regulator which can be switched from the normal position to admit more gas when operating under adverse conditions.

The trigger mechanism allows selection of single shots, three-round bursts, or full automatic fire, controlled by a selector switch on the left side. The box magazine is interchangeable with that of the U. S. M16A1 rifle, and both can be folded alongside the receiver either for transport or to make the weapon more compact for use in the submachine gun role.

The barrel is rifled one turn in 32 calibers, much tighter than previous 5.56mm weapons, and is optimized for use with the Belgian SS109 bullet, which has been selected as NATO standard. With this ammunition the three-round burst will deliver shots dispersed by 70cm at 500m range, and will penetrate the standard U.S. Army steel helmet at over 1000 yards. The standard sights consist of a front post and a flip aperture rear sight set for 250m and 400m, but the rifle can accept all types of telescope, image intensifying and thermal imaging sights for sniping or night use.

Finnbiathlon .22

Manufacturer Tampereen Asepaja Oy, SF-33100, Tampere 10, Finland
Type Bolt-action, magazine, rimfire
Caliber .22 Long Rifle RF
Barrel 22.8in (580mm)
Weight 9.25lbs (4.2kg)
Magazine Capacity 5 rounds

The Biathlon event is an Olympic contest which involves skiing across country and stopping four times to carry out target shooting in prone and standing positions; the whole affair is intended to simulate a hunting expedition in the frozen North. When it was first invented, by the Scandinavians many years ago, it probably did; the contestants used military rifles and fired at realistically varying ranges. Since it has been absorbed into the artificial world of Olympic sports, however, the rifle has become a .22 rimfire and the range is fixed at 50 yards. Needless to say, as soon as it became an organized sport, the sportsmen began looking for an edge and a highly specialized design of rifle has resulted.

The Finnbiathlon is a good example of this rare class, and it exhibits some unusual features. Its angular appearance makes it obvious that it is a target rifle, but the unusual collection of straps mark it out as something out of the ordinary. These are the carrying slings which allow it to be slung from both shoulders and worn in the middle of the back; pointing up, so as to be out of the way when skiing; the sling ends in cords which can be passed through any pair of eight holes in the butt, so adjusting the height of the carry.

The bolt action is also unusual, being a straight pull type; these are exceptionally rare in modern weapons. The T-shaped handle is simply pulled straight back and pushed forward again, a sleeve with cam track taking

Left: Galil sniper's rifle.

care of rotating the bolt. This leads to a very fast action and one which gives minimal aim disturbance when performed at the shoulder, both desirable features in the Biathlon where time is at a premium. Another unusual item is a 'snow guard' around the muzzle, which prevents the sights or barrel becoming blocked with snow during traveling or even when diving for the ground for the prone shoots. When the muzzle is closed off, so are the sights, so there is no danger of accidentally loosing off a round.

The trigger is adjustable for tension and position, and is a two-pressure military type. The rear sight is an aperture type, fully adjustable for elevation and windage, while the front sight is a hooded aperture. Weights can be fitted inside the fore end in order to achieve the desired balance, the maximum additions taking the overall weight of the rifle up to 11lbs. As a final touch, the fore end has four slots in its right side into which four loaded magazines can be fitted, their bases out, so that they can be rapidly reached and changed during the progress of the event.

The center ring of the Biathlon target is 40mm in diameter (1.56in) and the rifle is quite capable of putting a string of shots into this at 50 meters. Its accuracy is first class, giving half- to three-quarter-inch groups at that range when fired from a rest. But of course, shooting a string of five from the standing position after traveling across miles of snow isn't exactly shooting from a rest.

Galil Assault Rifle

Manufacturer Israeli Military Industries, Tel Aviv, Israel
Type Gas-operated, selective fire
Caliber 5.56mm (.223)
Barrel 20.6in (524mm)
Weight 8.8lbs (4.0kg)
Magazine Capacity 35 rounds
Cyclic rate of fire 650 rounds/minute

The Israeli Army decided to adopt the 5.56mm cartridge after the Six-Day War of 1967, and in the following two years every 5.56mm rifle in existence was bought and tested. In view of their location, much emphasis was placed on reliability under hot dusty conditions. Of the various models tested, the Galil, designed by Israel Galil and Yaacov Lior, most closely met the requirements and development went ahead; it was approved for adoption in 1972 but it was some time before it actually got into service and it is not, even now, a universal issue throughout the Israeli armed forces. It has been exported to some other countries, however.

The Galil has been designed to fill the place of three weapons – the rifle, the sub-machine gun and the squad automatic or light machine gun. It can also fire a variety of grenades, and a short-barreled version has been developed for use by Special Forces.

Mechanically, the Galil leans heavily on the Kalashnikov; it uses a similar method of gas operation, with a cylinder above the barrel, and a similar gas piston-cum-bolt carrier assembly. The bolt has two locking lugs and a cam pin which follows a track in the carrier which drives it to rotate for locking and unlocking. The cocking lever is attached to the bolt carrier so that it can be used for positive bolt closure in the event of fouling, and the change lever for single shot or automatic fire is on the right; when moved to the 'safe' position it closes up the cocking handle slot against dust and also restricts the movement of the handle and bolt. The trigger and firing mechanism use a hammer and are very reminiscent of the Garand design.

The Galil may be found with a wood or plastic stock and handguard (Model ARM), or with a folding metal stock and plastic handguard (Model AR); the ARM is fitted with bipod and carrying handle for use as the squad automatic. There is also the Model SAR which resembles the AR but has a shorter (13in – 332mm) barrel.

The foresight is a post, adjustable for elevation for zeroing and concealed within a ring shroud, and a flip-over rear sight set for 300m and 500m ranges. Both sights have auxiliary night sights folded down behind them; when raised, these exhibit three white or pale green spots of light, generated by 'Betalight' radiological sources. To sight the weapon the three dots are lined up horizontally and the centre one alined with the target. The barrel has a flash hider which doubles as a grenade launching spigot, and the bipod joint incorporates a wire-cutter.

In service the Galil appears to have lived up to its expectations; it is simple, robust and accurate and it can withstand desert conditions probably better than any other comparable rifle.

Gepard Heavy Sniping Rifle

Manufacturer Istvan Fellegi, Miskolo, Hungary
Type Bolt-action, single shot
Caliber 0.50in (12.7mm)
Barrel 43.3in (1100mm)
Weight 35.2lbs (16kg)

Right: The Advanced Combat Rifle version of Heckler & Koch's G-11.

Bottom: The Gepard Heavy Sniping Rifle.

The Hungarian Gepard rifle is a rather peculiar design which first appeared in the West in 1990. It is a single-shot weapon, without a magazine, so that firing each round is a slow business. The pistol grip actually acts as the handle of the breech bolt and contains a very simple hammer and firing pin mechanism. To load, the pistol grip is twisted sideways to unlock the lugs on the bolt from meting recesses in the barrel, and the grip and bolt are then removed completely from the weapon. The cartridge is then inserted into the exposed chamber and the grip and bolt are replaced and twisted back so as to lock the breech securely. The hammer is cocked and then the trigger is pressed to fire the round.

The cartridge is the ex-Soviet 12.7mm machine gun round, roughly equivalent to the U.S. .50 Browning machine gun cartridge. It delivers a heavy bullet, and, as a result, generates a heavy recoil in the gun. The Gepard's barrel is fitted with a high-efficiency muzzle brake, which helps to reduce the recoil to manageable proportions. There is also a resilient butt pad and cheek piece to avoid injury to the firer. The rifle is usually supported on a simple adjustable bipod, but standard Warsaw Pact machine gun tripods can also be used.

The cartridge is sufficiently accurate to give a 300mm (12 inch) group with five shots at 600 meters range. The bullet is capable of penetrating 30mm of rolled steel armor plate at 100 meters, dropping to 15mm at 600 meters. The effective range is claimed to be up to 2000 meters against vehicles and similar large targets, 1200 meters against personnel.

Heckler & Koch G-11

Manufacturer Heckler & Koch GmbH, Oberndorf Am Neckar, Germany
Type Gas-operated, selective fire
Caliber 4.73mm
Barrel 21.25in (540mm)
Weight 8lbs (3.65kg)
Magazine Capacity 45 rounds

This is probably the most revolutionary weapon to appear anywhere in the past 40 years or more, involving a totally new type of mechanism and a caseless cartridge. It was planned to be adopted by the West German Army in 1990, but events overtook it, and the G-11 and the company who developed it were among the first victims of the 'peace dividend'.

The design began in the late 1960s when the West German Army, looking ahead, asked for new rifle designs. They laid down few conditions except that it had to be able to fire a three-round burst with dispersion of not more than two mils between each bullet impact. This meant that at 500 metres the extreme spread between the three shots had to be under one metre – and we are talking abut a three-round burst, not three individual aimed shots. Heckler & Koch soon realized that this meant a rate of fire in excess of 2000 rounds a minute in order to get three rounds off before the barrel moved from the point of aim, and this, in turn, meant devising a totally new mechanical solution.

Their first move was to develop a caseless cartridge, in association with Dynamit Nobel. This has two advantages: it is lighter than a conventional brass-cased round, so the soldier can carry more of them; and the rifle mechanism no longer has to cater for the extraction and ejection of the spent case. This development took time; the first design was a block of nitro-cellulose propellant and plastic binder, with a bullet in the front and a combustible cap in the rear. It worked, but overheated the rifle, leading to cook-off problems in which a round loaded into a hot chamber suffered spontaneous combustion from the induced heat. The problem was eventually overcome by the development of a new 'High Ignition Temperature Propellant' which requires a temperature some 100 degrees C higher than nitro-cellulose before it cooks off.

The mechanism in the rifle is complex, but can be summed up by saying that it is a rotating breechblock with a chamber bored in it. This revolves in line with the barrel. By operating an external knob the chamber is turned vertically, and a cartridge is fed in from the magazine, which lies above the barrel. Another turn of the knob and the block is rotated so that the chamber lies behind the barrel. Pressing the trigger allows a firing pin to strike the cap; cap and propellant are entirely consumed and the bullet is driven out of the barrel. Gas is tapped from the barrel and the power used to rotate the breechblock, collect a fresh round and rotate it again ready for the next shot. To unload, the knob is turned backwards and the cartridge drops out through a hole in the bottom of the rifle.

As might be imagined, the greatest problem to be overcome in this design is sealing the breech so that all the gas drives the bullet out and does not escape between the chamber and the barrel; the precise details are secret, but they appear to be very similar to the sealing of a Wankel automobile engine.

The mechanism, together with the barrel, is completely concealed within an all-enveloping plastic casing. This is formed into a butt, into a pistol grip and into a carrying handle which also contains a low-power optical sight with illuminated reticle for night firing. When a shot is fired the entire mechanism recoils about an inch inside this casing, being damped by buffer springs. As a result the recoil is felt more as a gentle push than as a violent blow.

If the selector switch is turned to the three-round burst position, the sequence of events for the first shot is the same as for a single shot. But as the first shot is fired and the mechanism begins to move backwards in recoil, control is assumed by an automatic device which now operates the bolt to load and fire a second shot while the system is still moving backwards. The second shot adds to the rearward momentum, and the third shot is chambered and fired. Only then does the system complete the recoil stroke and return to the forward position. In this case the recoil is about 2.5 inches, but the blow to the firer's shoulder is still not excessive. The noise of the three shots merges into one rasping report and the three bullets have left the barrel before the firer feels any recoil and before the barrel has started to move off the aim.

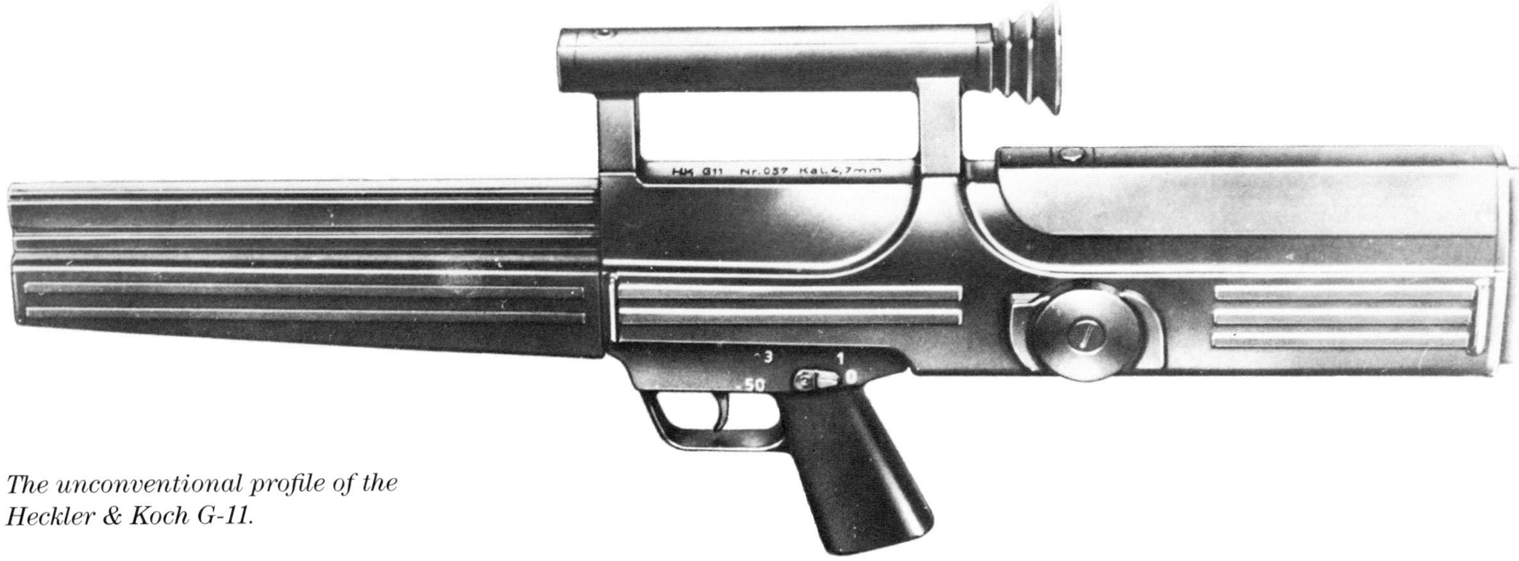

The unconventional profile of the Heckler & Koch G-11.

Left: The Heckler & Koch HK81 rifle.

In this way the demand for burst accuracy has been met.

At automatic fire the high-speed mechanism is out of action and the rifle merely repeats the single shot movement at a rate of about 600 rounds per minute. Here the individual recoils can be felt, but the internal buffering keeps most of the shots in the target area.

A slightly modified version of the G-11 was put forward as a candidate for the U.S. Army's Advanced Combat Rifle project. It performed well, but, as with all the other contestants, failed to provide the demanded 100 percent improvement over the M16A2. At much the same time as this trial was under way the re-unification of Germany took place, and the German government was faced with the problem of finding money to fund the economic recovery of the eastern provinces. As usual, the defense budget was the first target, and the contract for the G-11 was canceled. Instead of equipping the German Army with the new rifle, only about 1000 were purchased for use by Special Forces. Heckler & Koch had been relying upon this promised contract to recoup their enormous developmental expenses, and when the contract failed, so did the company. They were eventually bought by Royal Ordnance of Britain, and the G-11 rifle production was canceled. Whether this revolutionary weapon will ever see general issue is an open question; at the present time, it appears unlikely.

Heckler & Koch HK81 Rifle

Manufacturer Heckler & Koch GmbH, Oberndorf Am Neckar, Germany
Type Delayed blowback, selective fire
Caliber 7.62mm NATO
Barrel 17.7in (450mm)
Weight 19.05lbs (8.65kg) (with bipod and telescope sight)
Magazine Capacity 5, 20 or 30 rounds
Cyclic rate of fire 800 rounds/minute

European police forces now regularly confront armed criminals, so it is not surprising that the public's attitudes towards armed police are gradually changing.

The HK81 rifle is an interesting example of how gunmakers are tailoring their products to suit the special requirements of police forces, and it is also a lesson in how to acquire firepower without upsetting the populace at large.

On the face of it the HK81 is little more than the basic G3 military rifle with a few small changes. It uses the same two-part, roller-locked bolt which every H&K weapon shares, but the barrel is somewhat heavier than the military standard and is carefully fitted so that the rifle is capable of extremely high accuracy. There is also a light but strong bipod attached to the fore-end so that the rifle can be rested during long periods of surveillance. While iron sights (front hooded post and rear aperture) are fitted, the rifle is always supplied with a variable-power telescope sight. The trigger mechanism can be either a standard military two-stage trigger or an adjustable set trigger for increased accuracy. So the basic weapon is a robust and highly accurate sniping or general-purpose rifle.

Above the trigger, however, there is a change lever which allows automatic fire; and on the right side of the rifle there is a release for the quick-change barrel. So the HK81 can also function as a light machine gun, using the 30-round magazine. Thus while the police force has ostensibly bought rifles, it has in fact equipped itself with machine guns.

Further, by changing the barrel and bolt the gun can be rapidly converted to fire either the 7.62mm × 39 cartridge or the 5.56mm × 45 cartridge should the need arise. And by removing the magazine housing and replacing it with a belt adapter, it can be turned into a belt-fed machine gun in any of the three calibers. As if this were not enough, a laser projector can be fitted, placing a spot of light on the target to permit accurate aiming at night; image-intensifying sights can be fitted to the telescope mount; tear gas grenades can be projected from the flash hider (which doubles as a grenade-launching spigot), and there is even a tripod mount for heavy duty.

The HK81 is a remarkable example of versatility; it is also a depressing example of the lengths to which European police forces are being driven by political extremists.

Heckler & Koch HK91

Manufacturer Heckler & Koch GmbH, Oberndorf Am Neckar, Germany
Type Delayed blowback, semi-automatic
Caliber 7.62mm NATO (.308 Winchester)
Barrel 19in (482mm)
Weight 10.25lbs (4.65kg)
Magazine Capacity 20 rounds

The German Army's service rifle, the Heckler & Koch G3 is widely distributed throughout the world and enjoys a high reputation for serviceability. It is too well-known to warrant a separate entry here, but it is perhaps worth reminding readers that it is descended from the Mauser design of Sturmgewehr developed in 1945, whisked off to Spain to become the original CETME, and later returned to Germany and polished into G3 form. Like many military rifles of today, the G3 has a selective fire option which prevents it being legally acquired by sport shooters, and therefore Heckler & Koch have developed a semi-automatic-only version, which sells as the Model 91.

The HK91 is typical of today's military firearms, having a stamped steel receiver, plastic fore end, butt and pistol grip, and a very simple takedown procedure. The bolt moves on ribs formed in the receiver walls, and the barrel is pinned into the receiver. Above the barrel is a tubular sleeve carrying the cocking handle and bolt extension. The bolt is Heckler & Koch's renowned two-piece unit with roller locking, described elsewhere in these pages, which delays the opening of the breech long enough for the bullet to clear the muzzle, after which the action is straightforward blowback. One problem with blowback action is that the initial extraction of the cartridge tends to be somewhat abrupt, and this can cause trouble with necked high pressure cases. The HK91 uses a grooved chamber to allow gas to flow back down the grooves to the outside of the case and so 'float' it on a layer of gas, making extraction more easy and generally foolproof. The cases are ejected streaked with carbon and generally looking rather sorry, but experience has shown that they are perfectly safe to reload several times.

The sights are standard Bundeswehr service pattern, a post inside a ring for the foresight and a rotating rear sight with apertures for 200, 300 and 400 meters. There is also an open notch 'battle sight', and the entire rear sight unit can be adjusted to compensate for individual zeroing and for differences in ammunition.

The standard model uses a fixed plastic butt; there is also a version with telescoping metal buttstock. There is also the HK93, similar to the 91 but chambered for the 5.56mm cartridge.

The accuracy of the HK91 is rather better than average for this class of rifle; it will generally make four- to five-inch groups at 200 yards with European service ammunition, rather worse with other types. With handloaded ammunition it should be possible to get slightly under four inches if a telescope sight is used.

Heckler & Koch HK270

Manufacturer Heckler & Koch GmbH, Oberndorf Am Neckar, Germany
Type Blowback semi-automatic
Caliber .22 Long Rifle RF
Barrel 19.7in (500mm)
Weight 5.5lbs (2.5kg)
Magazine Capacity 2, 5 or 20 rounds

This sporting rifle from Heckler & Koch has an interesting amalgamation of civil and military features and there is a suggestion that it may have originated in a design for a military training rifle. However it started, the resulting rifle is one of their best, being light, rapid, accurate and extremely popular.

The 270 is a conventional sporting rimfire model, using a plain blowback bolt action. The stock is of walnut and might be called 'semi-Monte Carlo', since while the comb is fairly high there is no prominent cheek rest. Its finish is excellent and it complements the well-blued finish of the metalwork.

The magazine enters beneath the action; as with other German designs, regulations restrict the home market to a two-round box, but larger magazines are provided for export, the five-round as standard and the 20-round as an optional alternative or extra.

The foresight is a ring shroud containing a diaphragm unit carrying a central post; by removing a pin this diaphragm can be changed for different thicknesses and heights of post. The rear sight is the standard Germany Army G3 sight, which is the

Left: The Heckler & Koch G-3 rifle, the basis for the HK81.

Above: The Heckler & Koch HK270 semi-automatic rifle.

clue to its possible military training origin. This is an aperture sight which can be varied for set ranges by rotating an obliquely-set drum. The whole sight can be adjusted for elevation and windage very easily by use of a special tool supplied with the rifle. In addition, the receiver top is grooved for a telescope mount.

The 270 is by no means a target rifle, but on the other hand it should not be dismissed simply as a 'fun gun' either. Once zeroed it is capable of impressive accuracy and it makes an excellent hunting weapon for the vermin and small game found in Europe.

Heckler & Koch HK300

Manufacturer Heckler & Koch GmbH, Oberndorf Am Neckar, Germany
Type Blowback, semi-automatic
Caliber .22 Winchester Magnum RF
Barrel 19.7in (500mm)
Weight 5.7lbs (2.59kg)
Magazine Capacity 2, 5 or 15 rounds

The HK300 might be called a 'de luxe' version of the 270; it is built to take a more powerful cartridge, but retains the same basic blowback mechanism and is generally to a higher standard of fit and finish. The manufacturers claim that it is 'Specially intended for the close season and for hunting small predatory game and controlling stray domestic animals.'
The stock is of walnut, well checkered and oil-finished, and with a cheek rest on the butt. The barrel is somewhat heavier than that of the 270, as befits the heavier cartridge, but the bolt mechanism is basically the same. The sights comprise a front blade set on a ramp and adjustable for elevation, and an open blade rearsight adjustable for windage. The receiver top is slotted to take the HK05 universal telescope mount, which can be attached or removed in seconds, firmly locked in place by a lever, and retains the zero whenever replaced. As with other German designs, there is a two-round magazine for the domestic market and five or 15-round models for export.

The combination of heavier barrel and .22 Magnum cartridge have produced a rifle of superlative accuracy, capable of stretching most marksmen to their utmost ability.

Heckler & Koch HK770

Manufacturer Heckler & Koch GmbH, Oberndorf Am Neckar, Germany
Type Delayed blowback semi-automatic
Caliber .308 Winchester (7.62mm NATO)
Barrel 19.7in (500mm)
Weight 7.04lbs (3.20kg)
Magazine Capacity 2, 3 or 10 rounds

Thanks to somewhat more intelligent gun legislation than the rest of Europe and to their natural advantages in respect of forests and hunting areas, the Germans still have a thriving home market for firearms which helps to form a sound base for their export activities. Most German gunmakers, irrespective of their primary product, have an eye to this home market and ensure that they have a suitable product, if only to remind people of their existence. Thus it comes about that Heckler & Koch, generally associated in most non-German minds with military firearms, have an impressive range of sporting weapons, and the Model 770 is the civilian equipment of the well-known G3 military rifle.

In saying that we do not imply that it is a conversion for civil purposes; this role is played by the HK91 already discussed, but this sort of conversion is less popular in Europe than in the U.S.A. The HK770 is a well built sporting rifle and looks it; its military heri-

tage is only seen in the mechanical arrangements, which include the same two-part roller-locked breech block.

The 770 is a handsome weapon, with a graceful walnut stock, finely checkered and well finished. The receiver has a somewhat unusual steel cover over the bolt mechanism, and there is a folding cocking handle on the right side. A box magazine is inserted beneath the action; in Germany this is restricted to a model holding two rounds, to comply with various regulations, but for export, magazines holding 5 or 10 rounds can be provided. The magazine retaining catch is in the front of the trigger guard and the safety is on the left side, just above the trigger area.

The foresight is a flat-topped blade adjustable for elevation, while the rear sight is an open notch, adjustable for elevation and windage. The top surface of the 'upper receiver' (receiver top cover) is prepared for H&K's HK05 Claw Mount which will accept virtually any type of telescope mount.

On the range the 770 performs extremely well; those unaccustomed to

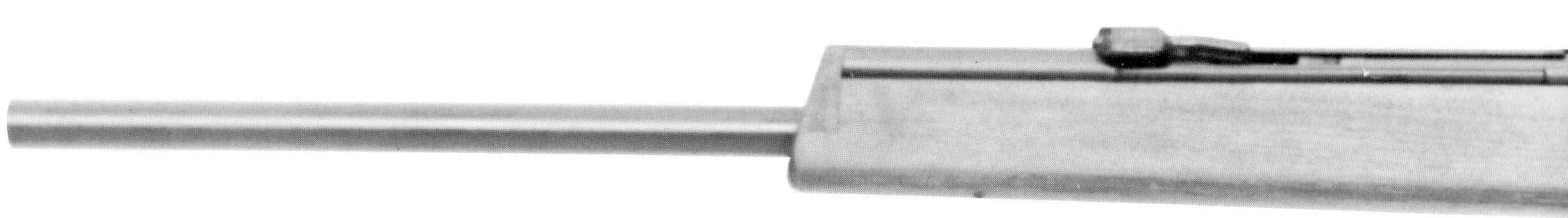

Above: The Heckler & Koch PSG-1 sniping rifle.

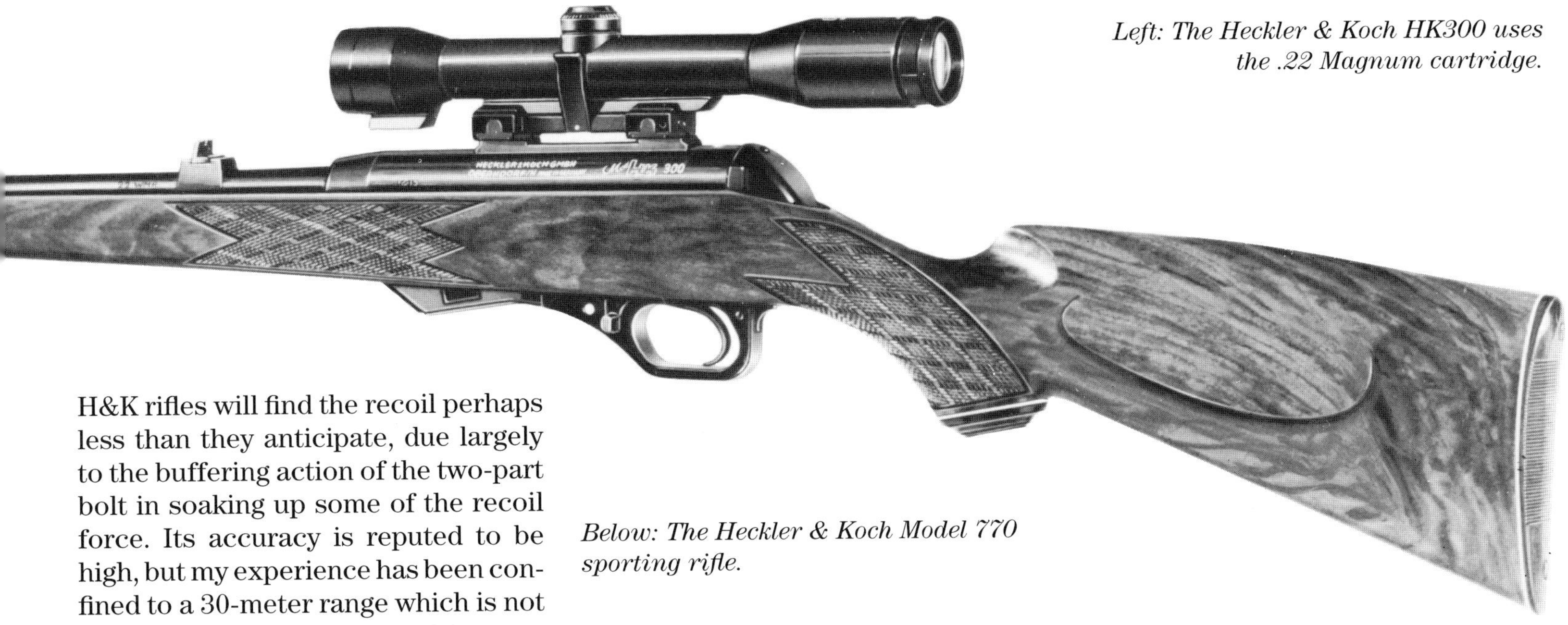

Left: The Heckler & Koch HK300 uses the .22 Magnum cartridge.

H&K rifles will find the recoil perhaps less than they anticipate, due largely to the buffering action of the two-part bolt in soaking up some of the recoil force. Its accuracy is reputed to be high, but my experience has been confined to a 30-meter range which is not sufficient for me to make fair comment. One major advantage over most semi-automatics derived from military design is that the vast production of the G3 and its allied models over the years enables this rifle to be turned out to a high standard of manufacture but at a most competitive price.

There are two parallel models to this; the HK630 is chambered for .223 Remington (5.56mm) cartridges, and the HK940 for the .30-06 cartridge. Apart from small differences in barrel length to accommodate the differing ballistics of the cartridges they are substantially the same as the 770.

Below: The Heckler & Koch Model 770 sporting rifle.

Heckler & Koch PSG-1 Sniping Rifle

Manufacturer Heckler & Koch GmbH, Oberndorf Am Neckar, Germany
Type Semi-automatic, delayed blowback, magazine
Caliber 7.62mm NATO (.308 Winchester)
Barrel 25.6in (650mm)
Weight 15.8lbs (7.2kg)
Magazine Capacity 5 rounds

This rifle has been developed by Heckler & Koch to satisfy the current demand from military and police authorities for a high-precision weapon for use by snipers and skilled marksmen. It uses the standard basic breech mechanism in which the bolt is a two-part unit and its opening is delayed by a roller-locking system. In this way the rifle's operation is already familiar to most service personnel and its repair and maintenance present no fresh problems.

Below: The ubiquitous AK-74.

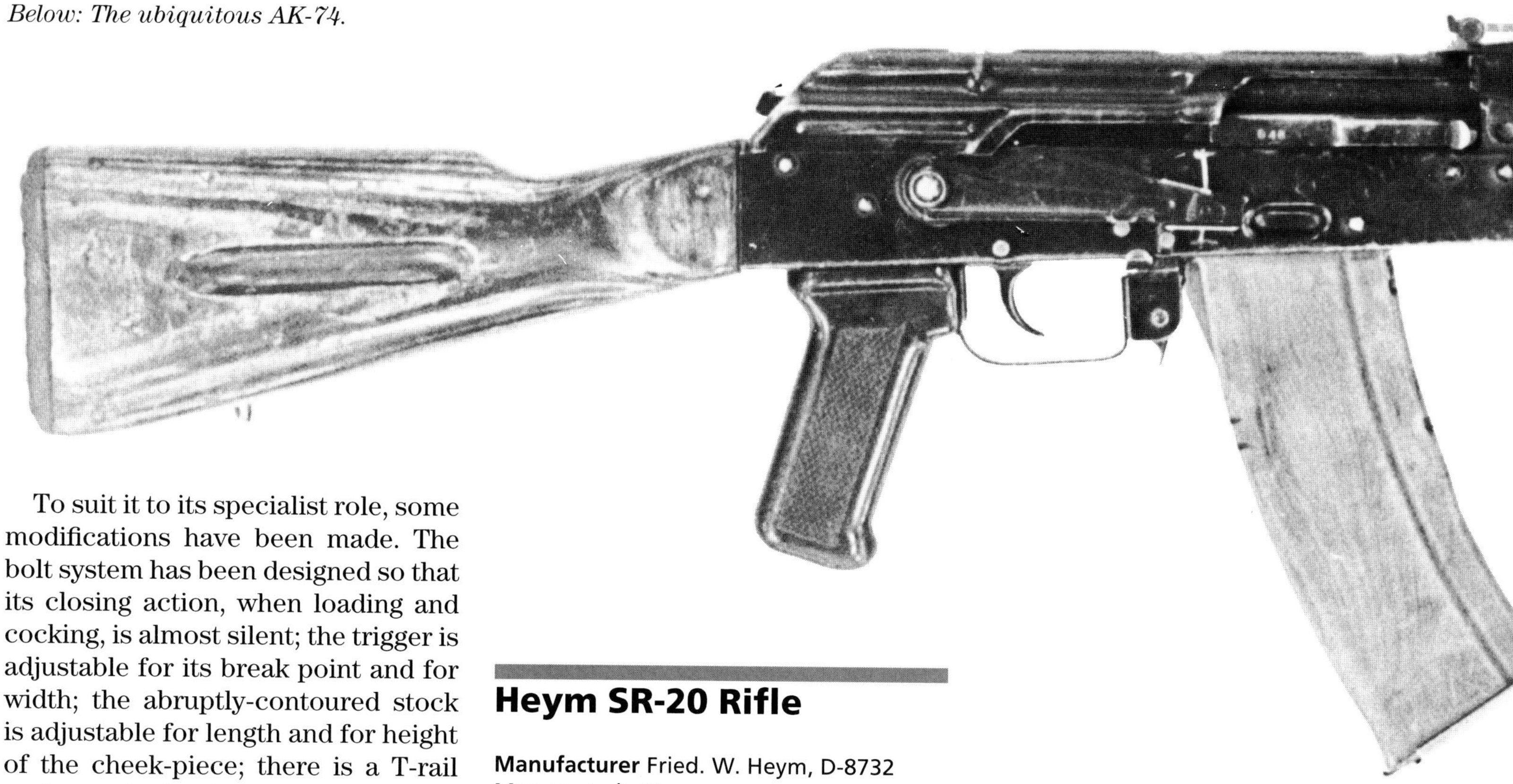

To suit it to its specialist role, some modifications have been made. The bolt system has been designed so that its closing action, when loading and cocking, is almost silent; the trigger is adjustable for its break point and for width; the abruptly-contoured stock is adjustable for length and for height of the cheek-piece; there is a T-rail underneath the fore end which permits the mounting of a hand-stop, a sling or even a light bipod or tripod; and the weapon is equipped with a telescope sight as standard. This has been carefully designed to suit the weapon and is unusual in that adjustments for elevation and azimuth are made by movement of the internal optical system, giving a high degree of precision; one click of either adjustment will move the bullet strike 1cm at 100m range.

The PSG-1 is heavy but well-balanced, and it shoots extremely accurately; 10 shots in a two-inch circle at 300 yards is well within its capabilities, though as with any other precision weapon it is best to test it with several makes of ammunition and bullet weights to find the one which suits it best. The PSG-1 has only recently been announced, and so far as I am aware there have been no major sales, though several German police authorities are evaluating it.

Heym SR-20 Rifle

Manufacturer Fried. W. Heym, D-8732 Munnerstadt, Germany
Type Bolt-action, center-fire, magazine
Caliber .270 Winchester
Barrel 20.5in (520mm)
Weight 6.5lb (2.94kg)
Magazine Capacity 5 rounds

Friedrich Heym is a long-established German gunmaker whose principal fame comes from his hand-built sporting guns – rifles, shotguns, drillings – which are virtually tailor-made for his clients. But for those with less wealth, he also makes a stock rifle which can be bought off the shelf – though even this has sufficient variations of barrel length and caliber to be able to suit almost all applicants.

The SR-20 is basically a Mauser action, but furnished in three lengths to suit short, medium and magnum cartridge lengths. It is assembled to three possible barrel lengths; 20.5in (520mm), 24in (610mm) and 26in (660mm); generally the three barrel lengths parallel the actions, the two shorter lengths being found with either of the two shorter actions and the 26in with the magnum action, but this is not immutable and Heym will marry whatever barrel and action you wish.

The shortest barrels are usually stocked to the muzzle in Mannlicher carbine style, while the longer ones are partially stocked in the usual sporting rifle manner. Whatever the stock type it will be of high-grade walnut, oil-finished and hand checkered, fitted to the barrel and action in a faultless manner. The sights are usually a front post with removable hood, and a rear notch fully adjustable for elevation and windage. The receivers are always drilled and tapped for telescope mounts. The trigger is fully adjustable, and the magazine has a hinged floor-plate released by a catch in the trigger guard. There is a three-position safety catch which gives the shooter a choice of 'bolt & trigger locked,' 'trigger only locked' and 'all free' positions.

Heym rifles will group to two minutes of arc as they come from the box. They are not inexpensive weapons by any standard of comparison, but the customer gets an accurate weapon, beautifully hand-finished and flawless in operation.

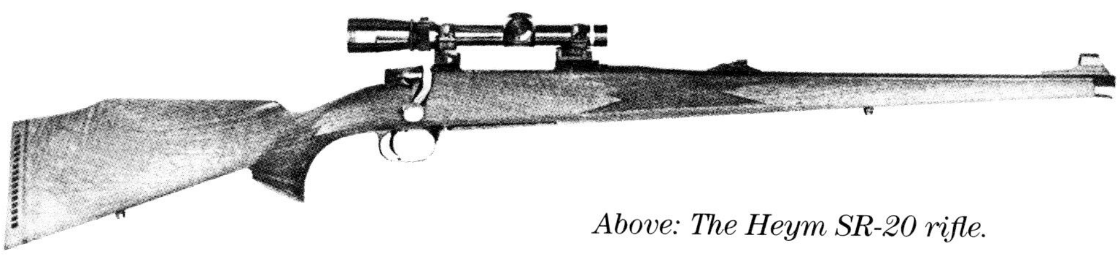

Above: The Heym SR-20 rifle.

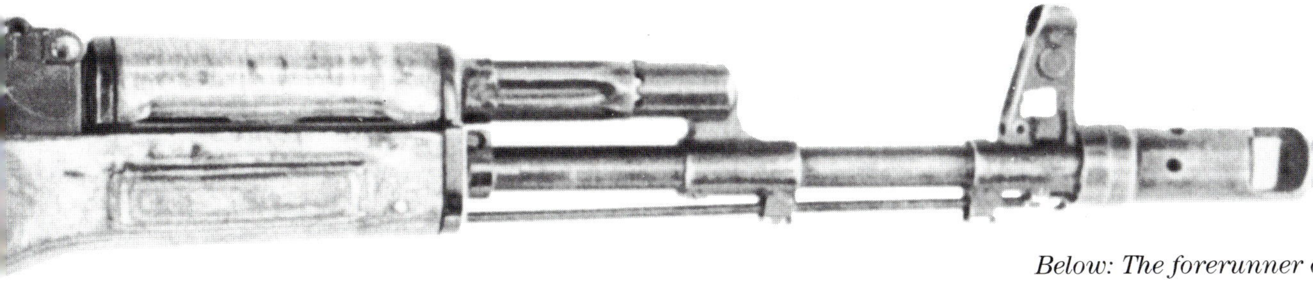

Below: The forerunner of the AK-74, the AK-47.

Kalashnikov AK-74

Manufacturer Soviet State Arsenals
Type Gas-operated, selective fire
Caliber 5.4mm
Barrel 15.75in (400mm)
Weight 7.93lbs (3.60kg)
Magazine Capacity 40 rounds
Cyclic rate of fire 650 rounds/minute

It was to be expected that with the western nations turning to small calibers for their military rifles, the Soviets would eventually follow suit. They had developed a necked-down version of their standard 7.62mm M43 cartridge with a 5.56mm bullet in the 1960s, though this appears never to have had any military applications other than as a research vehicle. What was also to be expected was that when they did move, it would be to a caliber and chambering entirely unlike anything in the west and totally incompatible with any capitalist weapon system.

The resulting rifle was first seen by outsiders in 1979, since when numbers of them have become available to western agencies (mainly from Afghanistan). In general the AK-74 is a modified AK-47 insofar as it uses the same receiver and stock, pistol grip, trigger unit and general configuration. The bolt is smaller, but the bolt carrier and gas piston are the same. The magazine is of thick and tough plastic, thick so that it can fit into the AK-47 magazine housing without demanding any modification. It holds 10 more of the smaller cartridges than did the AK-47 magazine. The wooden fore end grip has a horizontal groove, useful as a recognition feature if nothing else.

The most obvious change is in the addition of a muzzle brake, designed to divert some of the ejected gases sideways and upwards to counter recoil and upward climb during automatic fire. In this it appears to be very successful, since numbers of tests have shown that the rifle can be controlled quite well when firing automatic, the recoil force having been reduced to a level approximately that of a .22 rimfire sporting rifle. Unfortunately, muzzle brakes are a two-edged sword; they make life easier for the shooter, but they make life difficult for the men next to him, diverting the muzzle blast sideways, and Soviet medical publications have printed one or two articles on the dangers of ear damage on firing ranges with the new rifle.

The new cartridge is conventional enough, the case being slightly shorter and fatter than the .223. The bullet weighs 53 grains, is fully jacketed and boat-tailed and has a muzzle velocity of 900 meters/second (2950 ft/sec). This is rather low for this class of weapon, but appears to be adequate for combat purposes. Internally, the bullet is remarkable for having a vacant space in the nose; the major part of the core is mild steel, with a short lead section at the front. This combination appears to facilitate expansion, bent noses and tumbling on impact so as to deliver a severe wound. It is also somewhat complicated to mass-produce with any accuracy. The rifling twist is very steep – one turn in 26 calibers – and the rifling is bevelled on its leading edge so as not to incise the bullet jacket during its travel up the bore. Tracer and armor-piercing bullets have also been reported, though there is no information available on the penetration ability of the armor-piercing type.

Two types of rifle have been seen; the standard AK-74 has a wooden butt, while the AK-74S has a folding steel butt and appears to be issued to paratroopers and special forces only. The AK-74 replaced the AK-47 in Soviet service, and was adopted by other members of the former Warsaw Pact.

Kimber Model 82

Manufacturer Kimber of Oregon, Clackamas, OR 97015, U.S.A.
Type Bolt-action, rimfire, magazine
Caliber .22 Long Rifle RF
Barrel 22.5in (572mm)
Weight 6.56lbs (2.97kg)
Magazine Capacity 5 or 10 rounds

The bolt action .22 rifle was common in the U.S.A. in years gone by, but in the past decade American makers have become extremely scarce, and in order to remedy this the Kimber company was formed for the sole purpose of making and selling this rifle.

The Model 82 is well finished and elegantly checkered – even the buttplate. The receiver is tubular, milled from the solid, and attached firmly to the one-piece trigger and magazine housing. The bolt is sturdy and the handle positioned above the trigger, while the trigger is easily adjustable for pressure and over-travel. Five- or ten-round magazines are available; the five-round fits flush with the bottom of the fore end and is released by a small catch at its rear. Even the trigger guard has been milled from solid metal and not stamped from sheet steel as some sort of afterthought. The rifle can be supplied with sights to choice, but the normal case is for it to have no iron sights but grooves for Kimber telescope mounts. The barrel is heavy, extremely well finished inside and out, and with the chamber dimensions on the low side of the permitted tolerances. Accuracy is excellent; half-inch groups at 50 yards, firing from a rest, are easily attained, provided one takes the trouble to try various brands of ammunition to discover that which is best suited.

Marlin Model 375 Rifle

Manufacturer Marlin Firearms Co., North Haven, CT 06473, U.S.A.
Type Lever action, center fire, magazine
Caliber .375 Winchester
Barrel 20in (508mm)
Weight 6.75lbs (3.06kg)
Magazine Capacity 5 rounds

John Mahon Marlin began making lever-action rifles and carbines in 1881 and the fact that the company he founded is still making them is sufficient proof of the excellence. There have been some small changes, but since 1889 the significant feature of the Marlin has been the solid top to the receiver and the side ejection port.

The Marlin Model 375 gets its nomenclature from being chambered for the .375 Winchester cartridge, which was introduced specifically for use in lever-action rifles in order to give them a medium-to-high powered round for use in forests and close country. Note that it is a rifle rather than a carbine; the barrel is much longer than the magazine tube and the whole weapon is three to four inches longer than the average carbine.

The Marlin action retains the solid top receiver and has a cylindrical bolt which, on operating the lever, comes out from the rear of the receiver to cock the external hammer. At the same time the cartridge lifter pivots to raise a fresh round from the magazine, and on the return stroke the bolt chambers the round, is locked, and the rifle is ready to fire.

Below: The Marlin Model 375 rifle.

Above: The Kimber Model 82 bolt-action rifle.

Above: The Mauser SP66 sniper's rifle.

One advantage of the solid top and side ejection Marlin is that it makes life easier for fitting a telescope, and the receiver is factory drilled and tapped for a mount. Marlin have also aided telescope shooters by making an extension hammer spur which protrudes to one side (either side, to choice) so that there is no danger of trapping the thumb between hammer and telescope when cocking or lowering the hammer. Iron sights re fitted, a gold-bead foresight and a step-adjustable rear sight with a rotatable insert which provides a choice of four notches.

The short magazine makes the rifle somewhat lighter at the muzzle than one normally expects with lever-actions, though this certainly helps when attempting to follow a moving target. Accuracy leans heavily upon the ammunition in use, but with the correct choice made, then groups between two and three inches are possible at 100 yards for the moderately practised shooter.

Mauser SP66 Sniper's Rifle

Manufacturer Mauser-Werke Oberndorf GmbH, Oberndorf am Neckar, Germany
Type Bolt-action, magazine
Caliber 7.62mm NATO
Barrel 26.7in (670mm)
Magazine Capacity 3 rounds

When the armies of the world adopted semi-automatic rifles, most of them slapped a telescope on those which proved-out best in their acceptance tests and issued them to snipers. The theory was that semi-autos made good sniping weapons since the firer did not have to move his arm to operate the bolt and therefore was less likely to disclose his position. This seems to have arisen because of the Soviet Army's policy of giving semi-autos to snipers during World War Two, but in my view the reason for this was more that their semi-autos were somewhat temperamental unless properly looked after, and a sniper is more likely to devote care to his rifle than the average front line soldier. In any event, after some years the snipers of the Western armies began complaining that stealthy reloading was of little use unless you could hit the target in the first place, and that military semi-autos, no matter how good, were simply not accurate enough for sniping purposes. As a result, there has been a gradual move back to bolt action rifles for snipers, and this Mauser is the issue for the German and at least a dozen other armies.

In appearance you would be excused for thinking that it is a high quality match rifle; the stock is strictly functional and non-military, with a near-vertical pistol grip, thumb-hole, deep comb and adjustable cheek-rest and deep stippled fore end. All this, of course, simply permits the sniper to get the best 'hold' he possibly can, which is half the battle. The action is a short Mauser bolt locking into the receiver with forward lugs and feeding from an integral three-round magazine concealed within the depth of the fore end. The bolt handle is at the forward end of the bolt, just behind the locking lugs, so that it is close to the trigger and reduces the action length to about half the normal. The firing pin spring is stronger than normal to give a fast movement to the striker and the 'lock time' (the time between pressing the trigger and the exit of the bullet from the muzzle) is about half of that with a conventional Mauser action.

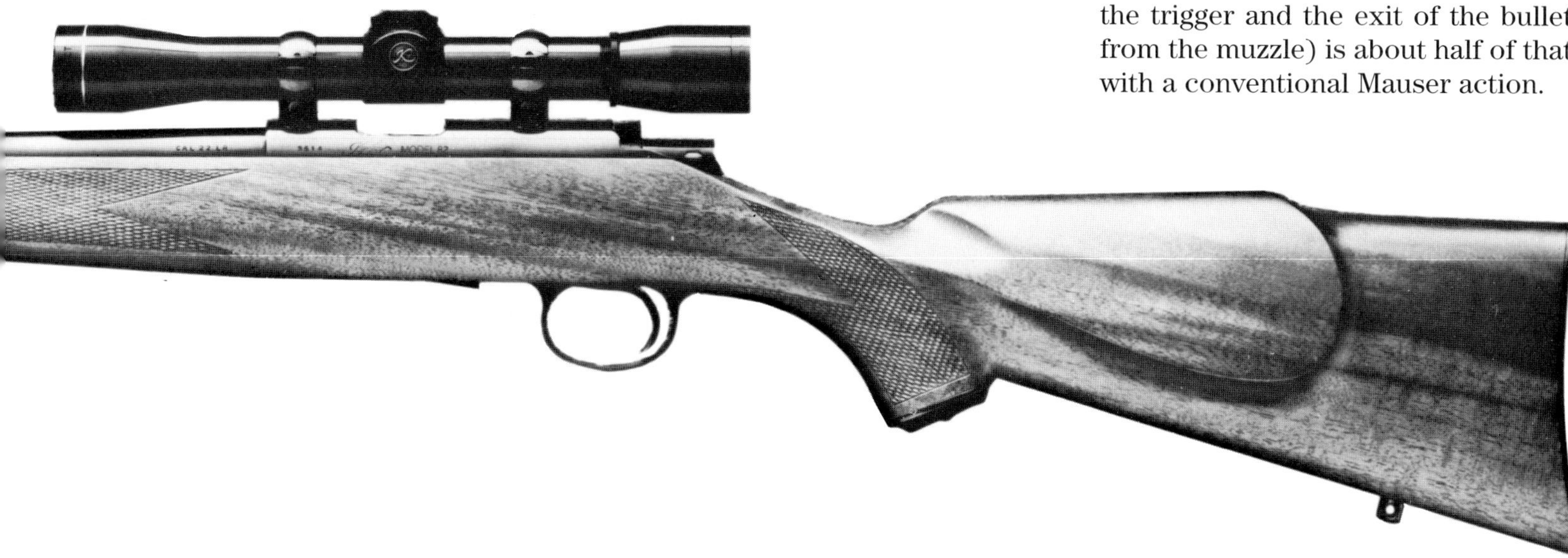

No sights are fitted; the user is expected to specify what he wants and the receiver is then adapted to it; Mauser recommend using a Zeiss Diavari optical telescope or a Varo or similar image-intensifying sight. The muzzle is fitted with a complex muzzle brake and flash hider which is designed to prevent the firer being dazzled by his own flash at night, a feature of particular importance when image-intensifying sights are in use.

I have been unable to fire the rifle, but reports indicate that its inherent accuracy is well in excess of the capabilities of stock military ammunition. Most countries are now taking steps to produce special batches of cartridges which have been more carefully assembled than the regular run-of-the mill issue ammunition, for use solely by snipers, and with this available, the Mauser will undoubtedly come into its own.

Mossberg RM-7

Manufacturer O. F. Mossberg & Sons, North Haven, CT 06473, U.S.A.
Type Bolt-action, center-fire, magazine
Caliber .30-06; 7mm Remington Magnum
Barrel 22in (560mm)
Weight 7.87lbs (3.57kg)
Magazine Capacity 4 rounds

Mossberg are well-known for the long series of shotguns and rimfire rifles produced by the company since before the turn of the century; their center-fire rifles are less well-known outside the U.S.A. This is their latest center-fire model, and one which repays study.

The appearance is conventional, with a conservatively styled walnut stock having a graceful pistol grip and good crisp checkering. Two heavy steel crosspins go through the stock behind the recoil shoulder and magazine in order to reinforce it.

The bolt is of Mossberg's own design using four front lugs for very positive locking and with the body fluted, with polished bearing surfaces, to ensure smooth action. The bolt knob is checkered for a firm grip, and there is a prominent safety catch on the bolt sleeve where it can be easily operated by the right thumb.

The magazine is unusual in being a rotary type, though not totally mechanical as, say, the Mannlicher-Schoenauer. The magazine has a curved inner wall against which the cartridges ride, propelled by a sprung follower arm which tracks them round their curved path to deliver them to the feedway. There is a magazine release lever which permits the contents to be emptied without having to work the bolt; the bolt is opened and the lever pressed, withdrawing the stop arm and allowing the follower to

push the cartridges out and into the feedway where they can be removed.

The foresight is a gold bead on a ramp; the rear sight an open folding leaf in the mid-position, capable of adjustment for elevation and windage. The receiver is factory drilled and tapped for telescope mounts.

Accuracy is good, averaging two-inch groups when rest-fired at 100 yards, and the rifle is well-balanced and handy in practical use.

Musgrave Model 90

Manufacturer Musgrave (Pty) Ltd, Bloemfontein, South Africa
Type Bolt-action repeater
Caliber Available in .243, .270, .308, .30-06, 7×57mm and 7×64mm
Barrel 24in (610mm)
Weight 9.25lb (4.2kg) approximately
Magazine Capacity 4 rounds

The Musgrave company was established in 1950 and soon built up a reputation for accurate, robust and elegant sporting rifles for South African hunters and target shooters. With the easing of the political situation, their rifles are now becoming available in other countries and are well worth consideration.

All their major-caliber sporting rifles are based upon a modified Mauser bolt system, machined from steel forgings and with sufficient strength to cater for the most powerful cartridges. The 'flagship' rifle is the Model 90, which is available in Standard, De Luxe, Light and Magnum models.

Some of the design features of the Model 90 are based on the Mauser K98 and Winchester Model 70. The Standard model is fitted with a sporter stock with cheek rest and butt pad. The bolt action is the Musgrave variation of the Mauser, notable for its safety catch being mounted on top of the striker cover at the rear of the bolt, where it is convenient to the thumb and easily visible. Iron sights are fitted, the adjustable rear sight ahead of the chamber and the front sight being hooded; the receiver is also drilled and tapped ready for a Weaver telescope sight mount.

Left: A quartet of Musgrave bolt-action rifles. From the top: The Model 90, Model 93, K98 de Luxe, and K98 light.

The magazine is, in Mauser style, integral within the rifle stock. As noted above, the rifle can be chambered for various popular sporting cartridges, though the magazine capacity remains the same for all.

The De Luxe Model 90 is mechanically the same as the Standard, but with a selected walnut stock and a generally higher quality of finish; the company can engrave virtually any form of decoration to order.

The Light Model 90 has a lightweight walnut stock with 'Schnabel' fore end and the barrel is some 50mm shorter than the standard rifle. Mechanically it is the same as the Standard, but weighs 2.2lbs (1kg) less.

The Magnum Model 92 differs in being chambered for the .375 H&H, .300 Winchester or 7mm Remington Magnum cartridges; it therefore has a longer action and trigger guard. Otherwise it uses the same type of bolt action as the Standard rifle, is fitted with a walnut stock with cheekpiece and recoil pad, and weighs 8.1lbs (3.66kg). This rifle has become very popular among big-game hunters in South Africa due to its combination of high power, accuracy and light weight.

Musgrave also manufacture a series of sporting rifles based on the Mauser Kar98 military bolt action rifle. These rifles are less expensive, more 'working' rifles than the Model 90, and are widely used throughout Africa.

Nikko Model 7000

Manufacturer Nikko Firearms Co., Tochigi, Japan
Type Bolt-action, center-fire, magazine
Caliber Various
Barrel 24in (610mm) or 26in (660mm)
Weight 8.5lbs (3.86kg) with 24in barrel
Magazine Capacity 3 (Magnum) or 5 (regular)

Although ostensibly manufactured in Japan, this is something of an international weapon; the action is made in Japan, the barrel in Belgium, and the wood for the stocks comes from the U.S.A. The whole design is very much tailored for the American market.

The action is a five-lug bolt having an opening arc of 60°, the lugs being at the rear end of the bolt. The bolt body is nicely engine-turned, the face is counterbored, and the firing pin cocks on opening. There is a sliding safety catch alongside the rear of the bolt which locks the trigger but leaves the bolt free to be operated.

The stock is quite heavy and amply-proportioned; there is a high Monte Carlo comb and cheekpiece and the finish is good, if glossy. The interior fit and finish is not so good.

The magazine has a spring-loaded floor plate and a release catch at the front of the trigger guard. Sights are provided only on two calibers, .375 and .458; all others are without sights and are drilled and tapped for telescope mounts. Calibers available run from .22-250 to .458 Winchester Magnum and include all the commercial standards currently available.

I have been unable to fire this rifle, and reports from other sources are mixed; the general opinion seems to be that as it comes, the barrel is not always well bedded, giving rise to inconsistent shooting, but that with a little adjustment this can be overcome, resulting in a very good hunting rifle at a reasonable price.

Parker-Hale M85

Manufacturer Gibbs Rifle Co. Inc., Martinsburg, West Virginia, U.S.A.
Type Bolt-action repeater
Caliber 7.62mm NATO (.308 Winchester)
Barrel 27.5in (700mm)
Weight 12.56lbs (5.7kg) with sight
Magazine Capacity 10 rounds

The Parker-Hale company of Birmingham, England, has a long history of making small arms and accessories for sporting shooters. In the early 1960s they began making major-caliber rifles based on Mauser-type actions purchased from Spain. In the early 1980s their 7.62mm Model 82 was selected as the service sniper rifle by Australia, Canada and New Zealand. They then developed the Model 85 for the British Army sniping rifle trials, but it was not selected. In 1990 the company decided to give up their rifle business and concentrate on other things, and the patents and rights to the Parker-Hale rifles were purchased by Navy Arms of the U.S.A., whose subsidiary, the Gibbs Rifle Company now manufactures the Parker-Hale range.

The M85 is a highly accurate and reliable rifle designed to give a 100 percent first round hit probability up to 600 yards range, and is capable of accurate shooting to ranges well in excess of that. The action is basically that of the Mauser 1898 rifle, immensely strong and thoroughly tested over the century. Iron sights for ranges up to 900 yards are fitted, and the receiver is prepared for a telescope or electro-optical night vision sight.

The muzzle is threaded to accept a suppressor which can be used with supersonic or reduced velocity ammunition and eliminates all muzzle flash and firing signature and also reduces the recoil. The butt-stock is fully adjustable and there is a quick-detach bipod attached to the fore end.

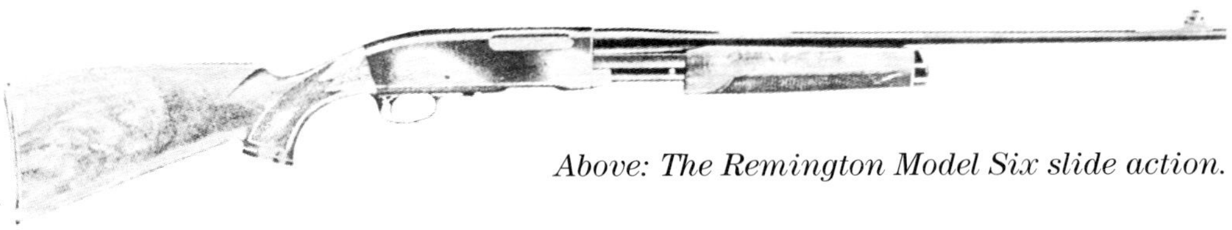

Above: The Remington Model Six slide action.

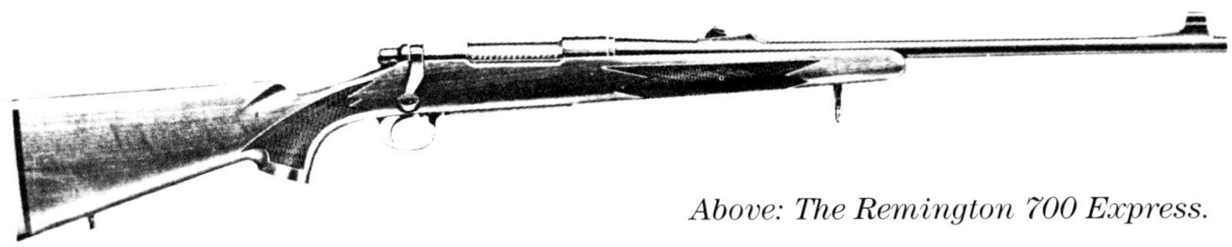

Above: The Remington 700 Express.

Remington Model Six Slide Action

Manufacturer Remington Arms Co., Ilion, New York, 13357, U.S.A.
Type Pump-action, center-fire, magazine
Caliber Various
Barrel 22in (560mm)
Weight 7.5lbs (3.40kg)
Magazine Capacity 4 rounds

Slide action guns ('pump guns' or 'trombone guns') are usually associated , at least in Europe, with low-powered .22 rimfire rifles or with shotguns, but providing the design is properly done there is no reason why the system should not be used with high powered rifles. Remington, though, seem to be the only people to have made a success of it, and they have featured a center-fire slide action rifle in their catalogs for several years. The Model Six is the latest version, introduced in 1981 and replacing the earlier Model 760.

One advantage of the slide action, if only a cosmetic one, is the 'streamlined' shape of the receiver, which flows from the line of the stock. This box-like receiver is immensely strong and has an ejection slot in the right side. The box magazine enters below the receiver. Below the barrel is a rod assembly which acts as a bearing surface for the slide grip to move upon. When the slide is operated, a connecting link cams the breech block out of engagement with a locking recess in the receiver, then withdraws it, ejecting the spent case. The forward stroke then propels the block forward to load the cartridge and cams the block into the locking recess. By careful design of the leverages the action can be made very smooth and it barely disturbs the aim; the only defect is that there is no mechanical gain to deal with the occasional sticky case.

The Model 760 has a checkered walnut Monte Carlo stock with pistol grip, and the slide grip is of similar material. The foresight is a gold beat on a matt ramp, while the rear sight is open, step-adjustable for elevation and also adjustable for windage. The receiver is factory drilled and tapped for telescope mounts.

The rifle is available in 6mm, .243, .270, .30-06 and .308 calibers, and its accuracy is good, with groups of just over two inches at 100 yards. In view of the extraction hazard, it pays to try a variety of ammunition to find which particular brand suits this rifle.

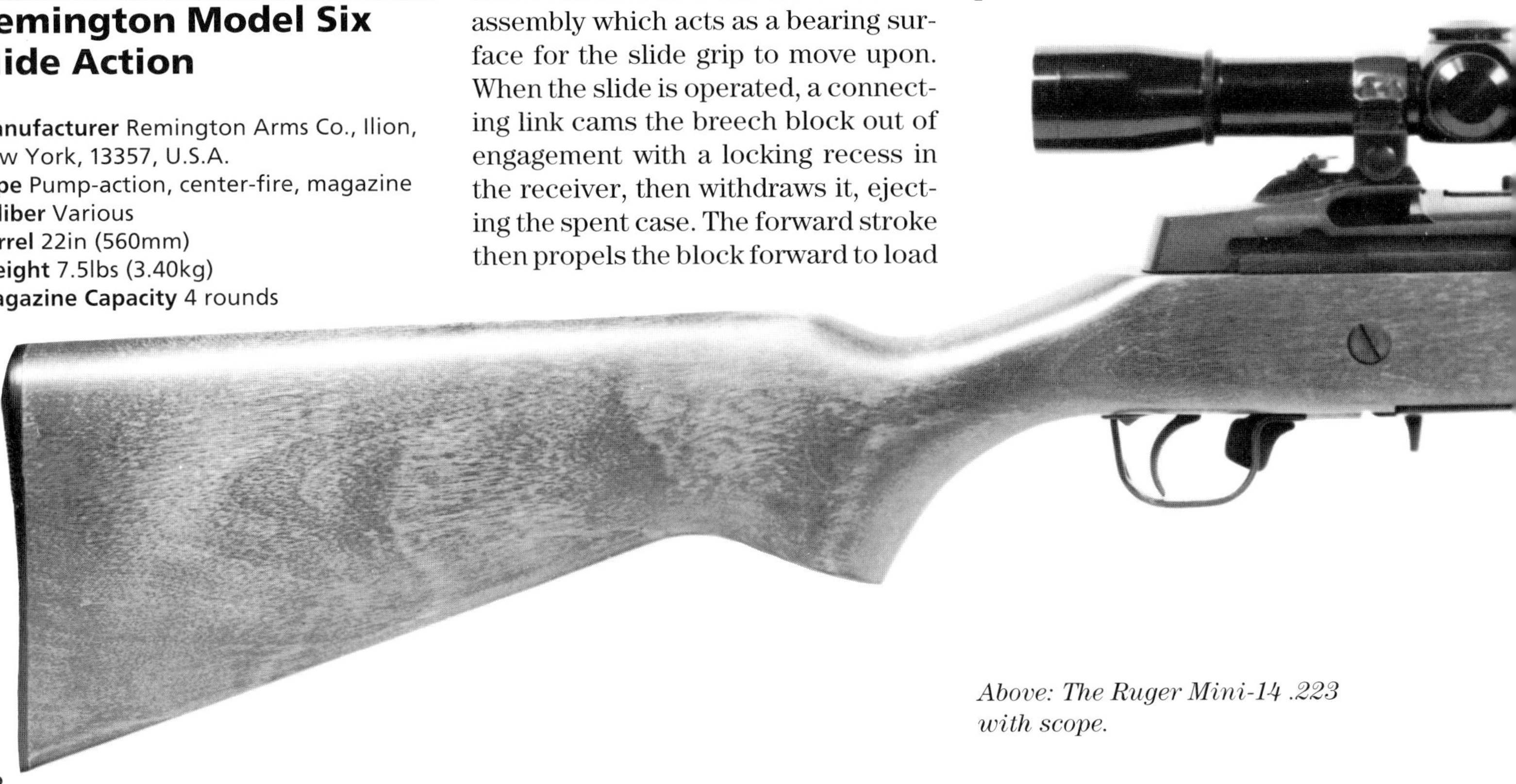

Above: The Ruger Mini-14 .223 with scope.

Remington Model 700 7mm Express

Manufacturer Remington Arms Co., Bridgeport, CT 06602, U.S.A.
Type Bolt-action, center-fire, magazine
Caliber 7mm Remington Express
Barrel 22in (559mm)
Weight 7.25lbs (3.29kg)
Magazine Capacity 5 rounds

The 7mm Remington Express cartridge is the new name for what used to be the .280 Remington; dimensionally identical, the new version has improved ballistics and Remington are promoting it as a long-range hunting cartridge. And the best way of doing that is to produce a good rifle to shoot it from, hence the Model 700 in 7mm Express.

The Model 700 has been in production for some time in a wide variety of calibers from .17 to .458, so it is a thoroughly proven design. Elegantly proportioned and well-finished, with a Monte-Carlo stock and inlaid fore end, the Model 700 balances well and comes easily to the shoulder. The action is basically a Mauser bolt, amply strong for this loading, while the barrel is smoothly tapered and appears to be light in weight, which probably accounts for the good balance.

The front sight is a post set on a ramp, hooded to obviate glare, and can be drift-set to compensate when zeroing. The rear sight is open, adjustable for elevation and windage. The receiver has been factory drilled and tapped for mounting any type of telescope sight mount base or for the addition of more specialized receiver sights.

The 7mm Express cartridge generates some 2800 feet per second (853 meters/sec) muzzle velocity in this rifle, and 200 meters is the theoretical cross-over point at which bullet and sight line should coincide. As a result the rifle shoots particularly well at that range and is capable of producing better than four-inch groups straight from the box and with factory ammunition.

Rossi Model 92SRC Carbine

Manufacturer Amadeo Rossi Lda., Sâo Leopoldo, Brazil
Type Lever-action, tubular magazine
Caliber .357 Magnum
Barrel 20in (508mm)
Weight (empty) 5.94lbs (2.69kg)
Magazine Capacity 8 rounds

In the days of the Old West the carbine chambered for a handgun cartridge (or vice versa, as you prefer) was the common saddle gun, but the concept seems to have withered over the years, with the riflemen looking to more exotic calibers and better ballistic efficiency. But there is still a good case for the combination, especially in those parts of the world where there is a need for a general-purpose rifle with no frills. Rossi's Carbine enjoys good sales.

The 92SRC makes no bones about being an almost identical copy of the Winchester Model of 1892 in appearance, though there are some minor differences internally. The receiver is an investment casting, attached to a steel barrel, and the woodwork is well-fitted and polished while the metalwork is well blued. The breech mechanism is the traditional Winchester lever action, feeding from the tubular magazine beneath the barrel. This holds 8 rounds of .357; but the weapon can be used with .38 Special cartridges, and nine of these can be accommodated in the magazine. The foresight is a blade, while the rear sight is open, with step adjustment for elevation and capable of being drifted sideways for windage and drift zeroing.

The carbine appears to be somewhat touchy about ammunition; naturally, with a tubular magazine only flat-nosed bullets should be used, but different brands appeared to have tolerances which did not mate well with the tolerances of, for example, the cartridge guides in the breech. Length is also fairly critical, and while factory loads mostly work well, handloads need to be tailored to suit the characteristics of the breech. The accuracy is adequate, with two-inch groups at 50 yards possible with the right ammunition.

Ruger Mini-14 Series

Manufacturer Sturm Ruger & Co., Southport, CT 06490, U.S.A.
Type Gas-operated, semi-auto or selective fire
Caliber .223 (5.56mm)
Barrel 18.5in (470mm)
Weight 6.39lbs (2.9kg)
Magazine Capacity 5, 10, 20 or 30 rounds
Cyclic rate of fire 750 rounds/min (AC556 &556K only)

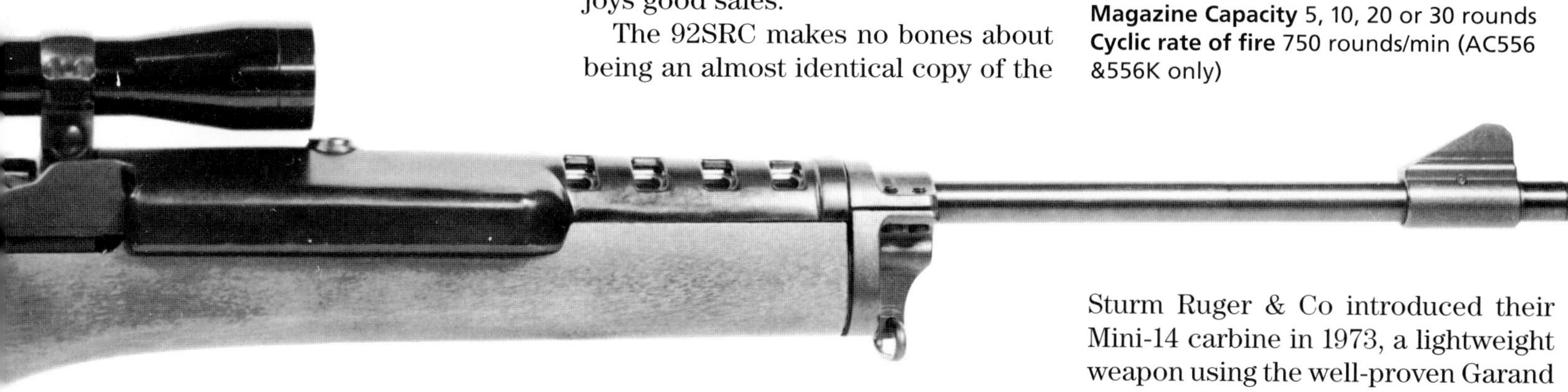

Sturm Ruger & Co introduced their Mini-14 carbine in 1973, a lightweight weapon using the well-proven Garand system of gas operation and rotating bolt, allied to the .223 cartridge. As might be imagined, such a useful combination of reliability and light weight, allied to a modern service cartridge, attracted several military and paramilitary forces to the extent that Sturm Ruger have developed some specific variants of the Mini-14 for use by such agencies. In the expectation that readers might be less familiar with these models, we append some notes on them.

The **Ruger Mini-14/20GB Infantry Rifle** is a conversion of the standard Mini-14 to meet general military standards. The front sight is protected, moved back on the barrel, and incorporates a bayonet lug; there is a flash hider on the muzzle, and the handguard is of heat-resistant glass-fiber reinforced plastic material. The flash hider is shaped so as to function as a grenade launching spigot. In other respects, and in general dimensions and weight, the Infantry Rifle version is the same as the commercial Mini-14 and is available in blued steel or stainless steel.

The **AC-556 Selective Fire Weapon** resembles the Mini-14/20 Infantry Rifle but incorporates modifications to the trigger mechanism to permit the firing of single shots, three-round bursts or full automatic fire.

The **AC-556K Selective Fire Weapon** is the AC-556 modified to have a steel folding stock, a pistol grip, and a shorter (16.7in or 425mm) barrel. Due to the added weight of the stock the complete weapon now weighs 6.9lbs (3.15kg). It is a particularly compact model, well suited to airborne or armored troops. These models are only for sale to law enforcement agencies or governments.

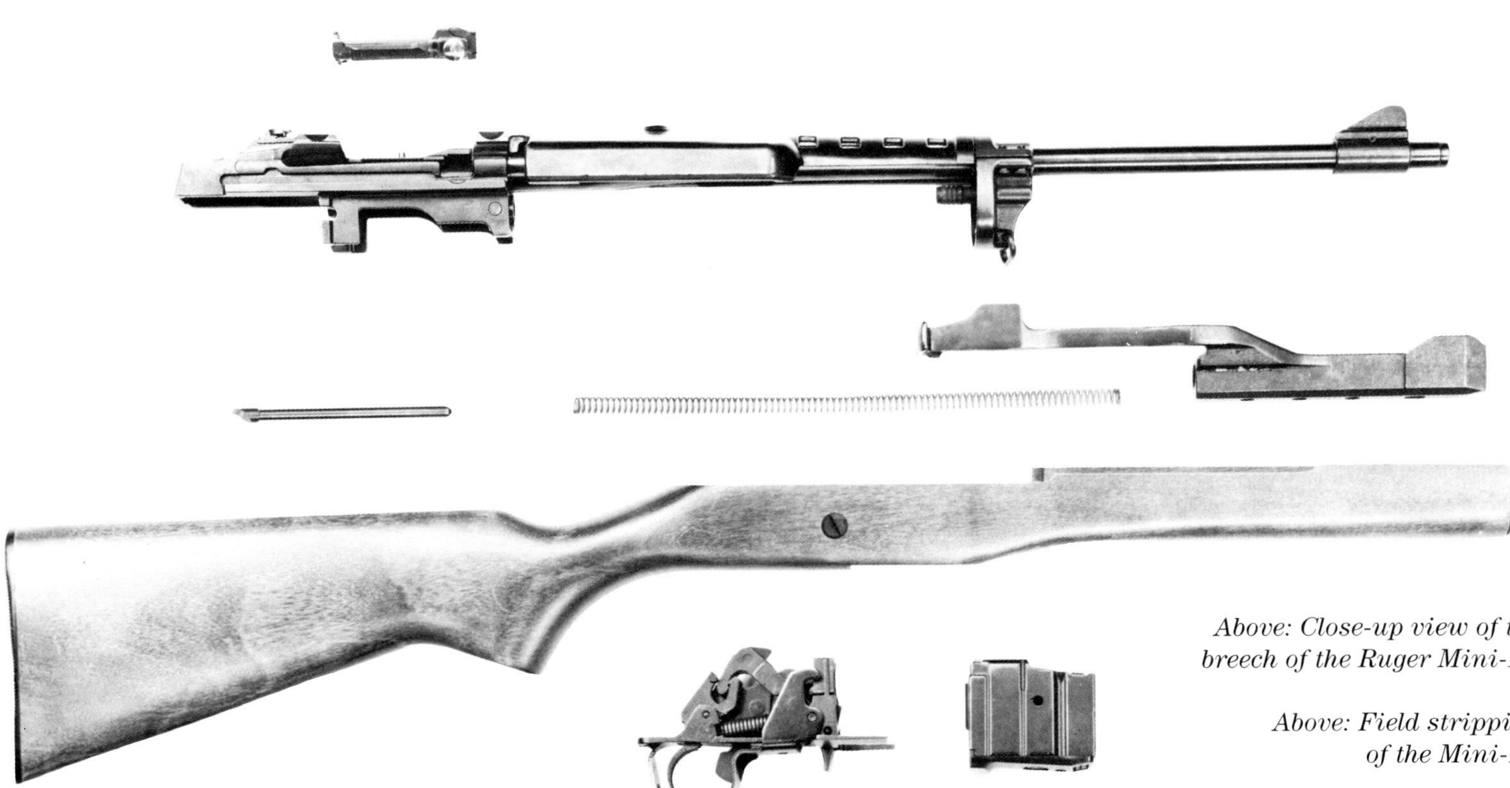

Above: Close-up view of the breech of the Ruger Mini-14.

Above: Field stripping of the Mini-14.

Above: The St. Etienne FA-MAS assault rifle.

St. Etienne 'FA-MAS' Assault Rifle

Manufacturer Manufacture d'Armes de St. Etienne, St. Etienne, France
Type Delayed blowback, selective fire
Caliber 5.56mm (.223)
Barrel 19.2in (488mm)
Weight 8.73lbs (3.96kg)
Magazine Capacity 25 rounds
Cyclic rate of fire 950 rounds/minute

The peculiar shape of this rifle has led to it being nicknamed 'The Trumpet' by today's *poilus*, and in the hands of a well-built soldier it looks like a toy. But it is a very efficient and ingenious design, and production at St. Etienne placed it in the hands of every French soldier by 1990. At first it was only seen in service use with paratroops, but infantry units are now being equipped and trained, and it eventually became the standard 'personal weapon' acting as rifle, carbine or submachine gun.

The system of operation relies upon delayed blowback of the breech block and carrier. The carrier has two 'delay arms' which, when the bolt is closed, contact a hardened steel rod lying across the receiver. When the rifle fires, the cartridge case attempts to move back against the face of the bolt; this movement is transferred to the carrier, but when this attempts to move, the delay arms, held against the cross-bar, resist. They now have to rotate on their pivot, so that their upper section moves back and, in doing so, begin to move the bolt carrier backwards. But the differing lengths of the two sections of the delay arms ensures a mechanical disadvantage which delays the movement. When the arms have moved about 45° they clear the cross-bar and the bolt and carrier now move to the rear, ejecting the spent case. In order to avoid hard extraction, the chamber has longitudinal grooves machined in it so that the fired case is 'floated' on a layer of gas during the extraction phase.

The rifle is a bullpup design, the bolt and chamber being alongside the firer's face and the trigger ahead of the magazine; this permits a long barrel in a short rifle, since the otherwise wasted length of a naked butt is avoided. The butt carries a buffer unit in its upper surface so as to cushion the recoil, and there is a rubber recoil pad. The bolt can have its extractor moved across, and the butt cheekpiece can also be moved, so that the rifle can be quickly adapted to left or right-handed firers. The cocking handle lies centrally, underneath the carrying handle; this handle is of plastic and grooved; within it lies the sights, a blade foresight and an adjustable aperture rear sight calibrated to 300 meters.

The firer can select single shots, three-round bursts or full automatic fire; the three-round burst mechanism is separate from the rest of the trigger

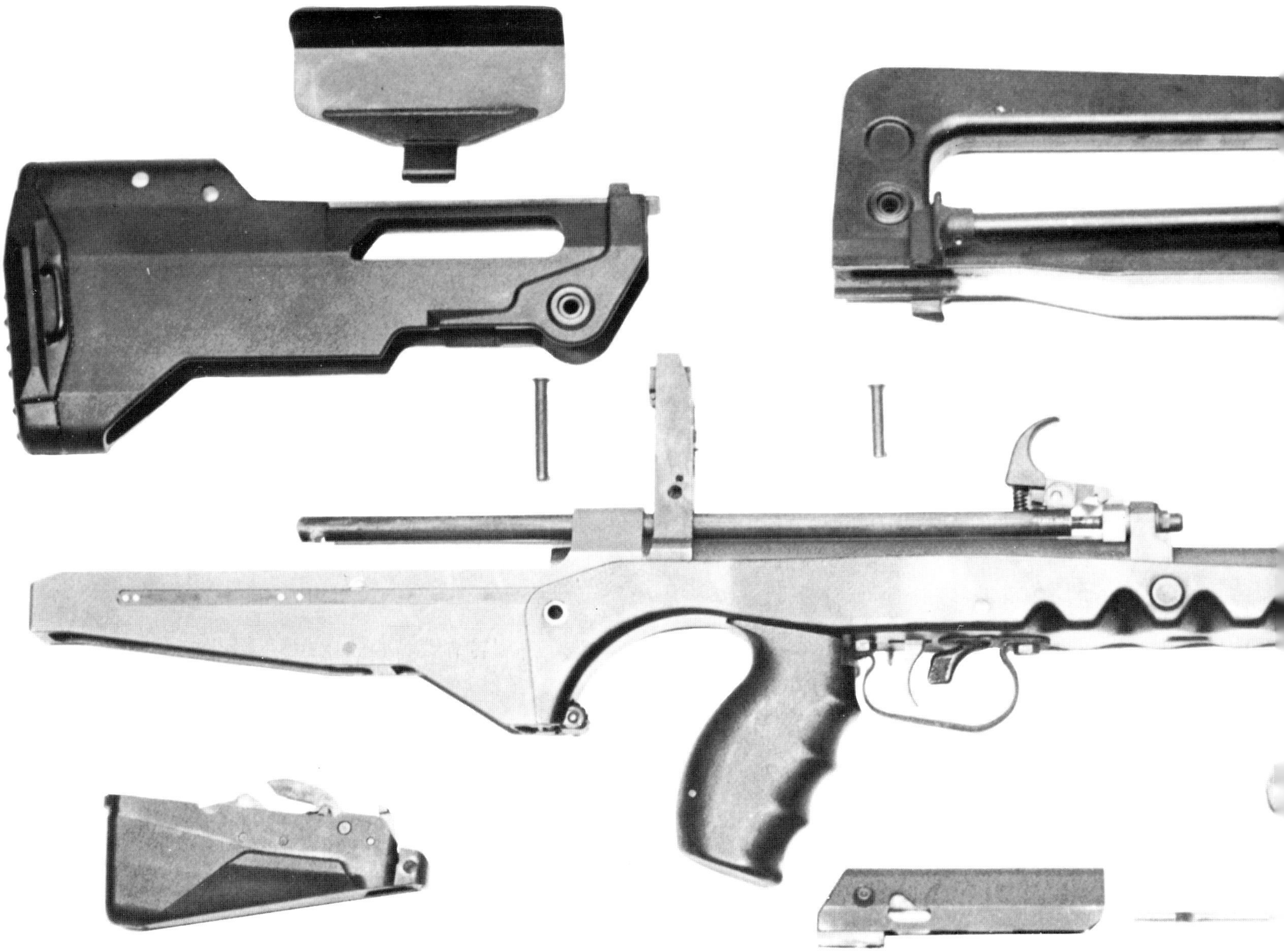

group so that should it fail the remaining options are still available. This means that there has to be two separate controls, one for fire selection and one for burst selection, but careful training avoids any problems with this. The rifle can also be readily adapted for firing grenades, and there is a light bipod which folds beneath the handle and steadies the rifle when firing automatic.

The FA-MAS (which means 'Fusil Automatique, Manufacture d'Armes St. Etienne) is comfortable to fire. It is very accurate at battle ranges and is easily controlled during burst fire. Its length allows it to be used in the submachine gun role quite effectively, and its adoption by the French Army increased the basic squad's fire power and also reduced the variety of weapons carried.

Sako P-72

Manufacturer Oy Sako AB, SF-11100 Riihimaki 10, Finland
Type Bolt-action, magazine
Caliber .22 Long Rifle RF
Barrel 23.375in (594mm)
Weight 6.53lbs (2.96kg)
Magazine Capacity 5 rounds

Sako have been making firearms for many years, concentrating particularly on center-fire sporting rifles in their export markets, but they have always made .22 rimfire rifles for home consumption. They have now begun exporting this rimfire rifle and, as well as making it in the standard .22 Long Rifle chambering, offer models in .22 Winchester Magnum RF and a center-fire version in .22 Hornet.

The general appearance echoes the lines of their larger-caliber sporting rifles, and the Sako is definitely not intended as a child's first gun or a plinker. The action gives the impression of immense strength, the bolt having two extractors and two locking lugs, while both receiver and bolt are large by conventional .22 rimfire

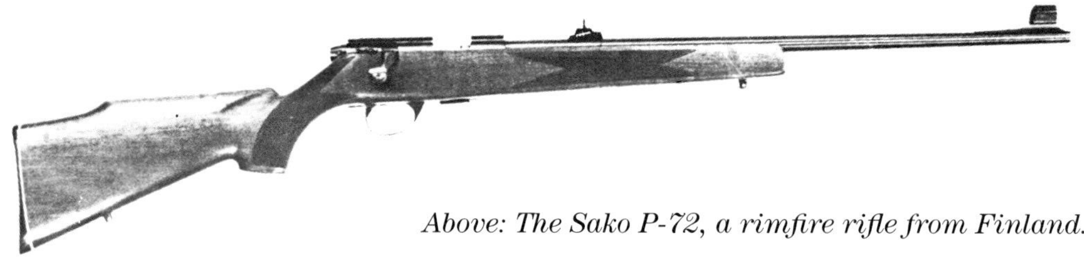

Above: The Sako P-72, a rimfire rifle from Finland.

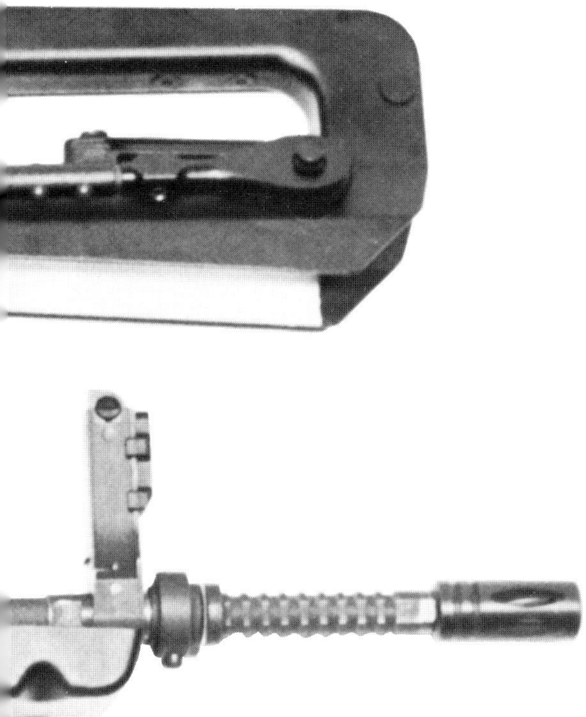

Left: The component parts of the FA-MAS assault rifle.

Right: The 'Headquarters Weapon' version of the SIG SG-541 rifle.

standards. The bolt is an interesting three-piece design in which the firing pin floats free, held back by its own spring, and the cocking piece, driven by the mainspring, is released by the sear to strike the pin. The cocking piece is retracted as the bolt lever is lifted to open the bolt, so that the firing pin spring moves the pin back before the chamber is opened.

The stock is checkered and oil-finished, and there is a substantial pistol grip; the comb of the Monte Carlo butt is somewhat low, though this may be an individual impression.

The sights incorporate the Williams Guide Line and comprise a ramped front sight with hooded bead and an open rear sight adjustable for windage and elevation; the receiver also has dovetail bases for a telescope.

Accuracy is good, one-inch groups at 50 yards being accomplished from a rest. I have seen reports of misfeeding but was unable to fire sufficient rounds to make any conclusions of my own.

SIG SG-550 Rifle

Manufacturer Schweizerische Industrie Gesellschaft (SIG), Neuhausen-Am-Rheinfalls, Switzerland
Type Gas-operated, automatic, magazine
Caliber 5.56mm (.223)
Barrel 14.05in (357mm); or 21in (533mm)
Weight (empty) 8.26lbs (3.75kg); or 7.36lbs (3.34kg)
Magazine Capacity 20, 25 or 30 rounds
Cyclic rate of fire 750 rounds/minute

The Swiss Army has used a powerful 7.5mm cartridge since the turn of the century, but in recent years it decided to investigate a lighter caliber and asked both its own Federal Arsenal at Berne and the SIG Company to develop some new rifles in smaller calibers. As a result both establishments produced prototypes in 5.56mm and in a new 6.45mm caliber; government testing eliminated the 6.45mm round and the SIG 550 became the Swiss service rifle in 1990.

The SIG 550 is their answer to the request and as well as being formally adopted it is now available for com-

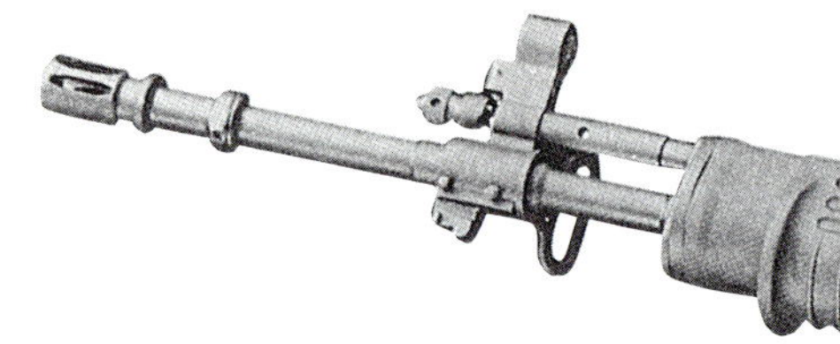

mercial sale to approved customers. It is a conventional gas-piston-operated rifle using a rotating bolt inside a bolt carrier. High-quality plastic material has been used for the folding stock and the fore-end guard, and also for the transparent magazine. Two lengths are available; the longer model is the 'Assault Rifle' while the shorter model is known as the 'Headquarters Weapon' and, with the butt folded, can be used in the submachine-gun role.

The sights are an aperture rear and blade front, with luminous dots for night sighting; there are mounting points for a telescope or for a variety of electro-optical sight units. There is a three-round burst facility, plus single shots or full automatic fire, and a light bipod can be fitted to steady the weapon when used in the squad automatic role.

Left: The SIG SG3000 sniper's rifle.

Below: The SIG SG551 assault rifle.

Left: The SR88A assault rifle.

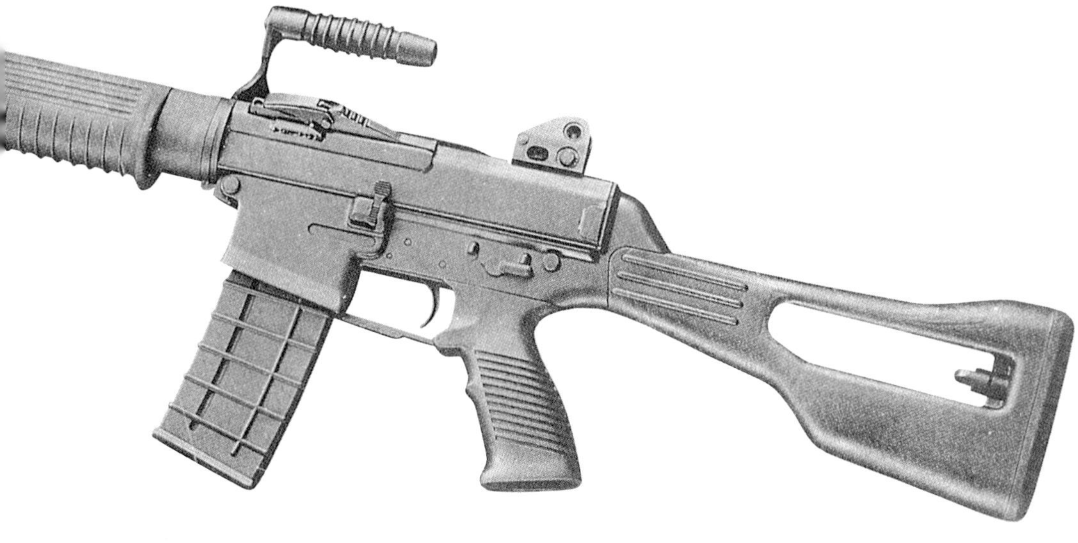

Singapore Assault Rifle SR88A

Manufacturer Chartered Firearms Industries Ltd, Singapore
Type Gas-operated, selective fire
Caliber 5.56mm (.223)
Barrel 18.1in (460mm)
Weight 8.11lbs (3.68kg)
Magazine Capacity 30 rounds

Chartered Firearms Industries began rifle manufacture by making the U.S. M16A1 rifle under license from Colt for the Singapore Armed Forces. They saw that there was a potential market in the Far East for a modern assault rifle, and since they could not market the M16, set about making a rifle of their own. In 1980 a design from Sterling Armaments of Britain went into production as the SAR80 rifle; it has gone through two stages of modification and improvement to reach the present SR88A model.

The SR88A, like its predecessors, uses the conventional gas piston, bolt carrier and rotating bolt method of operation. The lower receiver is an aluminum forging, the upper receiver a steel pressing, and the stock is of glass-fiber reinforced nylon. The bolt group assembly is in modular form and consists of the bolt, carrier, buffer springs and rods. The bolt has seven locking lugs, and the bolt is always kept forward in its carrier by the firing pin spring, a concept which allows for rapid assembly after cleaning and little risk of the bolt falling free during stripping.

The barrel is held to the receiver by a locknut and detent system and is oriented to the receiver by special slots in the barrel extension, so simplifying accurate assembly. The gas system consists of a chrome-plated regulator and a long-stroke piston assembly connected to the bolt carrier. The regulator has three positions, two which provide different amounts of gas and the third which shuts off the gas flow so that the rifle can be used for launching grenades.

The standard rifle has a fixed butt; where compactness is important it can be fitted with a telescoping butt. There is also a carbine version for airborne and other troops who need a more portable weapon. This has a 292mm barrel and a telescoping butt, but is otherwise to the same general design as the standard rifle. There is also an interesting sub-machine gun variant, chambered for the 9mm Parabellum cartridge and with a different barrel and bolt assembly. The bolt is not locked in this model and it operates as a simple blowback weapon. In appearance it is exactly the same as the short carbine, except for a thinner magazine which holds 32 rounds.

Squibman M-16 Rifle

Manufacturer Squires, Bingham Mfg. Co., Marikina, Philippines
Type Semi-automatic, blowback
Caliber .22 Long Rifle RF
Barrel 16in (406mm)
Weight 6lbs (2.72kg)
Magazine Capacity 15 rounds

'Squibman' is the brand name of the Squires Bingham Company and they have produced a variety of rifles, shotguns and pistols under this name. Their M-16 is one of several attempts to make a cheap rimfire weapon which resembles a combat rifle.

The configuration of the rifle is, as the title implies, based upon that of the American M-16, though the detail execution is considerably different. There is the 'straight-line' stock layout, the carrying handle with rear sight, the elevated foresight and the muzzle flash hider. But the mechanism is a simple blowback unit and the barrel and receiver are in a tubular assembly which simply drops into the stock. Below is the pistol grip and magazine housing assembly.

The stock is of mahogany, finished in ebony black, while the metal components are either blackened steel or anodized alloy. The rear sight is a fixed elevation aperture, adjustable for windage.

The M-16 shoots quite well, with acceptable accuracy, and makes a good general purpose 'fun gun' or vermin shooter. The design has not copied the M-16 so slavishly as to finish up with bad proportioning, as have some others, and there is sufficient length of butt to allow the rifle to be held comfortably and firmly.

Above: The Squibman M-16 rifle.

Steyr Advanced Combat Rifle

Manufacturer Steyr-Mannlicher GmbH, Steyr, Austria
Type Gas-operated, selective fire
Caliber 5.56mm synthetic case fléchette
Barrel 21.25in (540mm)
Weight 7.12lbs (3.23kg) without magazine and sight
Magazine Capacity 24 rounds

The Steyr-Mannlicher entrant for the U.S. Advanced Combat Rifle competition was considered to be an excellent example of modern technology, but, like the other entries it could not reach the 100 percent improvement over the M16A2 demanded by the U.S. Army. The company have said that it represents their view of the next generation of assault rifles and they will continue to develop it privately and will probably offer it for consideration some time early in the next century.

The rifle uses a gas system to actuate the breech mechanism, which is quite unusual and which is built around the special cartridge. This cartridge is of plastic, a plain cylinder with the priming composition arranged in a ring around the inside of the case, just ahead of the base. A fin-stabilized fléchette lies inside the case, its fins positioned by the primer ring and the body held by a polycarbonate sabot, and surrounded by propellant.

The breech consists of a block which carries the chamber. At the commencement of firing an operating arm is held back against a spring. On pulling the trigger this arm is released to run forward, take a cartridge from the magazine and load it into the chamber. The chamber then rises vertically to a position behind the barrel, where it is locked by a spring catch. Above the chamber is a fixed firing pin, pointing downwards, and as the chamber rises so this firing pin passes through a hole in the chamber block and, just as the chamber aligns with the barrel and locks, strikes the ring primer and fires the cartridge. The fléchette is driven up the barrel; gas, tapped from the barrel into a surrounding chamber, drives back a piston which is actually a sleeve around the barrel. This drives the operating arm back, unlocking the chamber and lowering it to the loading position. As the trigger is pressed for the next shot, so the arm goes forward again, and the cartridge entering the chamber pushes out the spent plastic case of the previous round, ejecting it forward from the weapon. There is no rim on the plastic case, so no obstacle to this forward ejection.

Above: Steyr's AMR 5075.

The rifle is a bullpup design, with the magazine almost at the rear of the stock. The mechanism is enclosed in a plastic outer casing, there being something of a family resemblance between this and their well-known AUG rifle. A carrying handle above the weapon is extended almost to the muzzle, so acting as a sighting rib for snap shooting, and iron sights are fitted; a telescope can be quickly attached to the carrying handle. The barrel is rifled with a twist of one turn in 85 inches, giving roll stabilization to the fléchette to improve accuracy.

The only real defect of the design, as revealed in the U.S. tests, is that the fléchette tends to leave the cartridge at varying chamber pressures, due to inconsistent strength in the plastic cartridge case. Varying pressures mean varying muzzle velocities and changes in trajectory from shot to shot, so that accuracy suffers. This, however, is simply a question of testing various materials and assembly methods until a consistent release pressure can be obtained, and it is probable that Steyr have already solved this, ready to offer the rifle to the next applicant.

Steyr AMR 5075 Anti-Matériel Rifle

Manufacturer Steyr-Mannlicher GmbH, Steyr, Austria
Type long recoil, semi-automatic
Caliber 14.5mm Special
Barrel 47.25in (1200mm) smoothbore
Weight 44lbs (20kg) approximately
Magazine Capacity 5 rounds

It will be recalled (see the Barrett rifle above) that the 1980s saw a sudden interest in the development of heavy sniping rifles, primarily intended for the destruction of vulnerable high-technology equipment. Unfortunately

the word 'sniping' suggests anti-personnel shooting, which gave many people a completely wrong idea about the function of these weapons. Steyr-Mannlicher avoided this by carefully calling this weapon an 'anti-matériel' rifle.

The AMR 5075 is a heavyweight precision rifle for a long-range attack of vulnerable equipment. It uses the long recoil system of operation; barrel and bolt recoil locked together for almost ten inches, after which the bolt is unlocked and held while the barrel runs back to the forward position. The bolt is then released to run forward, collect a cartridge, load it and then lock into the chamber by rotating.

This long recoil movement helps to absorb some of the recoil force; more is absorbed by a multi-baffle muzzle brake of high efficiency, and the entire barrel recoils inside a sleeve-type hydro-pneumatic recoil system which is more like the sort of thing found on artillery weapons than anything generally associated with rifles. All these reduction methods cut the felt recoil to a level which is little more than that of a conventional service rifle.

This is necessary, because the cartridge is a very powerful design. Instead of building the weapon around an existing cartridge, Steyr designed the cartridge to do what was wanted and then designed the weapon to suit. The cartridge case is of part-plastic construction and carries a 36-gram (1.25 ounce) tungsten fléchette which has a muzzle velocity of 4920 ft/sec (1500 m/sec) and an effective range up to 2000 meters, depending upon the type of target. At 800 meters range this fléchette has penetrated 40mm of rolled steel armor and then shattered behind the plate to give severe fragmentation damage.

The weapon is supported on a bipod, attached to the recoil cradle, and there is a 10-power telescope sight fitted as standard. A box magazine is inserted from the right side; on the prototype this held five rounds, but an eight-round magazine has since been developed. Other options for the future are automatic fire at a low rate, and the adoption of a rifled barrel so as to be able to take advantage of other ammunition designs.

The AMR 5075 was first shown publicly in 1990; this, unfortunately, was just the time when severe economies were beginning to be felt in the military world, and though a great deal of interest was expressed, no army has so far decided to adopt the weapon. Meanwhile Steyr go on refining it, and we may be sure that we have not heard the last of this potent design.

Steyr Armee-Universal-Gewehr

Manufacturer Steyr-Mannlicher GmbH, Steyr, Austria
Type Gas-operated, selective fire
Caliber 5.56mm (.223)
Barrel Various
Weight 7.9lbs (3.6kg) (508mm barrel)
Magazine Capacity 30 rounds
Cyclic rate of fire 650 rounds/minute

Below: The Steyr AUG assault rifle.

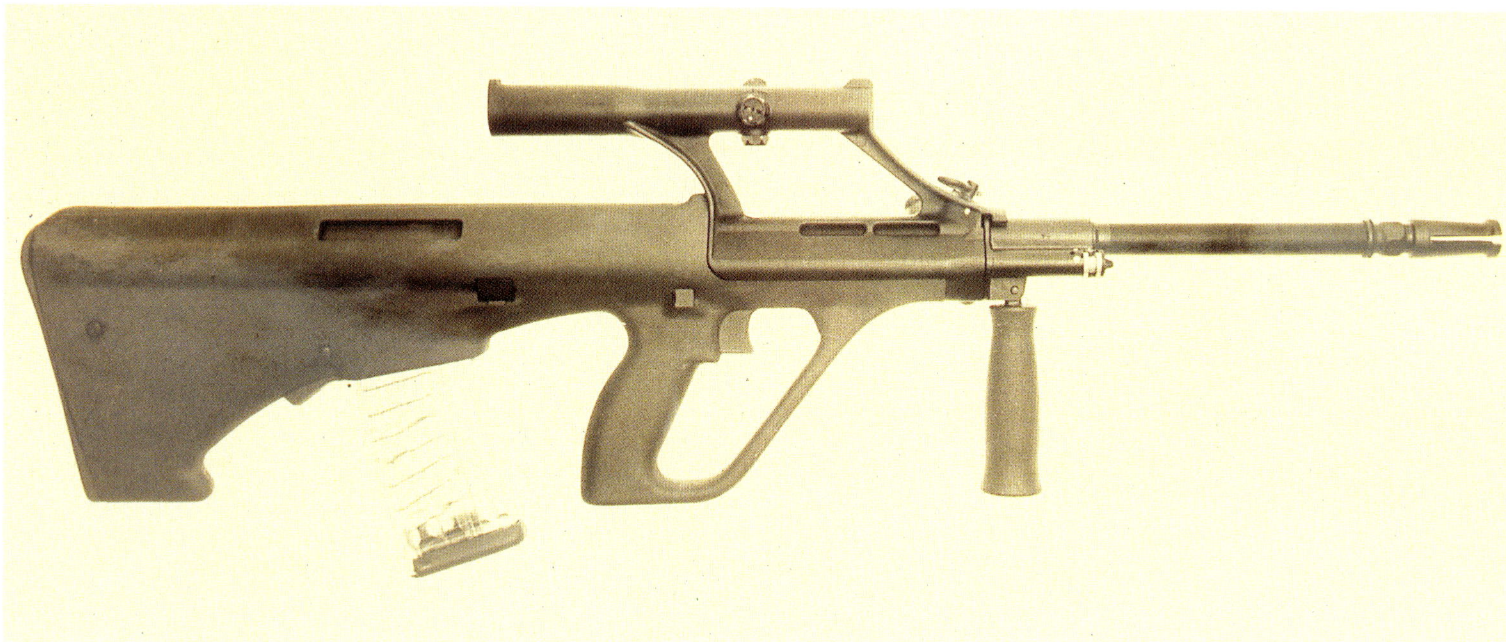

Above: Steyr's SSG-69 fitted with a suppressor.

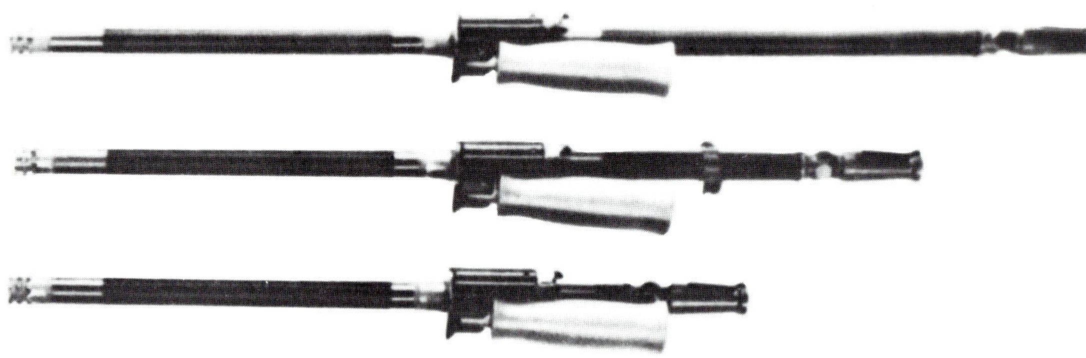

Right: The Steyr AUG with alternative barrels. From top to bottom: the squad machine gun, rifle, carbine, and submachine gun barrels.

Below, far right: The futuristic lines of the Steyr AUG.

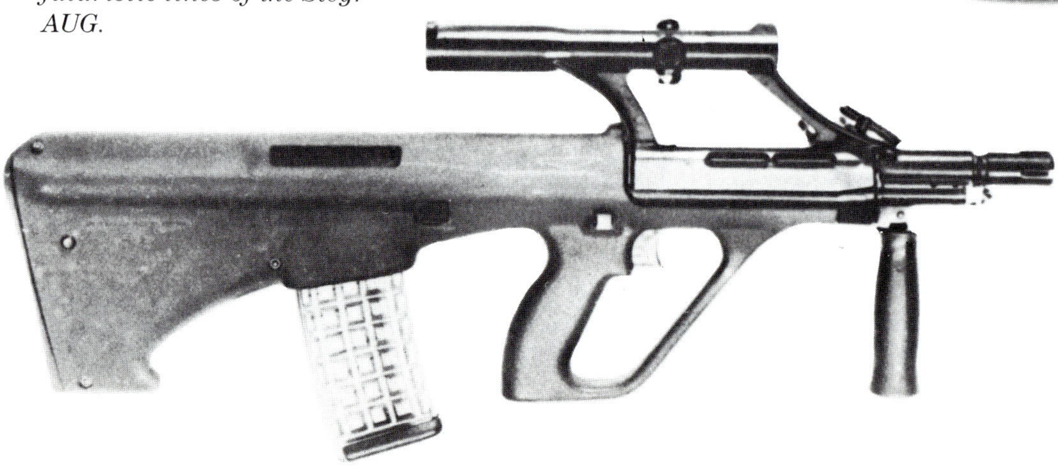

The Steyr AUG gets its name from its ability to be configured in four different ways, depending upon the length of the barrel and the presence or absence of a bipod. The basic mechanism, receiver and stock remain the same in all cases.

In appearance the AUG is, to say the least, futuristic, the plastic stock material and shape giving it the appearance of a toy or something from a space program. But its performance puts it well into the front rank of contemporary assault rifles and it has already been adopted by the armies of Austria, Argentina, Saudi Arabia and Tunisia, with others currently making evaluations and comparisons preparatory to possible orders.

The plastic stock unit forms a major part of the weapon; the principal feature is the main pistol grip with an enormous trigger guard which accepts the whole hand. Behind this is the magazine and its housing and release, and then the shoulder stock. It follows from this sequence that the AUG is a 'bullpup', having the action under the firer's cheek and the trigger well forward of the bolt and magazine.

The receiver unit is an aluminum die-casting which includes the seating for the barrel, bearings for the two bolt guides, the carrying handle and the optical sight. The bolt is the usual rotating multi-lug type held in a carrier, and this carrier moves back and forth on two machined steel bolt guide rods which are held in the receiver; thus there is no direct contact between receiver and bolt and therefore no need for expensive machining of the boltway. The return springs are concealed within the guide rods; in addition the left-hand rod acts with the cocking lever to operate the bolt when loading, and right-hand rod acts as the gas piston.

The barrel unit consists of the barrel, gas port and cylinder, gas regulator and a folding forward hand grip.

This grip can be used to change barrels, since the barrel locks into the receiver by interrupted lugs. Once the barrel is aligned, the gas cylinder unit, which carries a short-stroke piston, lines up with the right-hand bolt guide rod. One might expect some degree of imbalance with the gas impulse working off-axis, but in practice there is no torque effect and no deviation of shooting is detectable.

The magazine is a clear plastic unit, so that its contents can be seen at all times. The trigger group, containing the safety and selective fire mechanism, is a removable unit, much of it plastic. Selective fire is achieved by trigger pressure; a light pressure gives single shots, a harder pressure automatic fire. Again, this is something which, at first, one would expect to lead to inaccuracy, but once the technique is mastered it gives no trouble and automatic fire can be delivered as accurately with the AUG as with any other comparable rifle.

The various models are as follows: 'Commando' with 14in (315mm) barrel; 'Machine Carbine' with 16in (407mm) barrel; 'Assault Rifle' (the standard version) with 20in (508mm) barrel; and the 'Heavy Barrel Rifle' or 'Squad Automatic Weapon' with 24in (610mm) barrel and bipod. All models can be modified by removing the receiver casting and replacing it with another type which carries a low telescope mount instead of the optical sight and integral telescope; this is intended to cater for sniping telescopes or night vision sights.

Firing the AUG holds no surprises; it can be set up for left or right-hand firing very quickly by changing the ejector to one or other side of the bolt and rotating the ejection port cover in the butt to expose the port on the selected side. For those not accustomed to bullpup rifles, the weight distribution feels strange and distinctly light at the muzzle, but this is soon mastered and the rifle is extremely handy for use in quick combat situations. Accuracy is as good as, if not slightly better, than most other rifles of this caliber. The rifling is one turn in 41 calibers, tighter than the usual 1/54, which suggests that it will shoot equally well with a wide variety of service ammunition types.

Steyr-Mannlicher SSG-69 Sniper's Rifle

Manufacturer Steyr-Mannlicher GmbH, Steyr, Austria
Type Bolt-action, magazine
Caliber 7.62mm NATO
Barrel 25.6in (650mm)
Weight 8.6lbs (3.9kg)
Magazine Capacity 5 rounds

I have previously commented upon the recent rise in the use of bolt-action rifles for military sniping, replacing the earlier semi-automatics. One of the first to make this move was the Austrian Army, and the Steyr SSG-69 was the weapon developed to their specification.

When this rifle first appeared, most commentators suggested that it was simply the Greek Army Mannlicher-Schoenauer Model 1900 revived, but this was a gross simplification. In the first place the bolt is unusual in having its six locking lugs, in three pairs, at the rear and not in the front; in theory this is liable to give rise to compression stresses in the bolt and consequent inaccuracy, but in practice it seems not to matter. By way of compensation the barrel is set extremely deeply into the receiver and the receiver itself is strengthened, so that the whole assembly is rock-rigid.

The magazine is the Schoenauer rotating spool type, not seen on a military rifle since the aforementioned 1900 model, and it can be quickly removed from the bottom of the stock by squeezing in two grips on its base. The rear face of the magazine is closed by a transparent panel, so that the firer can slip the magazine out and, without moving it, can check on its contents and replace it. There is a specially-adapted 10-round box

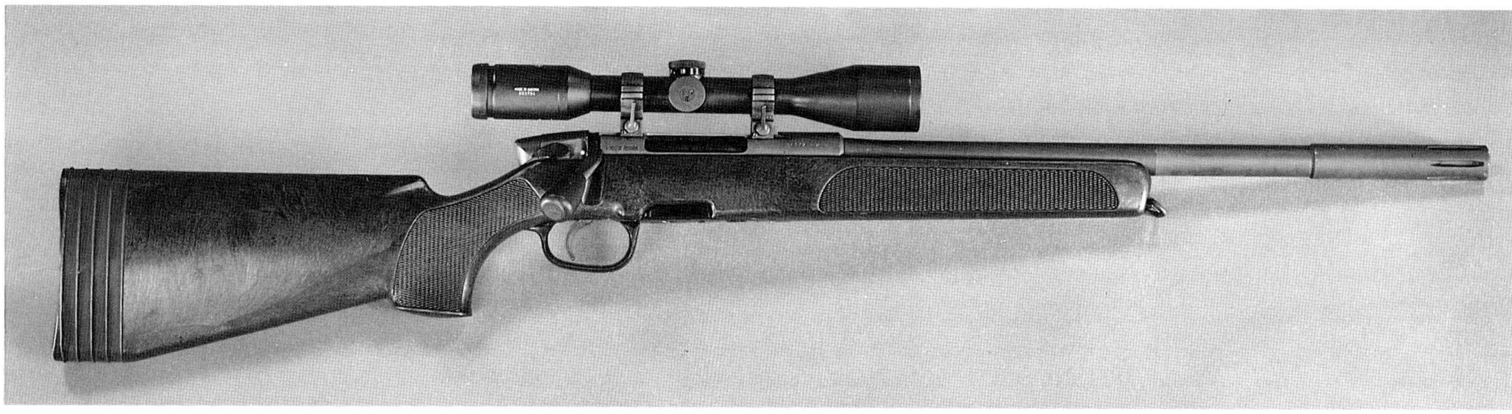

Above: The police version of the Steyr-Mannlicher SSG-69 sniper's rifle.

magazine which will fit in place of the spool should this be desired.

Iron sights are fitted for emergency use, a blade foresight and 'V' notch backsight. In normal use this weapon will be aimed by a telescope and the receiver is ribbed to take the Kahles 'Helia 6S2' which is standard issue. The same mounting can also be used for infra-red or image-intensifying night sights.

The stock and butt are made of olive-drab self-colored glass-reinforced fiber plastic material which is rot-resistant, impervious to rain, and fairly resistant to casual impact damage. It is also less likely to be seen than a wooden stock and has a matted surface which gives a good grip at all points, though the pistol grip and fore end have additional stippling.

In use this weapon is very accurate, giving 3½-inch groups at 30 yards, though as with most rifles of this type the accuracy relies greatly upon the quality of the military-grade ammunition. It is now available commercially, with a walnut stock and Walther match-grade adjustable sights; it makes an excellent full-bore match rifle.

Above: The Valmet M76 assault rifle.

Stirling M-20 Rifle

Manufacturer Squires, Bingham Mfg Co., Marikina, Philippines
Type Semi-automatic, blowback
Caliber .22 Long Rifle RF
Barrel 19.5in (495mm)
Weight 6lbs (2.72kg)
Magazine Capacity 15 rounds

The Stirling is another product of the Philippine Islands company of Squires Bingham. It is, in essence, the same blowback action used in their 'Squibman M-16' combat-style rifle but installed into a more conventional form of stock.

The stock is of Philippine mahogany; the standard model is sanded and oil finished while the De Luxe Model has the grain well figured and is with a polished finish. Both have machined checkering on pistol grip and fore end, and butt pads and pistol grip caps with

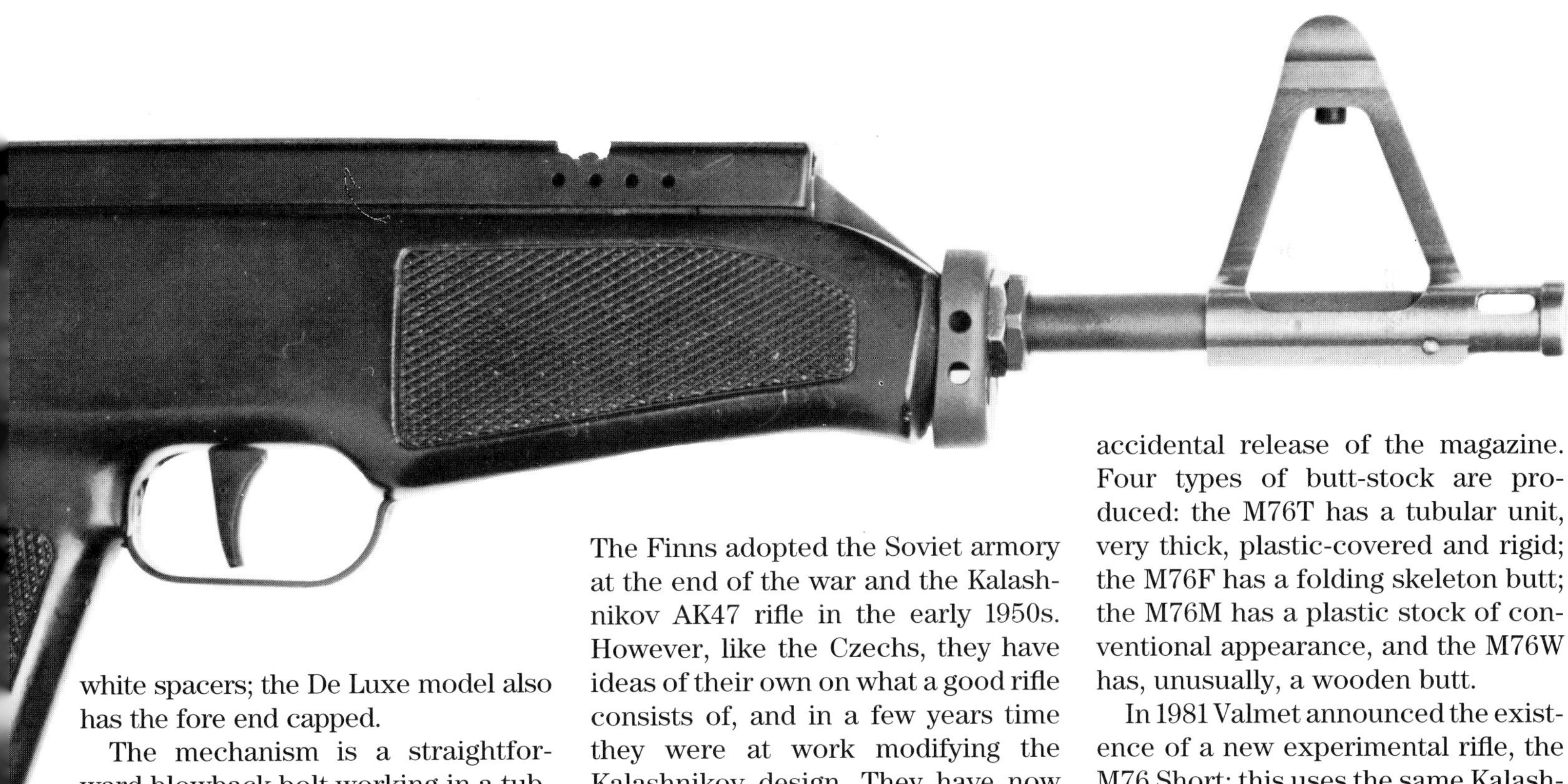

white spacers; the De Luxe model also has the fore end capped.

The mechanism is a straightforward blowback bolt working in a tubular receiver attached behind the barrel; the trigger mechanism and magazine housing are fitted through the stock, and the box magazine goes in from beneath. There is a combined muzzle brake and compensator, though just how much of its effect is practical and how much cosmetic is a moot point in this caliber. The whole of the mechanism can be removed from the stock by simply taking out one screw, after which disassembly into the various component parts for cleaning is very simple.

The Stirling is a sound little rifle, excellent for vermin and general plinking and sufficiently accurate for all practical purposes. It is well finished, and of first-class material, and the manufacture and assembly appears to be to a high standard for a reasonably-priced weapon.

Valmet M76 Rifle

Manufacturer Valmet Oy, Jyvaskyla, Finland
Type Gas-operated, selective fire
Caliber 7.62 × 39mm Soviet
Barrel 16.5in (420mm)
Weight 7.7lbs (3.5kg)
Magazine Capacity 15 or 30 rounds
Cyclic rate of fire 650 rounds/minute

The Finns adopted the Soviet armory at the end of the war and the Kalashnikov AK47 rifle in the early 1950s. However, like the Czechs, they have ideas of their own on what a good rifle consists of, and in a few years time they were at work modifying the Kalashnikov design. They have now gone through three stages of change and their latest version is known as the M-76. Though it looks like a standard Kalashnikov (though with far better exterior finish) there are some major differences. It has been adopted by the forces of Qatar, in the Middle East, and a semi-automatic-only version is sold as a sporting rifle in the U.S.A.

The receiver is of stamped steel rivetted together, and there is no wood whatever in the construction; the pistol grip and fore end are of steel, covered in plastic. Earlier versions (M60 and M62) have cooling holes in the fore end, but these have been omitted on the M76. There is a three-pronged flash hider on the muzzle, one prong of which carries a bayonet lug. The foresight is a hooded, adjustable, post, while the back sight is an aperture type protected by two wings. Instead of using the Soviet position in front of the chamber, the Finnish rear sight, being an aperture, is at the rear end of the receiver. It is also fitted with Tritium light beads for night aiming.

The trigger guard has no forward part, so that heavily-gloved fingers can get in to the trigger; there is a hinged bar at the front end to prevent accidental release of the magazine. Four types of butt-stock are produced: the M76T has a tubular unit, very thick, plastic-covered and rigid; the M76F has a folding skeleton butt; the M76M has a plastic stock of conventional appearance, and the M76W has, unusually, a wooden butt.

In 1981 Valmet announced the existence of a new experimental rifle, the M76 Short; this uses the same Kalashnikov mechanism of the M76 but fitted into a bullpup stock. It is chambered for the 5.56mm cartridge. The stock of the prototype is entirely of wood, but it is said that if the rifle were to go into production, then a plastic stock would be developed. However, the Finnish army showed no interest and the design was abandoned.

MACHINE GUNS

Previous pages: The Bushman 'Individual Defense Weapon; in action.

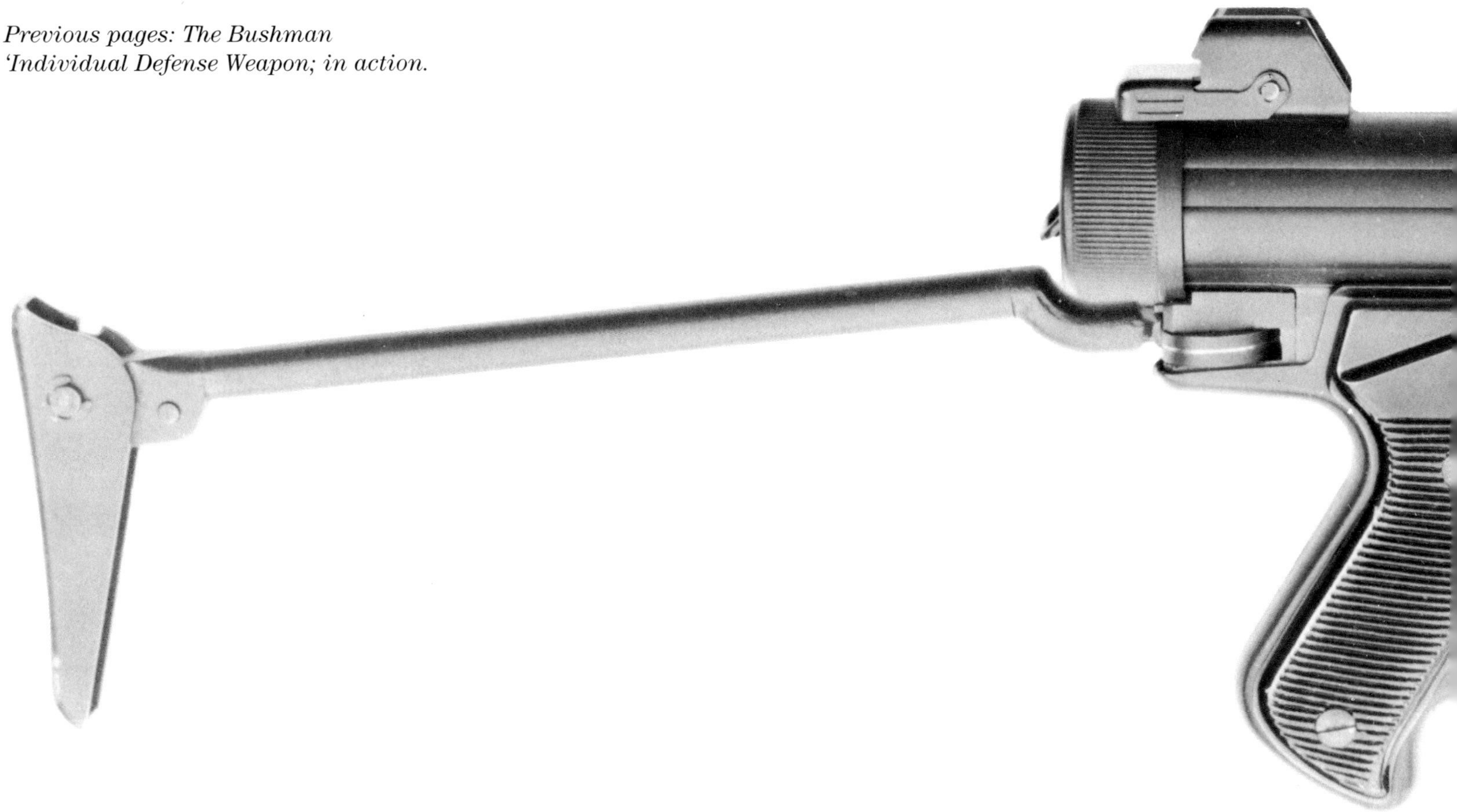

AKSU-74

Manufacturer State Rifle Factory, Izhevsk, Russia
Type Gas-operated, selective fire
Caliber 5.45mm
Barrel 7.87in (200mm)
Weight ca. 6.5lbs (3kg)
Magazine Capacity 30 rounds
Cyclic rate of fire 800 rounds/minute

When the Soviets adopted the Kalashnikov 7.62mm rifle, they abandoned their submachine guns, but in later years realized that they had been a little too hasty and needed a more compact weapon for occupants of vehicles. Their first attempt was to shorten the AK47 rifle, but this proved to be almost uncontrollable at automatic fire. At about this time they adopted the 5.45mm caliber for a new generation of Kalashnikov rifles and machine guns, and shortly afterwards set about making a compact model in the new caliber. The result was the AKSU-74, which was first revealed to the West in 1982 when a specimen was captured in Afghanistan.

The AKSU retains the basic method of operation of the familiar AK47 rifle, using a gas piston and a rotating bolt, but the shortening of the barrel introduced several complications. The 5.45mm cartridge was designed to be fired in a long-barrelled rifle, and the gas system of the Kalashnikov taps its gas from a position about two-thirds of the way up the barrel. Since the AKSU barrel is so short, all the gas generated in the cartridge would not have time to expend its energy and there would be a prominent muzzle flame and considerable blast. Therefore, a bulbous muzzle attachment can be seen, which acts as an expansion chamber for the emerging gas and muffles the flash and blast. It also helps to balance the internal pressure so that it is possible to tap off gas for the gas system closer to the breech than in other weapons.

A skeleton butt is fitted, which folds to the left side of the weapon, reducing the overall length to about 16.5 inches. The magazine is similar to that used with the AK-74 rifle, but has strengthening ribs molded into its front edge and is made of a lamination of sheet steel and plastic material. The receiver top cover is hinged to the gas block and lifts up to permit stripping the weapon; this differs from all other Kalashnikov designs, in which the top cover lifts off completely.

The AKSU is an ingenious design, but in many eyes somewhat overpowerful for the self-defense role for which it is intended. However, it does mean that the design and operation is already familiar to any soldier who knows the AK series of rifles – which was every Soviet soldier – and, unlike submachine guns, it does not require its own particular type of ammunition, happily firing the standard rifle cartridges.

Beretta Model 12S

Manufacturer Armi Beretta SpA, Gardone Val Trompia, Italy
Type Blowback, selective fire
Caliber 9mm Parabellum
Barrel 7.87in (200mm)
Weight (empty) 7.05lbs (3.2kg)
Magazine Capacity 20, 32 or 40 rounds
Cyclic rate of fire 550 rounds/minute

The Beretta Model 12 submachine gun has been in use by several armies since the late 1950s and has been produced under license in Indonesia and

Above: The Beretta 12A, a slight modification to a highly-respected design.

Below: The Model 12S field stripped.

Brazil. Beretta have now brought it up to date in a new and slightly modified version which has been issued to the Italian forces and has also been exported to Tunisia and other countries.

The basic Model 12 is a sheet steel submachine gun of outstanding robustness and simplicity. The breech block is of the 'overhung' type and surrounds the barrel at the moment of firing, while the pistol grips, magazine housing and trigger housing are all in one piece. There is a grip safety in the pistol grip which ensures that the bolt cannot move unless the weapon is being properly held in the firing position. It has a reputation for smooth action and controllable fire, largely

due to its balance and the fact that most of the barrel is inside the receiver so that the turning movement about the forward pistol grip is very small.

The Model 12S differs in having the fire selector and safety catch in a single lever unit, instead of two; the front sight has been made adjustable for windage and elevation; the attachment of the receiver rear cap has been strengthened and its locking catch moved to the top of the receiver for easier visual checking; the butt plate of the folding metal stock has been modified by the addition of a catch which ensures positive locking folded or unfolded position.

Though these are relatively small changes, they have made a positive difference to the weapon and turned a good design into a better one.

Top and right: The Beretta 12S is a weapon with a long service record. It was first introduced in the 1950s.

Above: The Model 12 with its butt folded.

9mm P.B. 39881

Bushman IDW

Manufacturer Bushman Ltd, Frogmore, St. Albans, England
Type Blowback, regulated
Caliber 9mm Parabellum
Barrel 3.25in (82.5mm)
Weight (empty) 6.4lbs (2.92kg)
Magazine Capacity 20, 28 or 32 rounds
Cyclic rate of fire 450 rounds/minute

The Bushman is described as an 'Individual Defense Weapon' (IDW) and is exceptionally small, no more than 10.8 inches (276mm) long. It can be easily concealed and carried, though it is rather heavier than might be expected from its size.

The Bushman introduced an entirely new idea into automatic weapons. Hitherto, it has been usual to build a weapon and then find out how fast it fires; if the rate of fire is too high or too low, then adjustments are made to the weight of the bolt, the strength of the return spring and other features in order to approach the desired figure. But the desired figure was no more than a figure which the designer felt was right; it had no scientific or technical origin. As a result most submachine guns are difficult to keep on target, since the vibration of the weapon and the muzzle blast combine to lift the muzzle during automatic fire, and the shots fly harmlessly into the air.

The designer of the Bushman reasoned that like most mechanical devices, a submachine gun would have a 'natural frequency' at which it would fire smoothly, without vibration and without the muzzle climbing. He developed an electronic control unit which arrested the bolt for a fraction of a second as it recoiled, and then released it. Being electronic, this device could be adjusted from infinitely slow to the full natural speed of the weapon, and it was simply a question of experimenting to find the natural frequency once the weapon had been designed.

Above left and left: Two views of the Bushman IDW, one of the smallest submachine guns in existence.

Above: The CETME Ameli 5.56mm machine gun.

The result is one of the smallest submachine guns in existence, little larger than an automatic pistol, which can be fired one-handed at a full automatic rate of 450 rounds a minute and which puts all the bullets into the target area. The weapon does not jump; it merely rocks slightly in the hand.

The Bushman is heavy for its size, being machined from forged steel, using modern computer-controlled machine tools. It is a blowback weapon, and without the delaying mechanism would have a natural rate of fire of about 1400 rounds per minute, at which rate it would be almost uncontrollable and certainly incapable of being fired one-handed. But the regulator arrests the bolt momentarily after each shot and then, instructed by a micro-chip, releases it at the correct time to give the desired rate of fire.

The electronic control principle has also been applied to some existing submachine gun designs, with equally good effect. At the time of writing the Bushman has just entered production, and it will be interesting to see where it will be adopted.

CETME Ameli 5.56mm Machine Gun

Manufacturer Santa Barbara SA, Madrid, Spain
Type Delayed blowback, automatic
Caliber 5.56mm
Barrel 15.75in (400mm)
Weight 11.5lbs (5.2kg)
Magazine Capacity 200-round belt
Cyclic rate of fire 900 rounds/minute

CETME (Centro de Estudios Tecnicos de Materiales Especiales) is a design and research establishment set up by the Spanish government in the early 1950s, and many of the original staff were refugees from Germany with experience in gun design. As a result, one can trace the original parentage of some of their designs right back to the Mauserwerke of 1943/45, and by the look of this weapon, to some other wartime design establishments as well: the Ameli looks very much like a miniaturised German MG42.

The Ameli was designed in the early 1980s for the Spanish Army, and it was one of the earliest 5.56mm machine

guns to enter service with any army. As with most of the weapons developed by CETME, it uses a delayed blowback system relying upon a roller locking system much the same as that used in the Model L rifle and in the Heckler & Koch rifles and machine guns. A two-part bolt is used, and as it closes, the rear section forces two rollers outwards into grooves in the receiver. On firing, the forward portion of the bolt cannot move back until these rollers have been withdrawn, which is done by pressure of inclined faces and delays the opening of the bolt long enough to let the bullet leave the muzzle.

The barrel lies within a perforated barrel jacket which has a long slot in the right side. A quick-release lever unlocks the barrel and forces the breech end out of the slot so that it can be grasped and pulled out of its front bearing. A fresh, cool, barrel can then be inserted, and a trained squad can change the barrel in under five seconds.

Feed is by means of a disintegrating-link belt; as each round is loaded from the belt the link falls free, so that there is no problem of what to do with the empty belt as it comes out of the gun. The rate of fire can be adjusted between 800 and 1200 rounds per minute to suit the particular role; the Ameli can be used either as a light squad automatic, when the high rate of fire is generally selected, or as a tripod-mounted company support weapon, where the low rate of fire is more appropriate.

The Ameli is currently in use by the Spanish Army, and has been assessed by several others. It is manufactured by Santa Barbara, the state armaments company, since, unusually, CETME do not possess any manufacturing capacity.

Chinese Type 64 Silenced

Manufacturer Chinese State Arsenal
Type Blowback, selective fire, silenced
Caliber 7.62mm Soviet Pistol
Barrel 9.6in (244mm)
Weight (empty) 7.5lbs (3.4kg)
Magazine Capacity 30 rounds
Cyclic rate of fire Not known

This weapon is far from new, its Type number being an indication of its date into service, but it was not generally known in the west until the latter 1970s. It is completely Chinese-designed and constructed and appears to be an amalgam of ideas taken from various European designs. So far as is known, the Type 64 is only used by the Chinese Communist Army.

The basic mechanism is that of the Soviet PPS-43, a plain blowback weapon using a stamped and welded steel receiver to house a very basic bolt and return spring. The trigger mechanism, which incorporates a selective fire mechanism, is a copy of that used on the Bren machine gun, several hundred of which, in 7.92mm Mauser caliber, were made in Canada and supplied to China during the 1939-45 war. The chamber is fluted, a step probably devised to ease extraction with the necked cartridge case, and the curved magazine fits into the bottom of the receiver.

The forward section of the barrel is perforated with four rows of holes which follow the rifling grooves, after which there are a series of disc-shaped baffles with a central hole through which the bullet passes. This whole assembly is surrounded by a jacket which forms the external 'barrel' section of the weapon. The result is unique because it is a rare example of a weapon designed from scratch as a silenced gun, and not one which has had the silencer added as an afterthought or modification. It is moderately effective, though not so efficient in silencing as the British Sterling or American Ingram designs, but it has the added bonus of being an efficient flash hider, so that the result is a useful weapon for ambushes and guerrilla operations. The principal drawback is the loss of velocity due to the escape of gas through the barrel vents; this is intended to reduce the bullet to subsonic speed, but obviously has a deleterious effect on its range and penetrative power.

Above and right: Two views of the Ameli 5.56 machine gun.

Above: The Chinese Type 64 silenced submachine gun, without magazine.

FAMAE SAF

Manufacturer FAMAE, Santiago, Chile
Type Blowback, selective fire
Caliber 9mm Parabellum
Barrel 7.87in (200mm)
Weight (empty) 6.4lbs (2.9kg)
Magazine Capacity 30 rounds
Cyclic rate of fire 1300 rounds/minute

Like the Steyr submachine gun, the SAF is based upon an assault rifle design, though in this case with much more modification. In the 1980s the FAMAE factory (the Chilean government small arms factory) obtained a license to manufacture the Swiss SIG 540 assault rifle. This is a 5.56mm locked-breech weapon of fairly conventional pattern, and is the standard

Left and below left: The Chilean-manufactured FAMAE SAF, available with either fixed or folding butt. Based on the Swiss SIG540 assault rifle, the SAF is standard Chilean army issue.

Chilean service rifle. Having set up the machinery to make this rifle, FAMAE looked at the design and decided to adapt what they could of the rifle to a submachine gun.

The general design, the receiver, stock and fore-end, is that of the rifle, though shortened. The rotating bolt breech closing system was modified to a simple blowback bolt, but the rifle's hammer mechanism was retained, so that, like the AUG 9 Para, this weapon fires from a closed bolt. The actual mechanism was altered, however, to allow for single shots, automatic fire or three-round bursts, the latter being somewhat unusual on submachine guns.

A new 9mm barrel was designed and fitted. The magazine was made in translucent plastic so that the contents can be seen at any time; it is also fitted with protruding lugs on one side and keyhole-like slots on the other, so that two or three magazines can be clipped together. One can be inserted into the magazine housing on the weapon, leaving the others exposed. When the first magazine is empty, it is simple to slip it out, shift the lot sideways and slip a fresh magazine into position – far quicker than withdrawing a fresh magazine from a pouch and fitting it in place, then having to pick up the old magazine.

Three models of the SAF are made; the standard model with a fixed plastic butt; standard with a side-folding tubular metal butt; and a silenced model with an integral silencer and folding butt.

There is also the 'Mini-SAF' with a much shorter barrel, no shoulder stock and a forward handgrip. It can use the standard 30-round magazine but a special 20-round magazine gives additional compactness. The whole weapon is only 12 inches long and is ideal for stealth work like bodyguard and covert operations.

FN P-90 Personal Defense Weapon

Manufacturer FN Herstal SA, Herstal, Belgium
Type Blowback, selective fire
Caliber 5.7 × 28mm SS90
Barrel
Weight 7lbs (3.02kg) with full magazine
Magazine Capacity 50 rounds
Cyclic rate of fire 900 rounds/minute

This unique weapon was developed by FN Herstal (originally, and perhaps better, known as Fabrique National of Liège) as a result of a very careful analysis of weapons usage in modern armies. This showed that only the assault infantry – which is perhaps about one-eighth of an army – actually needs a powerful (and expensive) assault rifle. The other seven-eighths are troops who serve other weapons – artillery, rockets or tanks, for example – or are service, communication or supply troops; none of these expect to use a rifle as their primary job, but they need a weapon for self-defense should the gun position be attacked or the ration column ambushed. Pistols and submachine guns are traditionally the weapon for these troops, but both these require training and constant practice to get the best out of them. A low-recoil weapon with a reasonable self-defense range and sufficient power to defeat body armor was required, one which was simple and instinctive in its use.

The P-90 broke new ground in weapon design. The shape is unusual, with a forward grip which can be held with both hands when the weapon is fired from the shoulder, or simply by one hand with the butt tucked into the hip. It is a blowback, firing a specially-designed cartridge which is more like a small rifle cartridge than the usual type of submachine gun round. The magazine lies on top of the receiver,

Below: The FN P-90 PDW.

with the cartridges lying across the axis of the weapon and feeding through a turntable which turns them through 90 degrees and guides them into the feedway in front of the bolt. Ejection is downwards, through the hollow pistol grip.

A collimating optical sight is fitted, which can be used with both eyes open and projects an image of a circle and central dot on to the view of the target. There are also two sets of iron sights, so that both right- and left-handed firers find it easy to aim.

The bullet has a synthetic core and metal jacket; it is capable of piercing 30 layers of Kevlar fabric (as used in bullet-proof vests) at 100 meters range and a standard steel helmet at 150 meters. In spite of this, the recoil energy is about two-thirds of the 9mm Parabellum round and the weapon is quite easily controlled during automatic fire.

The P-90 has been adopted by a number of military forces since its introduction in 1992.

Left and below: The compact FN P-90.

Top and above: Two views of the FN 'Minimi' machine gun.

FN 'Minimi' Machine Gun

Manufacturer Fabrique Nationale d'Armes de Guerre, Herstal, Belgium
Type Gas-operated light machine gun
Caliber 5.56mm (.223)
Barrel 18.3in (465mm)
Weight 14.32lbs (6.5kg)
Magazine Capacity 30 rounds, or belts
Cyclic rate of fire 850 rounds/minute

When Fabrique Nationale developed their 5.56mm CAL rifle in the late 1960s, they felt it logical to continue work and develop a 5.56mm machine gun to accompany it. In fact the CAL was somewhat ahead of its time, and has since been replaced by the FNC, an improved design, but the 'Minimi' machine gun appeared in 1974 and was well-timed to catch the first stirring of enthusiasm for the 5.56 caliber. It has been adopted by the armies of Belgium, Indonesia, Thailand and other countries and also approved for the U.S. Army as the M249 Squad Automatic Weapon (SAW).

The Minimi is of conventional type, using gas tapped from the barrel to drive a piston which propels a bolt carrier. This contains a rotating bolt which is unlocked by cam action. The unusual feature of the Minimi is its feed system; it is capable of feeding from a box magazine or from a belt. The bolt is provided with two sets of feed horns which will strip cartridges either from an overhead belt or from a side-mounted magazine, while a simple mechanism prevents any attempt to feed both at once. Thus the gun can be normally operated as a belt-feed weapon but in an emergency

Above: The 'Minimi' squad automatic weapon, as adopted by the U.S. armed forces.

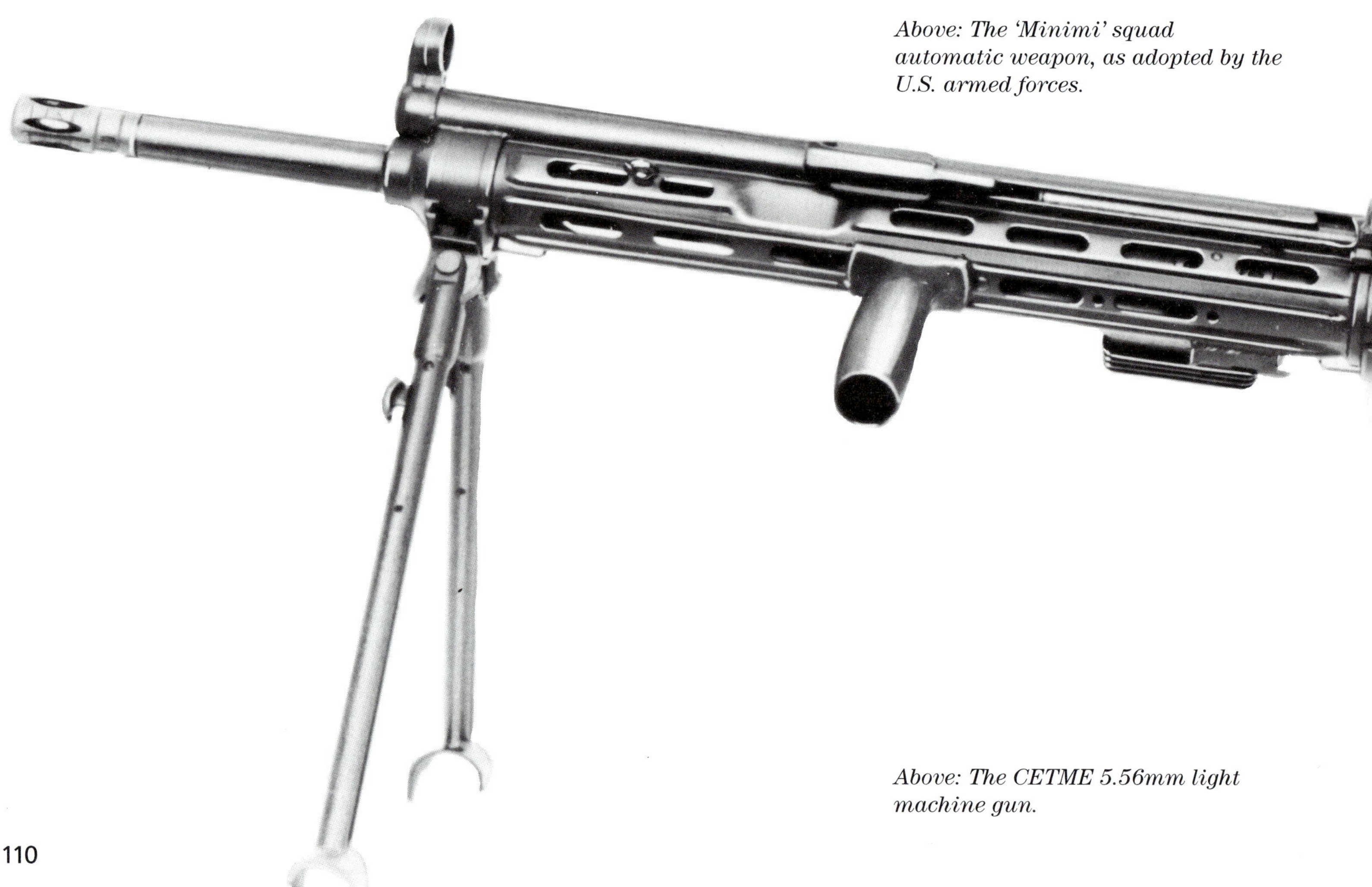

Above: The CETME 5.56mm light machine gun.

can be fed from the standard M16A1 30-round box. The belt is carried in a transparent box which acts as a carrier when not on the gun and then locks securely to the gun when installed for feeding. Two sizes are available, one for 100 rounds and one for 200 rounds.

The standard model has a fixed metal butt; there is a variant model for airborne or special forces which has a shorter barrel (335mm) and a folding metal butt. Both types have quick-release barrels so that they can be changed when over-heating. The standard sights consist of a protected blade mounted on the gas regulator and an elevation-adjustable aperture rear sight. The receiver will also accept NATO standard mounts for image-intensifying sights.

Trials by the U.S. Army, preparatory to accepting it for the SAWS program, showed the Minimi to be remarkably free from stoppages and breakages during prolonged firing. By adopting the Minimi the U.S. Army looks like having a good light machine gun for the first time in its history.

Above: The 'Minimi' in action.

Heckler & Koch HK21A1 GP Machine Gun

Manufacturer Heckler & Koch GmbH, Oberndorf-Am-Neckar, Germany
Type Delayed blowback general-purpose automatic
Caliber 7.62mm NATO
Barrel 17.7in (450mm)
Weight 17.63lbs (8kg)
Magazine Capacity Belt feed
Cyclic rate of fire 900 rounds/minute

The HK21A1 is the latest development of the HK21 gun, which has been in military service for some years, and the aim has been to produce a one-man machine gun which will improve the firepower of the infantry squad without adding to their logistic load. As well as being the squad light gun it can be tripod-mounted and used as a company support weapon.

The layout of the gun is similar to the company's rifle design, and it uses the same roller-locked delayed blowback breech mechanism. A major change has been to do away with the magazine-loading option and make

this a belt-fed-only gun. The belt feed unit has been redesigned to make belt loading much quicker than previously. The barrel can be quickly changed by cocking the weapon, releasing the barrel latch, and then easing the barrel forward and sideways through a slot in the ventilated barrel guard. There is a bipod which can be mounted in the usual place, at the front end of the jacket, or can be moved to a position just in front of the feed unit, at the center of balance, if preferred.

A variety of specialized mountings are available; there is a spring-buffered tripod with panoramic sight for support fire roles; a column mount which fits on light vehicles and uses spring balancing gear to take the weight of the gun; and two different 360° tracks for ground, vehicle or anti-aircraft defense.

The HK21A1 is understood to have been purchased by several African and Asian armies, but no firm details have been released.

Heckler & Koch MP5

Manufacturer Heckler & Koch GmbH, Oberndorf-Am-Neckar, Germany
Type Delayed blowback, selective fire
Caliber 9mm Parabellum
Barrel 8.8in (225mm)
Weight (empty) 5.4lbs (2.45kg)
Magazine Capacity 15 or 30 rounds
Cyclic rate of fire 650 rounds/minute

The Heckler & Koch company made their G3 rifle the foundation of their business and by adapating its mechanism they have parlayed it into a number of formats. This sub-machine gun is somewhat unusual in that it uses a delayed blowback mode of operation and incorporates the roller-locked breech mechanism used in the G3 rifle to do it. As a result several of the parts of the MP5 are common to the G3 rifle, a point which has attractions for military procurement officers. The MP5 is in use by German police and Border Guards, by the Swiss and Dutch and several other police and military forces, and has also been seen in the hands of the British Special Air Service operating against terrorists.

The two-part breech block of the MP5 locks the forward section by two rollers, forced out into recesses in the receiver by the forward motion of the rear section during the closing movement. The force on the cartridge base, on firing, attempts to drive the for-

This page: Two variants of the Heckler & Koch MP5: at top, with retractable stock; and the ultra-short type.

Above: The Hughes Chain Gun mounted on a Bradley infantry fighting vehicle.

ward section back, but it cannot move immediately, so keeping the breech closed, and does not move until the heavy rear section of the bolt has begun to move back and so left space for the rollers to be forced inwards by the inclined faces of their recesses. Once the bolt is free, it recoils backwards in the usual manner to complete the extracting and reloading cycle.

There are a number of variations on the basic model, which is known as the MP5A2 and has a plastic buttstock and fore end. The MP5A3 has a telescoping metal buttstock. The MP5SD has a permanently-fixed silencer around the barrel and sub-divides into three versions – MP5SD1 with no butt, MP5SD2 with fixed plastic butt, and MP5SD3 with telescoping butt. The MP5K is a specially shortened version for concealed use by anti-terrorist squads and similar people; it can also be fitted inside a special briefcase for use by bodyguards; it can be fired from this concealment and performs faultlessly, the empty cases being carefully channelled and collected so as not to bounce around and jam the weapon. There are also attachments to permit these various models to be fired from ball-mounts in armored vehicles or from specially-developed turrets.

Hughes Chain Gun® Machine Gun

Manufacturer Hughes Helicopters, Culver City, CA90230, U.S.A.
Type Mechanical, belt fed, machine gun
Caliber 7.62mm NATO
Barrel 22in (558mm)
Weight 29.1lbs (13.2kg)
Magazine Capacity Belt fed
Cyclic rate of fire Variable up to 600 rounds/minute

Mechanical machine guns are as old as the industry, names like Gatling, Gardner and Nordenfelt having been prominent in this field in the 1870s, but with the development of the self-powered Maxim they were rendered obsolescent. They reappeared when it became obvious that only mechanical solutions could provide the high rate of fire demanded by modern aerial combat, and the Gatling was revived as the electrically-driven 'Vulcan' aircraft cannon. But for land force use they seemed to be out of the question until Hughes perfected this design, one of the most significant developments in small arms technology in the last fifty years. It has been adopted in 7.62mm caliber as a tank and armored vehicle gun by the U.S. and British armies and is likely to be taken into use by several others in the future. In 25mm and 30mm caliber it is in use by the U.S. forces as a helicopter weapon and has also been evaluated by the British Army as armament for their 'Fox' armored car.

The heart of the Chain Gun is a loop of commercial roller chain which lies on the bottom of the receiver and is driven round by a gear, driven by an electric motor. Attached to this chain is a lug which engages in the bolt carrier, so that as the chain moves forward, along one side of the receiver, so the carrier is moved forward, a cartridge is fed into the breech, and the bolt is rotated and locked. As the chain lug moves, following the loop path, across the front of the receiver there is no motion of the bolt carrier; the breech stays locked and the cartridge is fired. Then as the chain lug turns the corner and begins to run back, down the other side of the receiver, the bolt is unlocked and opened, the carrier pulled back, the case ejected. As the chain lug makes its fourth side of the receiver, again there is no motion on the carrier and there is a brief pause which permits cooling of the open barrel.

The delay, or 'dwell', with the closed bolt acts as a safety in case of a hangfire (delayed ignition of the cartridge), and if the cartridge has not fired by the time the lug has made its crossing, the gun stops and the operator has to restart it, thus giving ample time for the longest hangfire to discharge itself safely. If the round is a misfire, then once the gun is re-started the dud round is extracted and ejected safely. Ejection is done down a forward-facing tube, since this gun is designed for use in armored vehicles and the empties (and any unfired rounds) are thrown clear of the turret. Since the gun is sealed, fumes cannot escape into the vehicle but are ejected either through a jacket sleeve around the barrel or through the ejector tube, keeping the air in the tank relatively clean.

It will be apparent that the rate of fire is infinitely variable by simply controlling the speed of the drive motor, though in practice the controls are such that either single shots or 600 rpm are available. The Chain Gun also has the advantage of providing positive mechanical lift for the ammunition belt, instead of relying upon recoil of the gun's moving parts to actuate the feed. This, together with the precise control and inter-operation of the entire operating cycle, makes the Chain Gun one of the most reliable and smoothly-operating machine guns in existence.

M60E3 Lightweight Assault Machine Gun

Manufacturer Saco Defense Inc, Saco, Maine, U.S.A.
Type Gas-operated, automatic
Caliber 7.62mm
Barrel 22in (560mm)
Weight 19.4lbs (8.8kg)
Magazine Capacity unlimited link belt
Cyclic rate of fire 500-650 rounds/minute

The M60 machine gun was adopted by the U.S. Army in the late 1950s and served as a general-purpose machine gun, bipod-mounted as the squad automatic, or tripod-mounted as the company support gun. It was somewhat heavy and had a number of design faults which took some time to cure, and in the 1980s the U.S. forces requested a lighter version for use by rapid intervention troops and light infantry. The M60E3 was developed to fill this requirement, which it has done with considerable success.

The weapon uses a rotating bolt which is mounted on a post at the end of the gas piston assembly. As the piston is driven back, this post, acting in

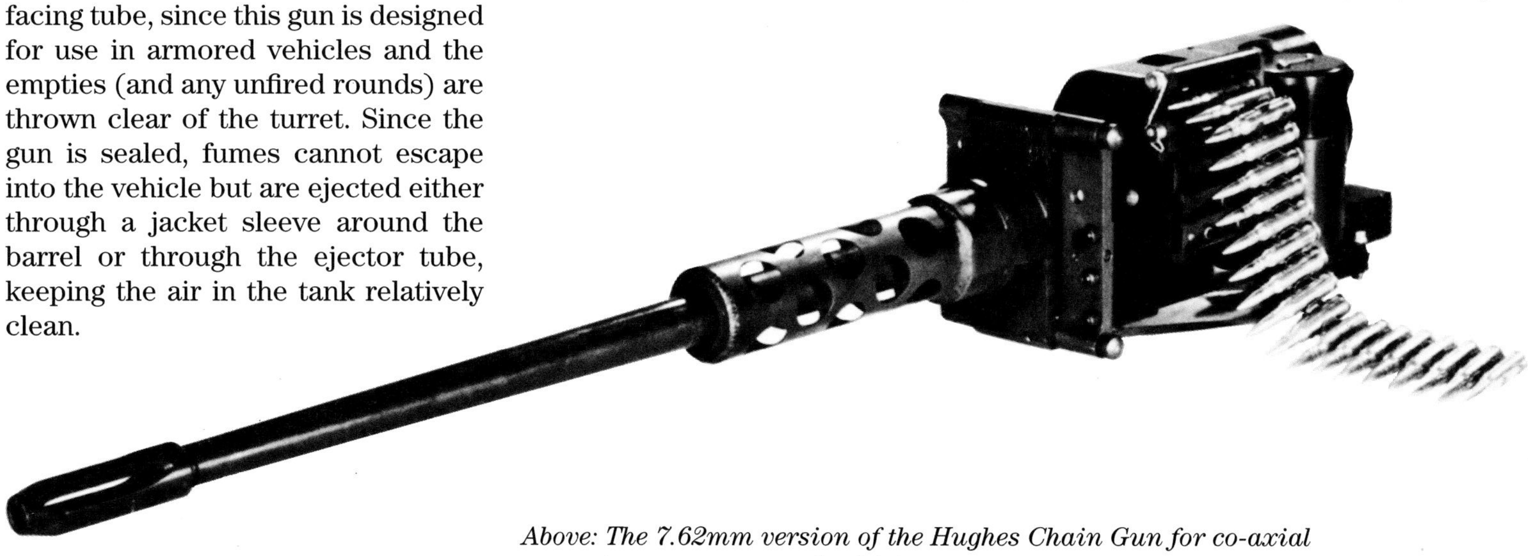

Above: The 7.62mm version of the Hughes Chain Gun for co-axial mounting on an armored vehicle.

Above: The M60E3 lightweight assault machine gun.

a curved camway in the body of the bolt, rotates the bolt to unlock it from the chamber. It then drives the bolt back; it is prevented from rotating by the locking lugs riding in grooves in the receiver. A buffer spring halts the rearward movement, and then the assembly runs forward, the bolt collecting a fresh round from the feedway and loading it into the chamber. As the bolt reaches the end of the grooves, the post and cam path rotate it to lock, and the post, continuing forward, strikes the firing pin in the bolt and fires the round. The backward and forward movement of the bolt is also used to grip the feed belt and move it across the gun.

The changes in the basic M60 design which turned it into the M60E3 are the fitting of a lightweight barrel, adding a light bipod, a carrying handle attached to the barrel, a forward hand grip for firing from the hip or shoulder, and some improvements to the feed and gas systems. Two optional barrels are also available, a lightweight short barrel for the utmost compactness, and a heavy barrel for missions which demand sustained firing. These may be interchanged with the standard barrel without the need for any further adjustment. There is also a conversion kit which allows any older M60 to be converted to the M60E3 specification.

In 1992 the Saco company announced the development of the 'M60E3 Enhanced' machine gun. This is generally similar to the M60E3 but has an improved bipod, improved forward hand grip and heat shield, a hinged shoulder rest to give the firer better control when firing from the bipod, and a new design of sling attachment to prevent the sling coming into contact with a hot barrel.

A variety of fire control systems are available for these weapons, including optical and electro-optical sights for night or day use, laser aiming spotlights, laser rangefinders and similar devices. All these can be attached to or detached from the gun without loss of zero, using specially-developed U.S. Army mounts.

Model 62 Machine Gun

Manufacturer Sumitomo Heavy Industries, Tokyo, Japan
Type Gas-operated, automatic
Caliber 7.62mm
Barrel 20.6in (524mm)
Weight 23.6lbs (10.7kg)
Magazine Capacity Belt
Cyclic rate of fire 600 rounds/minute

The Model 62 is the standard machine gun of the Japanese Self-Defense Force and has some unusual features. It is a general-purpose gun, used on a

Above: Israel's Negev light machine gun.

bipod as the squad automatic and on a tripod as a heavy-support weapon.

The gun is gas-operated, having the usual cylinder and piston below the barrel. The rear end of the piston rod carries a vertical post, to which is attached the firing pin. This post fits into a slot in the breech-block and thus as the piston moves, so it drives the block backwards and forwards. As the block closes the breech, the piston rod continues moving, and a ramp on the end of the rod forces up the rear end of the breech-block until two lugs on its sides are wedged into recesses in the side of the receiver, so locking the breech firmly closed. The last forward movement of the piston carries the firing pin forward to strike the cap and fire the cartridge.

The quick-change barrel is automatically locked in place so long as the top cover of the receiver is closed. Opening the cover unlocks the barrel, so that it can be removed and a new barrel inserted; it also prevents the bolt from rising in order to lock, so that there is no chance that the firing pin can possibly line up with the chamber and thus accidentally fire a shot while the barrel is being removed or the cover open.

Extraction of the spent case is not done by the usual sort of spring-loaded extractor; the cartridge is located in the chamber by a spring-loaded stud which presses into the extractor groove from below. As the bolt is unlocked, so a claw-like arm drops and engages with the cartridge rim, and as the bolt moves back so the cartridge is pulled out of the chamber and ejected.

Feed is from a disintegrating-link belt. A feed arm inside the top cover is driven by the movement of the bolt, and pulls the belt across in two steps, corresponding to the backward and forward movement of the bolt as each shot is fired.

A somewhat heavier version of this weapon, known as the Model 74, is used as a co-axial machine gun in armored vehicles.

Negev Light Machine Gun

Manufacturer Ta'as Israel Industries, Ramat Hasharon, Israel
Type Gas-operated, selective fire
Caliber 5.56mm
Barrel 18.1in (460mm)
Weight 15.9lbs (7.2kg) empty
Magazine Capacity 30-round magazine or belt
Cyclic rate of fire 650-950 rounds/minute

The Israel Defense Force adopted a heavy-barrelled version of their standard Galil rifle as their squad automatic weapon and used it for several years, but in the late 1980s decided that a more purpose-built light machine gun would be preferable. One drawback of the heavy Galil was its fixed barrel, which made overheating, particularly in the Middle Eastern climate, an ever-present problem.

The Negev is a conventional enough weapon, using gas to drive a bolt

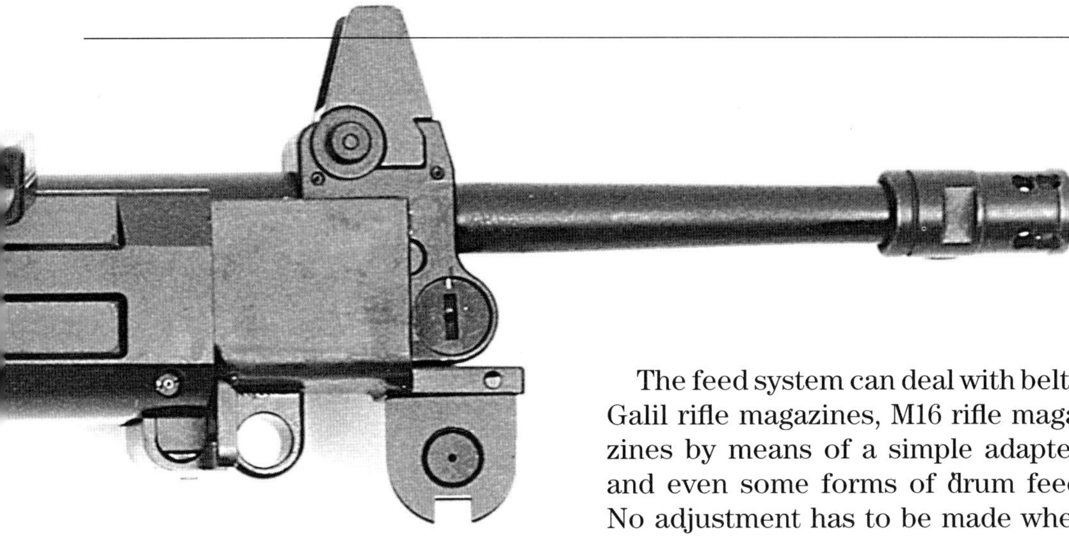

carrier which contains a cam-operated rotating bolt. The bolt locks into a barrel extension, to which a quick-change barrel is attached by interrupted lugs. Thus, as soon as the barrel begins to overheat it can be rapidly changed for a fresh one, and the hot barrel allowed to cool. It also fires from an open bolt; the bolt is kept back by the trigger mechanism when the trigger is released, so that air can flow through the barrel and into the interior of the receiver and thus assist in cooling between bursts of fire.

The feed system can deal with belts, Galil rifle magazines, M16 rifle magazines by means of a simple adapter, and even some forms of drum feed. No adjustment has to be made when changing from one system to another, and there are safeguards to ensure that in the heat of battle, nobody tries to load from two sorts of feed at once.

The gas regulator has three positions; in normal conditions position one gives a rate of fire of 650-800 rounds per minute; position two gives a rate of 800-950 rounds per minute, or, in dusty or dirty conditions, can be used to give more power to overcome fouling. The third position shuts off the gas to the gas system in order to permit grenades to be launched from the muzzle.

The Negev can be used as a light machine gun or it can be fitted with a shorter (330mm) barrel to act as an assault machine gun or rifle. The gun can be easily and quickly stripped into six sub-assemblies, including the bipod. All parts, including the quick-change barrels, are fully interchangeable, and the receiver is prepared for sight mounts to accept any kind of optical or electro-optical sight.

'Scorpion' Machine Pistol

Manufacturer Czech State Arsenals
Type Blowback, selective fire
Caliber .32 ACP (7.65mm) (but see text)
Barrel 4.4in (112mm)
Weight 3.50lbs (1.59kg)
Magazine Capacity 10 or 20 rounds
Cyclic rate of fire 840 rounds/minute

Like the Czech CZ58 rifle mentioned elsewhere, this is not a new weapon but it deserves a mention for two reasons; firstly because it is a unique miniature submachine gun, and secondly because it is appearing more

Above: The Czech 'Scorpion' machine pistol in .32ACP caliber.
Left: The silenced version of the 'Scorpion.'

and more often in the hands of terrorists and revolutionaries, largely because of its small size and concentrated firepower. In its original form it was of somewhat limited legitimate application; it was then increased in caliber to give it a wider military role, and was adopted and manufactured in Yugoslavia. (The two are easily distinguished, since Czech production has a wooden pistol grip and Yugoslavian models have plastic grips.) It equipped various units of the Czech and Yugoslavian armies and has been exported to various African states with Communist connections. How these weapons find their way into terrorist hands is not for us to suggest.

The original Scorpion (or CZ61) is the .32 caliber model, and it was designed as a light weapon capable of being holster-carried by crews of armored vehicles, as a self-defense weapon. The small bullet is hardly a combat projectile, but as a last-ditch weapon for use by the crew of a stalled tank, it has some validity. The mechanism is a simple blowback bolt, and a change lever allows single shots or automatic fire. In either mode it can be fired one-handed, or the wire stock can be unfolded to allow its use as a shoulder weapon. It is unpleasant to fire from the hip since the empty cases are ejected vertically and usually hit the firer in the face.

The light bolt and weak recoil spring would led to an unacceptably high rate of fire if left to themselves, and so a rate reducer is fitted into the pistol grip. As the bolt reaches the end of its rearward travel it is held by a catch; during the rearward movement the bolt trips a light plunger and drives it down inside the pistol grip, against a spring. This light plunger passes through a heavy weight and passes some of its energy to the weight, causing it to begin to move down. The plunger reaches the bottom of the grip and its spring sends it back, where it meets the descending weight and passes through it; this acts as a retardant to the plunger. Eventually the plunger reaches the top of the grip once more and releases the bolt catch, allowing it to go forward and fire the next round. This all sounds very time-consuming, but in fact it cuts the rate down to 840 rounds per minute, so the travel of the plunger is all over in about .0012 of a second.

Later models of the Scorpion were chambered for different cartridges; the CZ64 fires the .380 Auto (9mm Short) cartridge; the CZ65 fires the 9mm Soviet (Makarov) cartridge; and the CZ68 is chambered for the 9mm Parabellum round. There has been little published about these variants and few have been seen outside Czechoslovakia. The CZ68 is, as might be expected, somewhat larger than the other models.

Singapore Ultimax 100

Manufacturer Chartered Industries of Singapore, Singapore
Type Gas-operated, automatic
Caliber 5.56mm (.223)
Barrel 20in (508mm)
Weight 10.8lbs (4.9kg) with bipod
Magazine Capacity 20, 30 or 100 rounds
Cyclic rate of fire 520 rounds/minute

Having successfully manufactured M16 rifles, M203 grenade launchers and then their own rifle (described elsewhere in these pages), CIS of Singapore, moved by the U.S. Army's SAW (Squad Automatic Weapon) program of the 1970s, decided to make their own machine gun and offer it for test. They originally called it the SAW, though in this case it meant 'Section Machine Gun', but this was soon changed to 'Ultimax 100', largely because of the unusual 100-round magazine. Work began in 1980, but before the design could be perfected the U.S. Army had selected the FN Minimi as their light machine gun. Nevertheless, the Ultimax proved to be an excellent weapon and was

Right: The Ultimax 100, named after its 100-round magazine.

Below: The Ultimax 100 fitted with drum magazine.

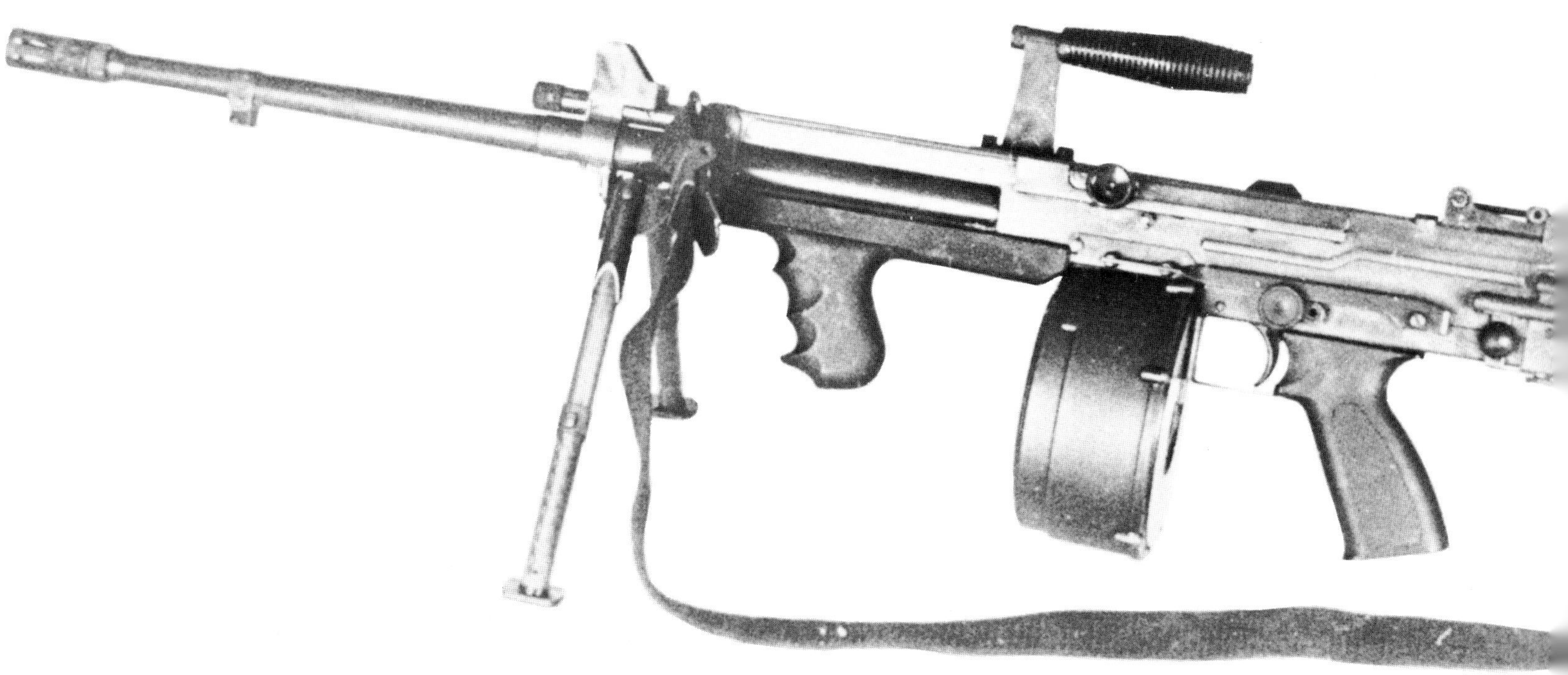

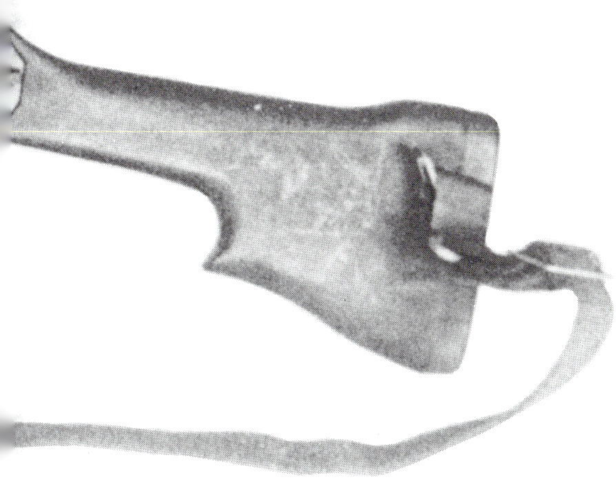

adopted by the Singapore Armed Forces and has been sold to various countries in the Far East where it has performed well.

The Ultimax 100 is a fairly conventional gas-operated gun, using a piston to drive a bolt carrier which holds a rotating bolt. It fires from the open bolt position and only fires automatic – single shots are not possible except by careful taps on the trigger, the slow rate of fire helping here. The first model (Mark I) had a quick-change barrel which proved not to be very quick in practice, and it has been dropped. The Mark II uses a heavy fixed barrel capable of firing 500 continuous rounds without heat damage problems. The Mark III has a similarly heavy barrel but one which can be quickly changed when circumstances dictate.

There are various magazines; 20- or 30-round box magazines can be used, or a special 100-round plastic drum. With any of these the weapon can be fired from the shoulder or the hip under complete control. The sights are fully adjustable for windage and elevation and are graduated up to 1000 meters, a somewhat optimistic marking with 5.56mm ammunition. At shorter ranges to 400-500 meters, though, it is steady, holds well on the target and is as accurate as any of its competitors.

Soviet PK Machine Gun

Manufacturer Soviet State Arsenals
Type Gas-operated, belt fed, machine gun
Caliber 7.62mm Soviet Nagant M1891
Barrel 25.9in (658mm)
Weight 19.84lbs (9kg)
Magazine Capacity 100, 200 or 250-round belt
Cyclic rate of fire 700 rounds/minute

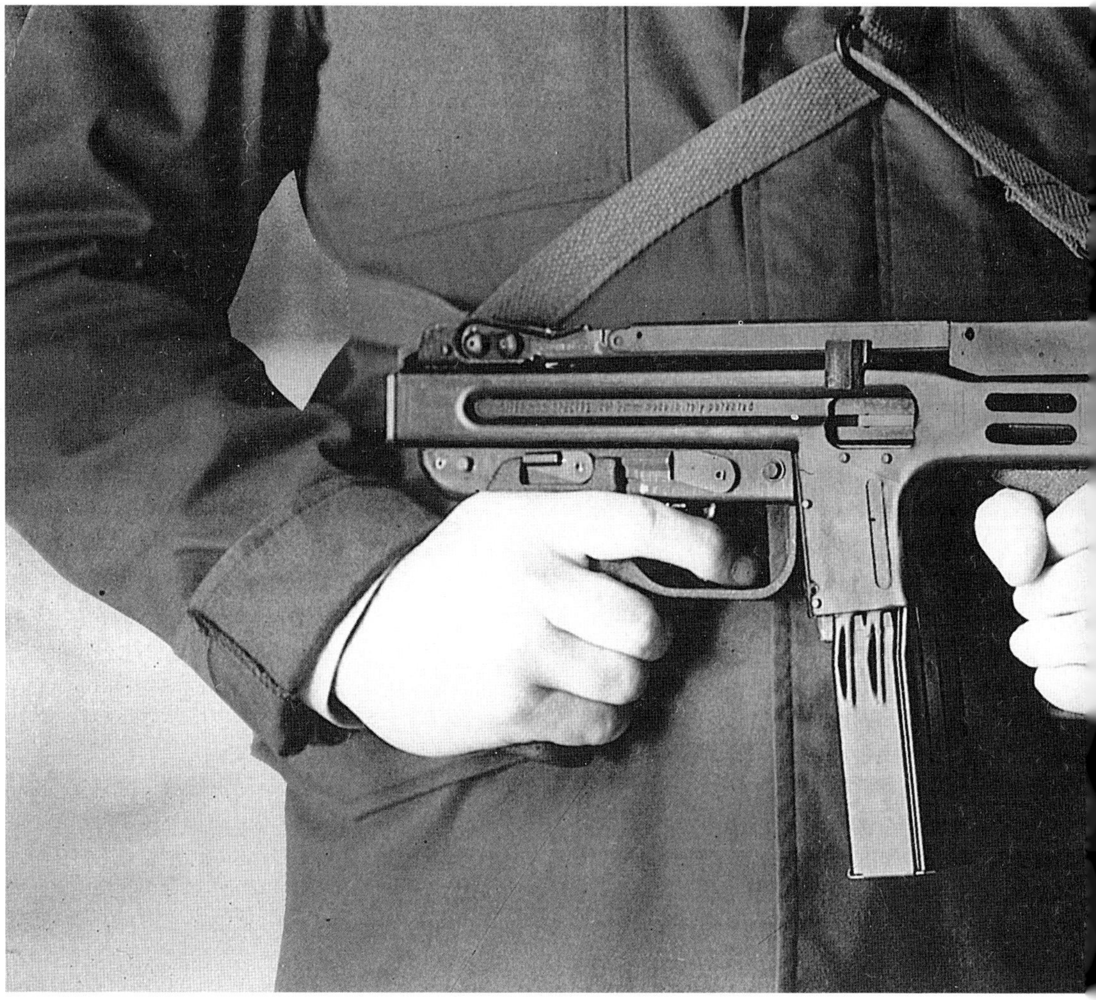

Since the 1920s the principal Soviet infantry machine gun was a Degtyarev design, using a locking system based on flaps forced into notches in the receiver by the forward movement of the firing pin. But when the Kalashnikov rifle became the Soviet standard, it was thought advisable to develop a Kalashnikov-based machine gun, if only for commonality of parts and manufacture. As a result, the 'PK' series ('Pulyemet Kalashnikova') appeared in the mid-1960s and was in universal use throughout the armies of the former Warsaw Pact.

In fact, although the PK uses the same type of bolt carrier and rotating bolt as the Kalashnikov rifle, other parts of the mechanism have been 'borrowed' from other designs; thus, the feed system has been taken from the Goryunov machine gun, as has the method of changing the barrel; the method of using the gas piston to drive the belt feed mechanism comes from a Czechoslovakian design; and the trigger has been taken from the

older Degtyarev guns. One benefit of this is that the various parts should all be well understood by the troops and armorers, and the result is a useful weapon, but it would have probably been better had it been designed for a more modern, rimless, cartridge instead of the ancient rimmed round dating from 1891. Nevertheless, this is a good long range cartridge and it gives the weapon ample power to reach out with accuracy.

The PK was the Soviet Army's first 'general purpose' machine gun, a concept widely adopted elsewhere but long resisted by the Soviets since they were reluctant to discard anything and had a vast collection of old medium machine guns to wear out before adopting the PK. The basic design has been parlayed into several versions, each slightly different and for a specific role; the PK is the basic gun on a bipod, the squad automatic; the PKS is the same gun but with a light tripod, making it the company medium machine gun; the PKT is the PK altered for installation as the coaxial gun in a tank; the sights, stock, pistol grip and trigger, and bipod are removed and a solenoid firing mechanism installed; the PKM is a 'product improved' PK with stamped metal feed cover, unfluted and lighter barrel and a hinged butt rest; the PKMS is the PKM on a tripod; and the PKB is the PKM with bipod, butt and trigger mechanism removed and twin spade grips fitted, for use as a pintle-mounted gun on armored vehicles.

Left: The Spectre M-4 first appeared in the early 1980s.

Above: The Russian PK squad machine gun.

Spectre M-4

Manufacturer Sites SpA, Turin, Italy
Type Blowback, selective fire, double-action
Caliber 9mm Parabellum
Barrel 5.12in (130mm)
Weight 6.4lbs (2.9kg)
Magazine Capacity 30 or 50 rounds
Cyclic rate of fire 850 rounds/minute

This submachine gun appeared in 1983 and has a number of unusual features. The designer set out to develop a weapon which could be used in an instinctive and automatic manner, so that the user could open fire instantly without having to consider the safety condition or perform any action other than pulling the trigger. The intention was to provide a weapon for anti-terrorist police and others who need to carry a weapon daily but may not be called upon to use it except at rare intervals; and when that time comes, it has to be ready for use without hesitation.

The Spectre looks conventional enough, with a pressed steel receiver and barrel jacket, and a butt which folds to lie along the top of the receiver. The magazine fits into a housing ahead of the trigger and is the first unusual feature; it contains four columns of cartridges instead of the usual two. This means that the 30-round magazine is no longer than a conventional 20-round, and the 50-round no longer than a normal 30-round.

The operation is also unusual. After inserting a magazine, the cocking handle is pulled back and released in the normal way. But instead of the bolt remaining back, it runs forward and chambers a cartridge. A 'hammer unit' remains at the rear of the receiver; but pressing a de-cocking lever allows this unit to run forward under control and stop a short distance behind the bolt. The weapon is now perfectly safe to carry, and will not fire if dropped or mishandled. But as soon

Above: The compact look of the M-4.

Left: The Spectre M-4 in action on the firing range.

Below left: A stripped-down view of the M-4.

Above: The long-barreled version of the M-4, the Spectre Carbine.

as it becomes necessary to fire, all that needs to be done is to squeeze the trigger. This will retract the hammer unit from its rest position and then release it with sufficient force to hit the firing pin in the bolt and fire the cartridge in the chamber, after which the action is automatic until the trigger is released.

Since the bolt is always closed when the gun is at rest, it might be expected that the barrel will heat up when firing and not cool very quickly; this is countered by a forced draught air system, operated by the movement of the bolt, which pumps air through and around the barrel while firing.

The basic Spectre submachine gun is accompanied by three variant models; the 'Spectre PCC' (Police Compact Carbine) which fires single shots only and has a longer barrel; it can also be fitted with a silencer. The Spectre Carbine is long-barreled and fires only single shots. And the Spectre Pistol is the basic Spectre but without a stock or fore-grip, and fires single shots only. The Police Carbine and Pistol versions are available in .40 Smith & Wesson caliber as well as in 9mm Parabellum.

Star Z-84

Manufacturer Star Bonifacio Echeverria & Cia, Eibar, Spain
Type Blowback, selective fire
Caliber 9mm Parabellum
Barrel 8.45in (215mm)
Weight 6.6lbs (3kg)
Magazine Capacity 25 or 30 rounds
Cyclic rate of fire 600 rounds/minute

Star is one of the oldest of Spanish small arms manufacturers, and they have been making submachine guns since the 1930s. Since 1945 a succession of their weapons has equipped the Spanish armed forces, and the latest of these is the Z-84, introduced in the mid-1980s.

The Z-84 was developed with a view to correcting one or two deficiencies in earlier models and also to reduce the cost and complexity of manufacture. Much use has been made of steel stampings and investment casting. The feed system has been carefully engineered so that it will feed both jacketed and soft-point bullets without faltering, and its resistance to water damage has led to it being adopted as an assault weapon by Spanish marine and commando units.

The gun fires from an open bolt, using the system of 'advanced primer ignition' in which the cartridge is actually fired while the bolt is still loading it into the breech. This means that the explosion force must first arrest the forward movement of the bolt, then reverse it, and then blow it to the rear. Without this feature the bolt would have to be much heavier and the weapon correspondingly larger.

The bolt is recessed, so that it wraps around the chamber end of the barrel at the instant of firing; this allows for a maximum barrel length in a compact overall length and also reduces the distance needed for the bolt to recoil. The center of balance is above the pistol grip, so that it is possible to fire the weapon single-handed with good stability. The magazine fits into the pistol grip, so that the balance of the weapon does not change as the ammunition is used and it is possible to change magazines, even in the dark, very quickly.

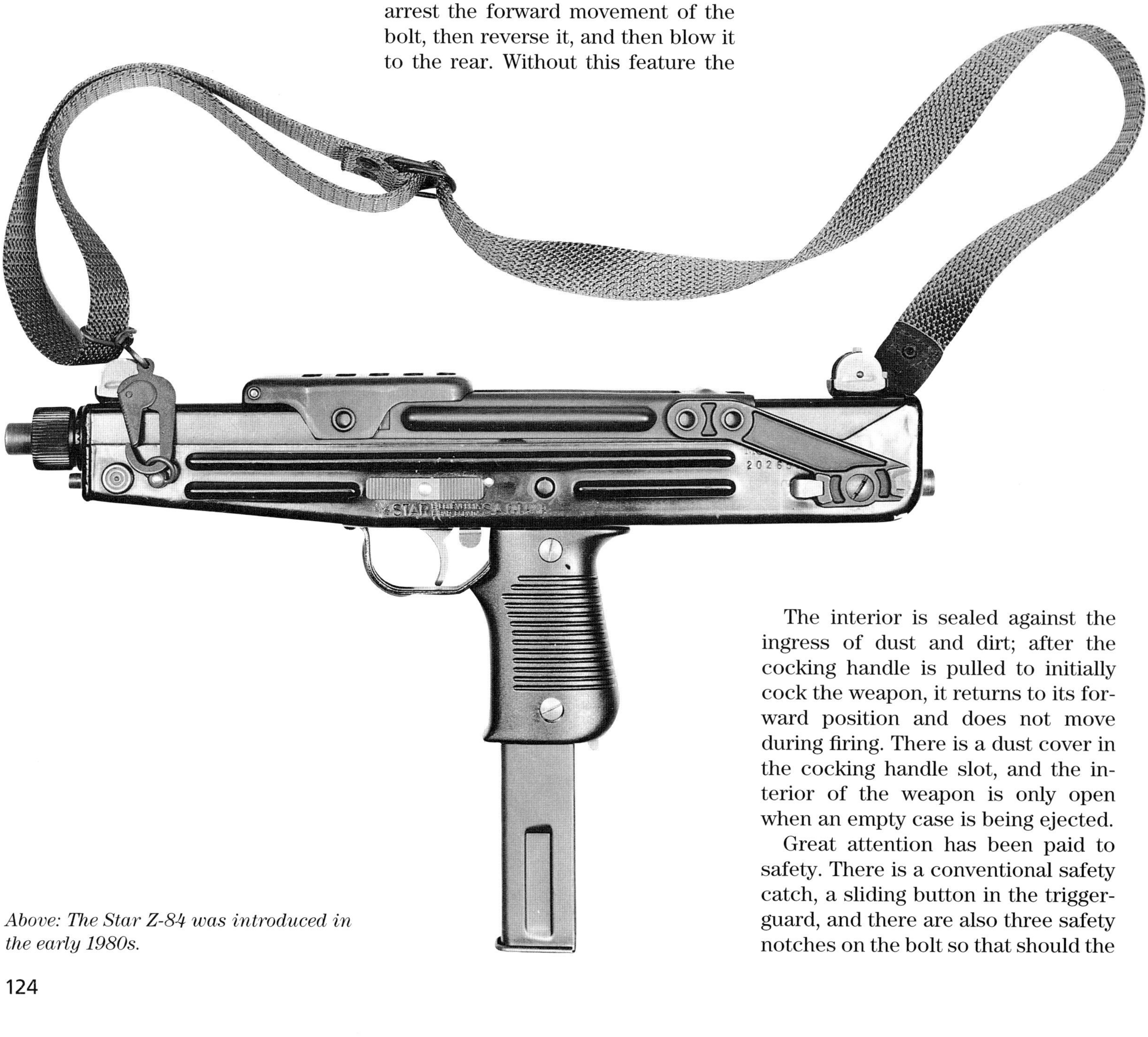

Above: The Star Z-84 was introduced in the early 1980s.

The interior is sealed against the ingress of dust and dirt; after the cocking handle is pulled to initially cock the weapon, it returns to its forward position and does not move during firing. There is a dust cover in the cocking handle slot, and the interior of the weapon is only open when an empty case is being ejected.

Great attention has been paid to safety. There is a conventional safety catch, a sliding button in the trigger-guard, and there are also three safety notches on the bolt so that should the hand slip while cocking, the bolt cannot run forward and load a cartridge. An automatic safety lock is applied whenever the bolt is at rest, so that dropping the weapon cannot jar the bolt into loading and firing; this is automatically withdrawn when the weapon is cocked and remains out of action while firing.

The Z-84 is a well-thought-out design and has been sold to numerous military and security forces outside Spain.

Steyr AUG 9 Para

Manufacturer Steyr-Mannlicher GmbH, Steyr, Austria
Type Blowback, selective fire
Caliber 9mm Parabellum
Barrel 16.5in (420mm)
Weight (empty) 7.25lbs (3.3kg)
Magazine Capacity 25 or 32 rounds
Cyclic rate of fire 650-750 rounds/minute

The Steyr AUG rifle was the first 'modular' design: the barrel, receiver, firing mechanism can all be changed to configure the weapon into whatever sort of rifle is wanted. By an extension of this principle, Steyr pioneered a trend which is now becoming more common, of converting what is basically a locked-breech rifle into a blowback submachine gun.

The AUG 9 Para is based on the standard AUG rifle by changing the barrel for one of 9mm caliber; changing the bolt assembly for a simple blowback unit; and changing the magazine housing by fitting an adapter to take a narrower magazine holding the 9mm Parabellum pistol cartridge.

The result is a submachine gun with a longer barrel than normal for this type of weapon, and one which fires from a closed bolt. Both these features improve accuracy, and the longer barrel produces a rather higher muzzle velocity than is usual in this caliber.

The 'closed bolt' feature means that when the magazine is inserted and the cocking handle pulled back and released, the bolt runs forward and chambers a cartridge, leaving the hammer cocked ready to fire. On pulling the trigger in the usual type of submachine gun, the bolt runs forward, loads the chamber and then fires. There is therefore a sudden shift of balance due to the movement of the bolt and, as a result, a first-round hit is unlikely. With the AUG 9 Para, pulling the trigger simply releases the hammer; nothing else moves and the weapon stays steady at the aim, so that first-round hits are the rule rather than the exception.

The company originally marketed a conversion kit, allowing anyone with an AUG to convert it to a submachine gun. Later, however, this was withdrawn and only brand-new weapons were sold, since it appeared that even a simple conversion was beyond the skill of some users.

A separate barrel fitted with an efficient silencer is also available; this can be exchanged for the normal barrel by simply pressing a catch and twisting the front handle sideways to unlock the interrupted lugs of the barrel from the receiver. As with the rifle, the basic model has a carrying handle with a low-power optical sight, but it is possible to change the receiver to one with a sight mount and thus fit night vision or other specialist sights.

Above: The Steyr AUG 9 Para, based on the standard AUG rifle, is shown here with a silencer.

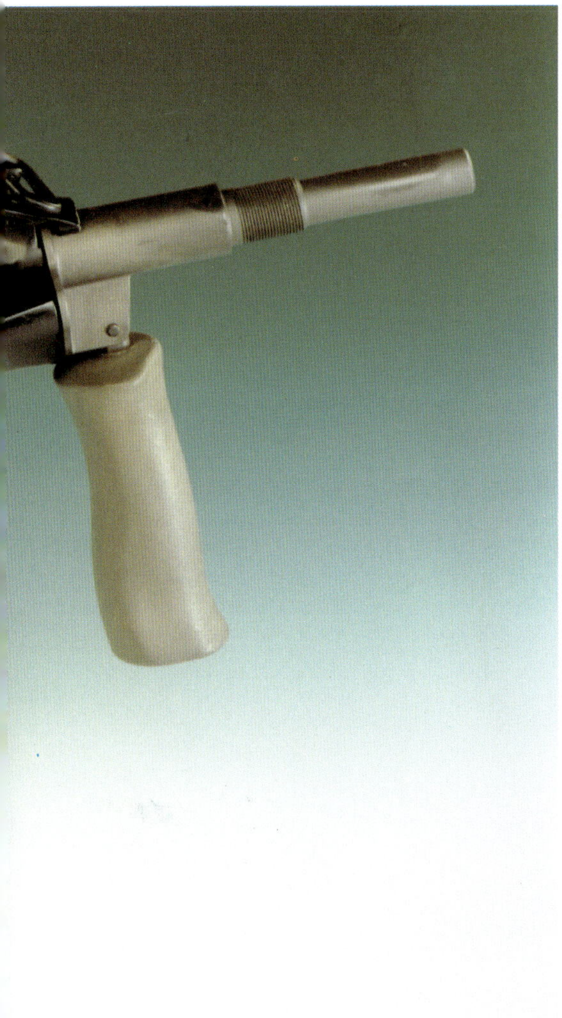

machine gun. Indeed, a variant model which does away with the front handgrip and only fires single shots is called the 'Special Purpose Pistol' (SPP) and is classed as a pistol.

The TMP is a locked-breech weapon firing the 9mm Parabellum cartridge. There are only 41 component parts, and the frame and top cover are made from a synthetic plastic which is sufficiently strong to be able to do without steel inserts to support the bolt. The breech is locked and unlocked by rotation of the barrel, a system which Steyr pioneered in the early years of the century but which they ceased to use after 1918. A lug beneath the barrel engages in a groove in the frame. On firing, the barrel and breech block recoil still locked together, the lug sliding down the groove. The groove then spirals, and as the cam follows this track, so the barrel is revolved until the bolt lugs are unlocked from the chamber. The barrel is then held while the bolt runs back and then forward again to chamber a fresh round. Bolt and barrel then go forward, and the cam track again revolves the barrel to lock the breech.

Single shots or automatic fire are provided by a two-stage trigger, similar to that used on the Steyr AUG rifle. The first pressure on the trigger fires single shots; pulling through against the pressure of an auxiliary spring delivers automatic fire. There is a three-position cross-bolt safety catch which has a central position giving semi-automatic fire only, so providing additional control.

Although there is no butt-stock, and no provision for fitting one, the forward handgrip permits adequate control of the weapon, and short bursts can be fired with considerable accuracy after a little practice. Single shots can be fired with one hand quite easily; it is only slightly heavier than a Colt .45 automatic pistol and somewhat lighter than most larger-caliber revolvers.

Initially made in 9mm caliber, production in .40 Smith & Wesson caliber has now begun, and there are plans for a modular system of interchangeable parts which will allow the TMP to be converted to fire 9mm Steyr, 10mm Auto or .41 Action Express cartridges.

Above: The Steyr AUG 9 Para in standard configuration.

Left: Indonesian troops get to grips with the Steyr AUG on the firing range.

Steyr TMP (Tactical Machine Pistol)

Manufacturer Steyr-Mannlicher AG, Steyr, Austria
Type Recoil-operated, selective fire
Caliber 9mm Parabellum
Barrel 5.12in (130mm)
Weight 2.86lbs (1.3kg)
Magazine Capacity 15 or 20 rounds
Cyclic rate of fire ca 600 rounds/minute

The Steyr Tactical Machine Pistol belongs in the emerging group of 'Personal Defense Weapons' – short, stockless, and closer to being an enlarged pistol than a down-sized sub-

Above: The Steyr TMP (Tactical Machine Pistol).

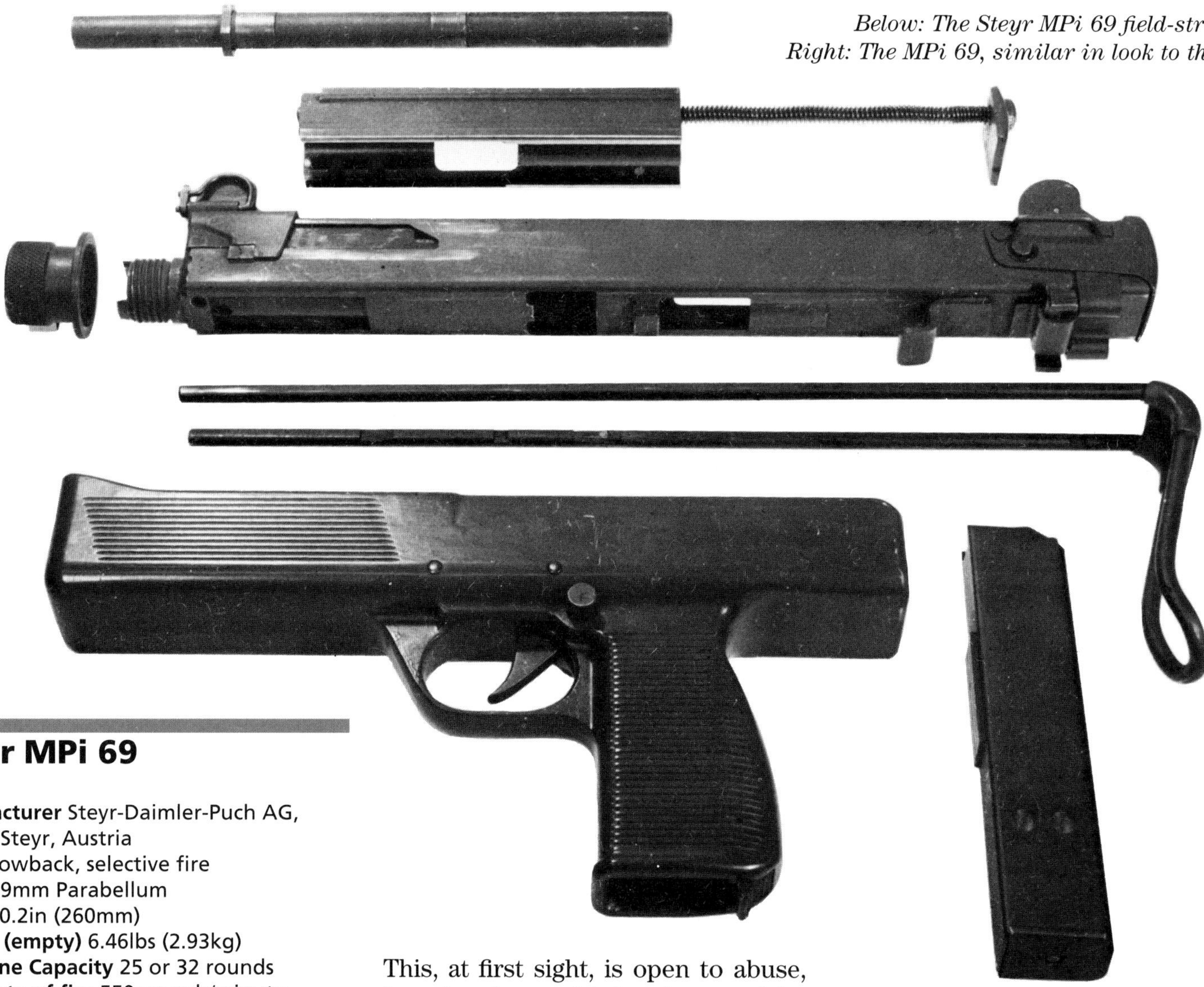

Below: The Steyr MPi 69 field-stripped.
Right: The MPi 69, similar in look to the Uzi.

Steyr MPi 69

Manufacturer Steyr-Daimler-Puch AG, A-4400 Steyr, Austria
Type Blowback, selective fire
Caliber 9mm Parabellum
Barrel 10.2in (260mm)
Weight (empty) 6.46lbs (2.93kg)
Magazine Capacity 25 or 32 rounds
Cyclic rate of fire 550 rounds/minute

This submachine gun resembles the Uzi in some respects, but is a totally different and rather simpler design. It is currently in use by a number or armies and police forces throughout Europe and the rest of the world.

The receiver is formed from bent and welded sheet steel and is carried in the frame unit, steel with a molded nylon covering. The magazine feeds in through the pistol grip, a convenient system in the dark, and the bolt is of the 'wrap-around' or 'telescoped' type in which the actual bolt face is well back within the bolt and much of the bolt mass is in front of the breech at the moment of firing. This system allows the maximum mass for the minimum bolt stroke and assists in producing a compact weapon. Cocking is performed by pulling on the carrying sling, which is attached, at the forward end, to the cocking knob. This, at first sight, is open to abuse, but a bracket, welded to the top of the receiver, ensures that the cocking action can only be performed when the sling is held at right-angles to the receiver, on the left-hand side. The normal pull from the top of the weapon, as when slinging it over the shoulder, cannot move the cocking-piece.

There is a safety catch in the form of a cross-bolt above the trigger which locks the trigger when set to safe; it is a three-position bolt; when pushed across to the right, so that a white 'S' protrudes, it is safe; when pushed across to the left so that a red 'F' protrudes, it is set for automatic fire. There is also a half-way position in which single shots are possible. This safety catch is a weak piece of design in my view since except by memorizing, it is impossible to know what the state is in darkness; it would be better to have one end ribbed or knurled.

The third position is, in any case, superfluous; with the selector set for automatic fire a light squeeze on the trigger fires a single shot, and this can be repeated as often as wanted. To fire bursts, a heavier squeeze is required. There is no need to reset the selector lever at all, and I can only assume that the central position has been put there as a safety feature during initial training, so that an over-enthusiastic squeeze will not produce a runaway gun. This two-stage trigger is also to be found on the Steyr AUG rifle, and takes some getting used to; I have found it a hindrance to accurate shooting in the automatic mode.

The MPi 69 is easy to strip and reassemble, taking no more than 15 seconds in either direction for a trained soldier. Strictures on the safety and trigger apart, it is a well-designed, simple and robust weapon, and provided soldiers are trained to its peculiarities, a highly effective one.

Uzi Semi-automatic Carbine

Manufacturer Israeli Military Industries, Tel Aviv, Israel
Type Blowback, semi-automatic
Caliber 9mm Parabellum
Barrel 16.1in (410mm)
Weight 8.5lbs (3.85kg)
Magazine Capacity 25 or 32 rounds

The Israeli-developed and manufactured 'Uzi' submachine gun is probably one of the best-known modern weapons of its class. During its 30 years of military service many countries have bought it for their armies and even more for their police and security services. Undoubtedly many less well-connected gun buffs would like to have one for their collections, but the law tends to frown upon privately-owned machine guns; as a result IMI spent a good deal of time in redesigning the Uzi so that it became a repeater, firing single shots only, and yet was impossible to modify back into full-automatic form.

The resulting weapon came on the market in 1981 and the only visual difference from a service Uzi is the length of the barrel, some six inches longer than the military version. There are internal differences, within the receiver, which change the method of operation and which also prevent substitution of standard military components, so that it is impossible to swap parts and so change it back into a full-automatic weapon. In addition the mechanism is now altered so that the Uzi fires from a closed bolt, instead of an open bolt; this makes good sense for a single-shot weapon since it helps accuracy, and there is no need to have the bolt stay open so as to allow cooling air to go through the barrel during pauses in firing.

The Uzi is built up from steel pressings and turnings, with grip and fore-end in black plastic. The folding steel butt is used, and stripping the weapon is extremely simple. The foresight is a post which is adjustable for windage and elevation for purposes of zeroing, and there is a special tool for this pur-

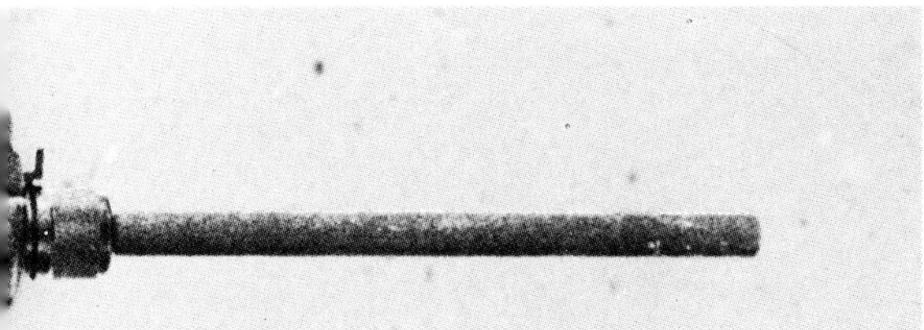

Left: The folding stock version of the Uzi.

Below: Uzis with fixed stocks.

Above: The Uzi in German hands.

pose. The rear sight is a simple two-position flip aperture with settings for 100 and 200 meters.

Although the 9mm Parabellum cartridge is not one which would instinctively commend itself to anyone searching for the ultimate in accuracy, it has to be said that this long-bareled Uzi performs remarkably well, consistently making five-shot groups around one-and-a-half inches at 25 yards. As a home defense weapon it has an authoritative air and the accuracy to back it up, and when not in use the makers provide a dummy barrel of service length.

SHOT GUNS

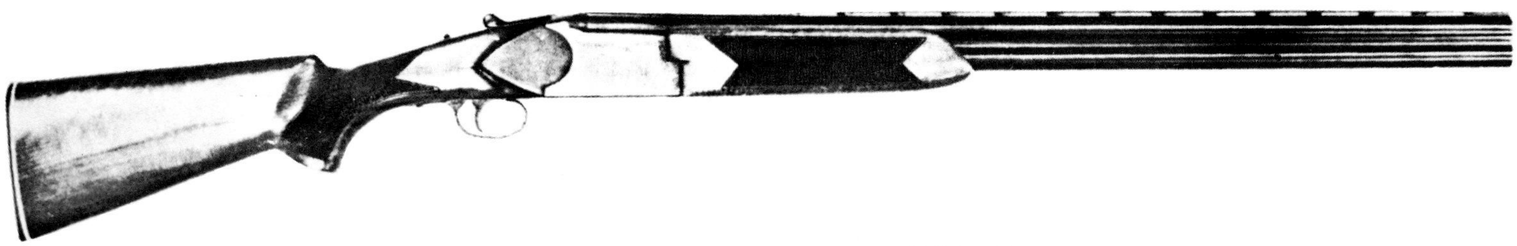

Astra Models 650 & 750 Shotguns

Manufacturer Astra-Unceta y Cia, Guernica, Spain
Type Superposed, single or double trigger
Gage 12
Barrel 28in (711mm)
Weight 7.34lbs (3.33kg)

Astra-Unceta are widely-known for their pistols, but rather less well-known outside Europe for their sporting guns, a state of affairs they are now seeking to remedy. Their home market has been satisfied by conventional single and double guns for some years, but they have now developed an over-and-under specifically for export.

The Models 650 and 750 differ in their trigger arrangement; the 650 has double triggers, while the 750 has a single trigger with a selector to permit firing either barrel first. Either can be had with automatic ejectors or with manual extractors. The barrels are bored to modified and full choke.

The gun is well-finished, with a walnut stock with pistol grip, and well-executed checkering on stock and fore end. The receiver is neatly roll-engraved, the fit of metal to wood is first-class, and the barrels are well polished and blued. The receiver body is somewhat deep, due to the use of bottom bolting, but this leaves ample room for the hammers and firing pins and the selective trigger mechanism, so that the component parts are robustly proportioned and easily reached for repair or adjustment. The firing pin holes in the standing breech have removable bushings. The barrels are surmounted by a ventilated rib with a gold bead front sight.

The Astra gun handles well and delivers consistent patterns. For its price it is a sound and reliable gun which should give long service.

AYA Model 25 Shotgun

Manufacturer Aguirre & Aranzabal, Eibar, Spain
Type Double, side-by-side
Gage 12
Barrels 25in (635mm)
Weight 6.25lbs (2.83kg)

AYA have a long and good reputation for the production of shotguns to a wide variety of specifications, ranging from 'working guns' to 'best guns', and their Model 25 is a classic side-by-side in the English tradition.

The walnut stock is straight, without a pistol grip, and is lightened by two longitudinal holes plugged at the butt end; both it and the short and tapering fore end are well finished and carefully checkered. The barrels are light and shorter than is usual, so that the principal weight lies in the center of the gun and it balances well.

The action uses internal hammers and double triggers, and the smooth stock permits the hand to be moved rapidly to shift triggers between shots. The top lever opens the gun and sets the automatic safety, while the action of opening the gun cocks the hammers. As the gun is closed, so the ejectors are cocked and the double underbolt locks the gun firmly. The barrels are usually provided with modified choke on the right and full on the left, and these produce tight patterns.

These short, light, and centrally-balanced guns are not to everyone's taste; in broad terms this gun has been based on, if not copied from, the Churchill Model XXV of London, and Churchill had his own ideas on what constituted a good gun and on how to shoot it.

Benelli Auto-loading Shotgun

Manufacturer Benelli Armi SpA, I-61029 Urbino, Italy
Type Recoil-operated auto-loader
Gage 12 or 20
Barrel 25.6in (650mm), 27.6in (700mm)
Weight 7lbs (3.18kg)
(12-ga, 27.6in barrel)
Magazine capacity 3 or 4 rounds

The Benelli looks like any other automatic shotgun, but underneath the skin is a most unusual mechanism, much different to the usual long-recoil system pioneered by Browning and copied by almost everybody since then. It is well-known in Europe but a recent newcomer to the U.S.A. and deserves closer inspection.

The breech bolt of the Benelli is a two-part unit, the two being separated

Pages 132-133: Hunting in the Alps with a Beretta over-and-under shotgun.
Above left: The Astra 750 over-and-under 12-gage.
Below left: The Spanish AYA Model 25.

Below: The Benelli M3 Super 90.

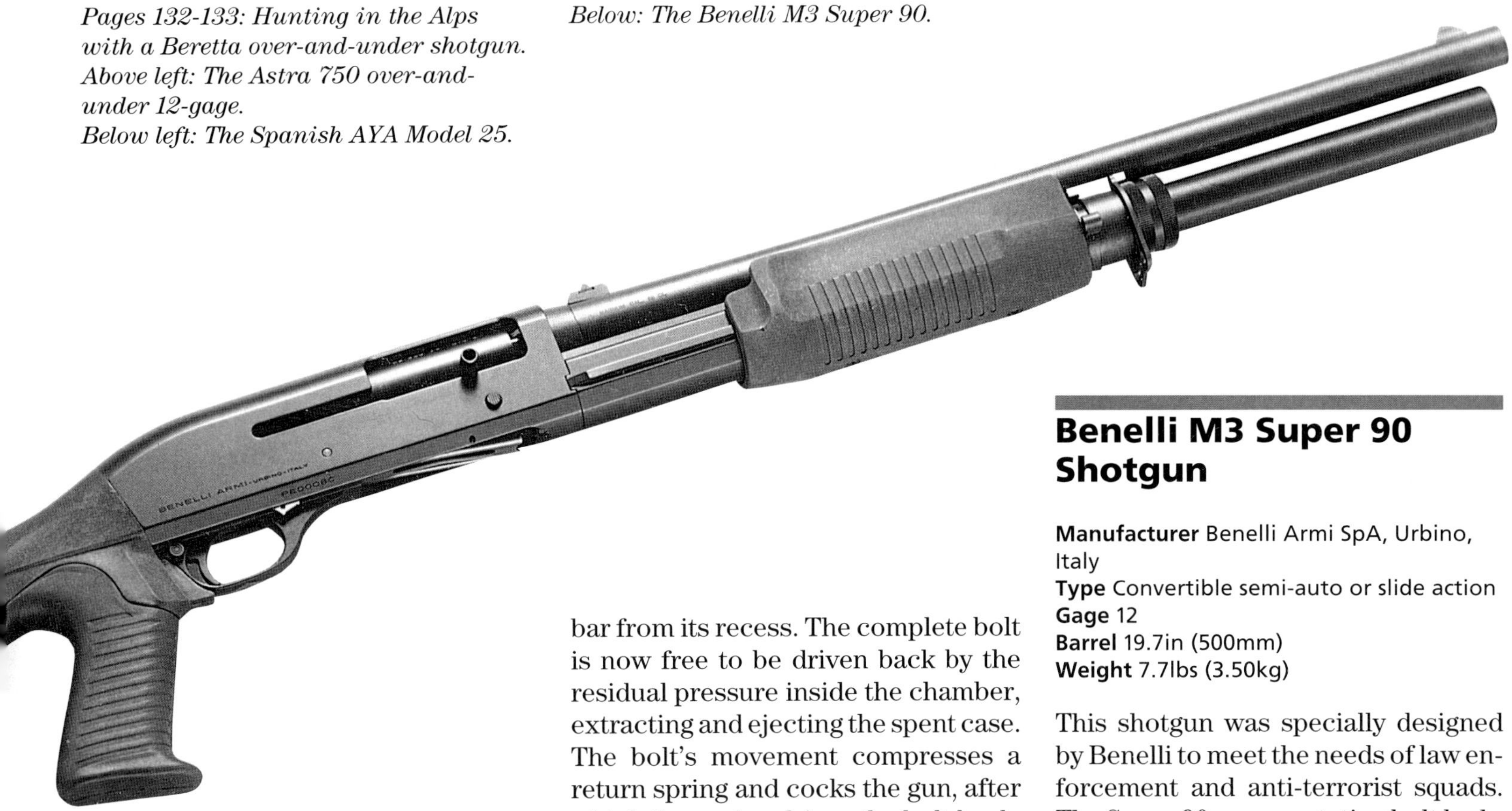

by a coil spring. Attached to the bolt head is a locking bar which trails beneath the bolt assembly and drops into a recess in the receiver so as to hold the breech closed during firing. When the shot is fired, the recoil drives the gun backwards; the bolt body's inertia causes it to remain stationary in space, so that it actually moves forward in relation to the rest of the gun. This compresses the spring and also holds the locking bar firmly down. This movement occupies the time during which the shot charge is passing up the barrel and leaving the muzzle, so that by the time the spring is fully compressed and the bolt body has stopped moving, breech pressure has dropped to a safe level. Now the spring reasserts itself, forces the bolt body back, and this lifts the locking bar from its recess. The complete bolt is now free to be driven back by the residual pressure inside the chamber, extracting and ejecting the spent case. The bolt's movement compresses a return spring and cocks the gun, after which the spring drives the bolt back, loading the next cartridge, the locking bar drops into place and the gun is ready again.

An interesting bonus of this system is that if cartridges with different loadings are used, the recoil force changes and so does the relative compression of the bolt spring, so that there is a self-regulating effect which gives fractionally greater delay in opening for heavier charges.

The Benelli is well-finished, with an aluminum lower section to the receiver, a steel upper section, and well-checkered walnut stock and fore end. The steel parts are highly polished and well blued, while the aluminum portion of the receiver is finished in matching black. The gun handles well and delivers a good pattern. Various choices of choke are available in the two barrel lengths.

Benelli M3 Super 90 Shotgun

Manufacturer Benelli Armi SpA, Urbino, Italy
Type Convertible semi-auto or slide action
Gage 12
Barrel 19.7in (500mm)
Weight 7.7lbs (3.50kg)

This shotgun was specially designed by Benelli to meet the needs of law enforcement and anti-terrorist squads. The Super 90 uses a rotating bolt locking system and works in such a way that the user can select either semi-automatic fire or manual pump action by simply pressing the command lever set into the front of the handguard. To fire in the semi-automatic mode this lever is turned anti-clockwise and moved forward so as to lock the handguard to the barrel connecting ring. Once set in this mode, the gun operates using the two-part inertia bolt mechanism described elsewhere.

For pump action the command lever is turned anti-clockwise and pulled backwards. This frees the handguard so that it can be pushed back and forwards in the usual slide or pump action manner to load and unload the gun. When set in the slide-action mode, the inertia spring is locked out of action and it is impossible for the gun to fire semi-automatically.

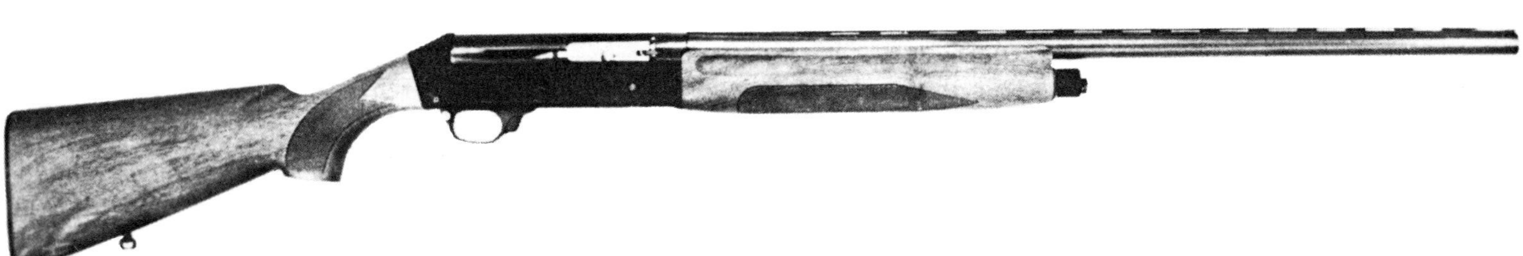

Above: The Benelli auto-loader.

Above: The M3T Convertible variant of Benelli's Super 90.

Below: The firing mechanism of the M3T.

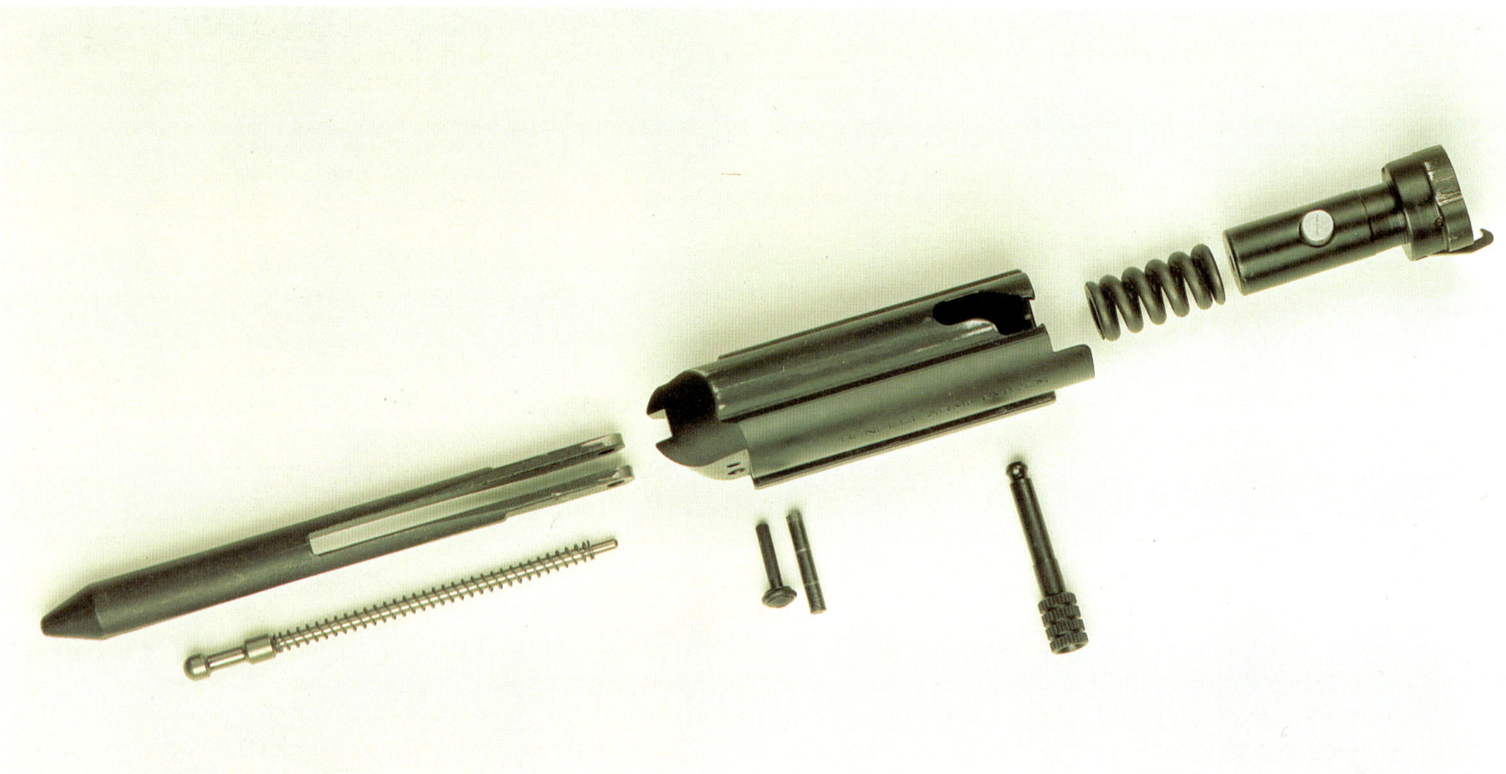

As with other slide-action shotguns, the bolt of the Super 90 remains open after the last round in the magazine had been fired, both in semi-automatic and slide modes.

The upper receiver is of alloy steel, the lower receiver of 'Ergal' special aluminum alloy. The alloy steel barrel is cylinder bored and chromium plated, the outer surface being blued. The stock and handguard are in Rilsan synthetic material, reinforced with glassfiber. The foresight is fixed, and the rearsight is adjustable for windage.

In addition to the standard Super 90, there are a number of variant models. The Super 90 Combat is the same as the Super 90 standard but has special 'ghost ring' sights which allows the shooter to keep both eyes open while taking aim. He focuses on the foresight, and the rear sight becomes a softly defined 'ghost ring' image around it. This new sighting system ensures fast and accurate target acquisition and is now in use by many law enforcement agencies.

The 'Special Application' Model 90 is intended for easy carriage in cars; the barrel is shortened to 14 inches (355mm) and the magazine capacity reduced to five rounds. It also has a folding skeleton stock which folds forward, across the top of the receiver, to act as a carrying handle.

The most recent variation is the M3T Convertible, which is the standard Super 90 with the folding stock of the Special Application model. It is normally supplied with the 500mm barrel and 7-shot magazine, but on special order can be built with a 13.3 inch (340mm) barrel and 5-shot magazine, making it even more compact than the Special Application model. The M3 Super 90 family is extremely versatile, being capable of firing rifled slugs, buckshot (lead or rubber) or birdshot cartridges, CS or CN tear gas grenades, smoke bombs and signaling flares.

Bentley Model 30 Shotgun

Manufacturer Squires, Bingham Mfg. Co., Marikina, Philippines
Type Slide action repeater
Gage 12
Barrel 30in (762mm) (but see text)
Weight 7lbs (2.17kg)
Magazine capacity 5 rounds

The Bentley is another trade name of the Philippine Company of Squires Bingham. The Model 30 is the basic term for three quite distinctly different models.

The 'Model 30 Standard' is a conventional hunting slide-action gun, rather long in the barrel but otherwise unremarkable. The length of barrel does give it a useful long-range capability, which may well be useful on its home ground. The stock and fore end are of figured Philippine mahogany, oil-finished, while the receiver and barrel are blacked and polished, the bolt showing an engine-turned finish through the ejection port. The action is normal slide, a tilting bolt locking into the roof of the receiver. The standard form of barrel is with full choke, but a 26in. barrel bored improved cylinder or a 28in. modified choke can be obtained to special order.

The Model 30 Skeet has the same mechanism but uses a 24in. barrel, with a muzzle compensator and a special 'skeet choke' designed to get the optimum pattern at skeet ranges. The finish is to a higher standard than on the hunting gun, with a polished and varnished surface to the woodwork, a more hand-filling fore end, and checkering on pistol grip and fore end. This appears to be a very handy gun for rapid movement, and the muzzle compensator would diminish the throw-off and blast from such a short barrel.

The third model is somewhat specialized, the 'Model 30 Riot'. In general form this resembles the hunting gun, with plain stock and fore end (though with vertical ribbing to assist grip) but with a shorter 20in barrel which is cylindrical bored. This also has sling swivels on butt and magazine tube nose to permit it being carried slung.

All three Bentley guns are soundly made of good material and would appear to be good working guns in their particular roles.

Beretta 304 Semi-Automatic Shotgun

Manufacturer Pietro Beretta SpA, Gardone Val Trompia, Italy
Type Semi-automatic, gas-operated
Gage 12
Barrel 28in (711mm)
Weight 6.4lbs (2.9kg)
Magazine capacity 3 rounds

The Beretta family have been in the arms business since the 15th century, starting as barrel-makers and moving into making complete guns. Their work was divided between sporting and military, though biased towards the latter, but after the fall of Napoleon and in the years of the 'Long Peace' in Europe, the company moved into the mass manufacture of sporting weapons. Today, they are one of the largest firearms manufacturers in the world, and they have adopted the most up-to-date technology to ensure that their products combine the high-

Below: The Beretta 304 semi-automatic.

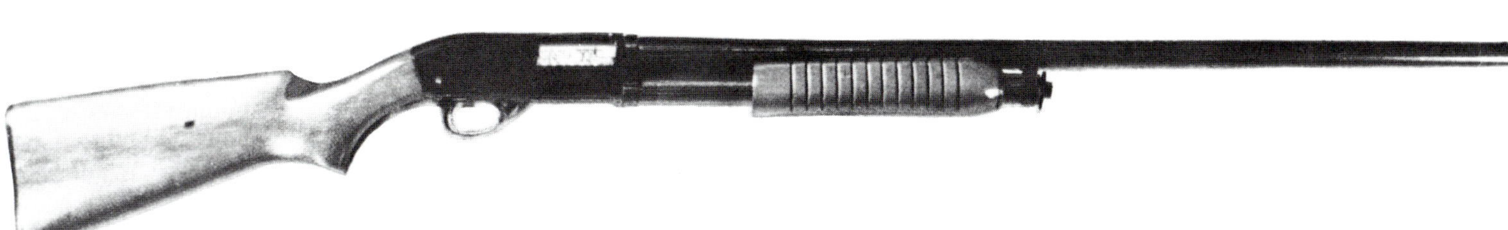

Above: The Bentley Model 30 slide-action gun from the Philippines.

est quality with attractive price.

The 304 is a lightweight gas-actuated weapon using a light alloy (aluminum/zirconium) which it is claimed, is as strong as steel, but only 65 percent of the weight. The barrel is, of course, cold hammer-forged from high-grade Cr-Mo-Ni steel and is internally chrome-plated, which should give it a very long life. The barrels are fitted with the Beretta style of interchangeable chokes so that the user can adjust the shot pattern to his own preference.

When the gun is fired, some of the propellant gas is tapped off to drive a stainless steel gas piston; this operates a rod sleeve which unlocks the breech bolt by means of a falling block. The bolt goes back against a recoil spring while the block actuates a lifter to bring the next cartridge in line with the breech. The spring then drives the bolt forward and loads the cartridge, the block rises and the bolt is securely locked ready for the next shot. The gas system is self-regulating, so that cartridges of varying power can be used without affecting the regularity or reliability of the reloading operation. There is a safety catch in the trigger guard, and there is also a cut-off which isolates the magazine, turning the weapon into a single-shot action.

The stock and fore end are well-finished and fit the hand comfortably; the stock can be adjusted for drop and cast-off by a spacer which fits between the stock and the receiver, so that it should be possible to adjust the fit of the gun to virtually any user.

There are a number of variants of the 304 either on the market or in course of development, including various barrel lengths, varying degrees of finish, and field, sporter and trap configurations.

Beretta 687 EELL Shotgun

Manufacturer Pietro Beretta SpA, Gardone Val Trompia, Italy
Type Double barrel, superposed
Gage 12
Barrel 30in (762mm)
Weight 7.05lbs (3.20kg)

The Beretta 680-series family of over-and-under guns is a most prolific one, with choices of 12 or 20-gage, 28 or 30 inch (710 or 762mm) barrels, and a variety of degrees of decoration and finish. The 687 EELL is the top-of-the-line gun.

The two barrels are forged from Cr-Mo-Ni steel, joined by a ventilated rib and surmounted by a flat sighting rib. They are fitted with the Beretta Mobilchoke which allows the user to change the degree of choke to suit his own

Below: The Beretta 687 EELL.

Right: The beautifully-finished Beretta 687 EELL.

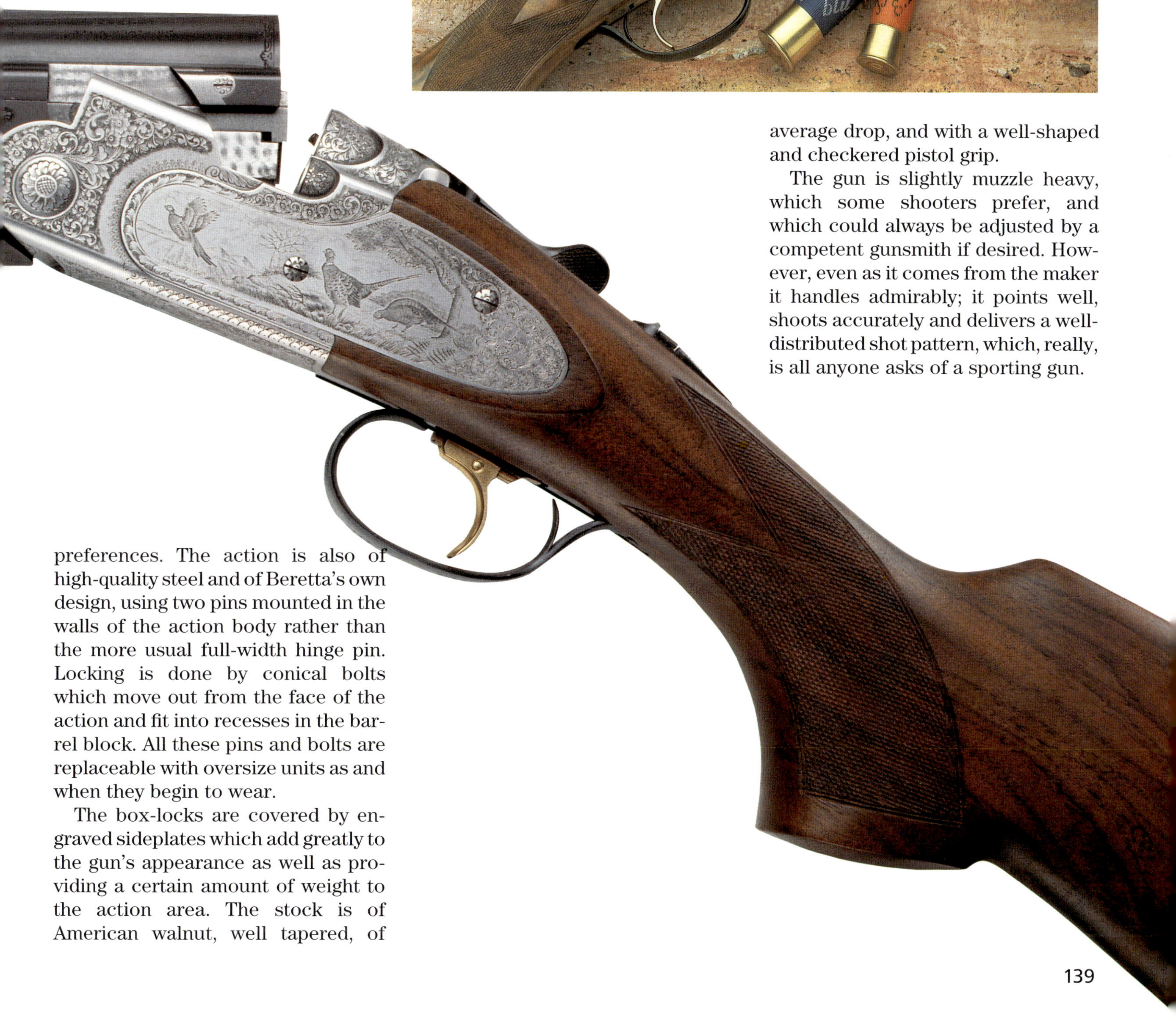

preferences. The action is also of high-quality steel and of Beretta's own design, using two pins mounted in the walls of the action body rather than the more usual full-width hinge pin. Locking is done by conical bolts which move out from the face of the action and fit into recesses in the barrel block. All these pins and bolts are replaceable with oversize units as and when they begin to wear.

The box-locks are covered by engraved sideplates which add greatly to the gun's appearance as well as providing a certain amount of weight to the action area. The stock is of American walnut, well tapered, of average drop, and with a well-shaped and checkered pistol grip.

The gun is slightly muzzle heavy, which some shooters prefer, and which could always be adjusted by a competent gunsmith if desired. However, even as it comes from the maker it handles admirably; it points well, shoots accurately and delivers a well-distributed shot pattern, which, really, is all anyone asks of a sporting gun.

Above: The Beretta 687 EELL.

Browning Custom 325 Shotgun

Manufacturer Miroku Firearms Co., Kochi, Japan
Type Double-barreled, superposed
Gage 12
Barrels 30in (762mm)
Weight 7.5lbs (3.4kg)

The question of who invented the over-and-under shotgun will be argued until Doomsday, but the parentage of this one is firmly established; it is the latest in a long line of similar guns stemming from the one designed by John M. Browning in the early 1920s and, in one variation or another, made by Browning ever since.

The Custom 325 is a well-built and well-finished gun, equally suited to trap or field use. The stock has a full pistol grip and a 'Schnabel' fore-end (with a little lip which positions the hand and prevents it slipping forward). There is a safety catch on the top strap which also acts as a barrel selector for the single-trigger mechanism, which utilizes recoil to re-set after the first shot.

The gun balances well, the center of balance being approximately in the hinge pin, making it quick to point and easily handled. The barrels are surmounted by a wide rib with a shallow center channel, giving a good visual aid to aiming and, as is usual with Browning products, the rich blue finish is immaculate. The chambers are for 2.25in. cartridges, and the shot pattern is even and well-distributed.

Above right and right: Browning designs have been acquired by a number of companies around the world. The Browning Custom 325 is made in Japan and possesses the high-quality finish and attention to detail for which the Browning name is justly famous.

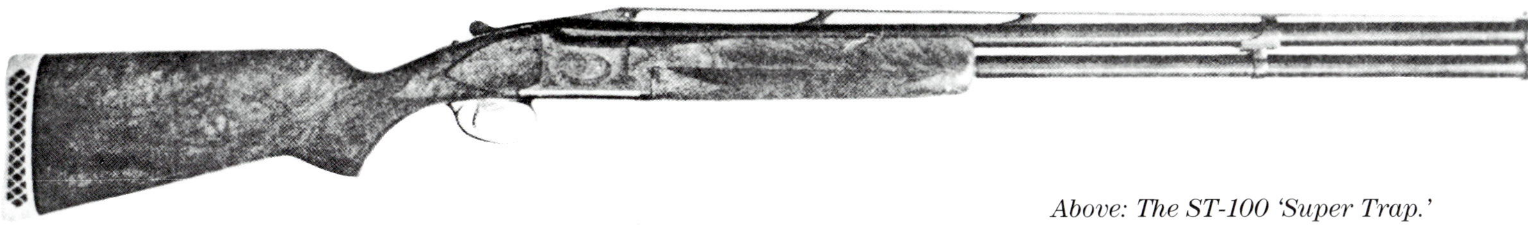

Above: The ST-100 'Super Trap.'

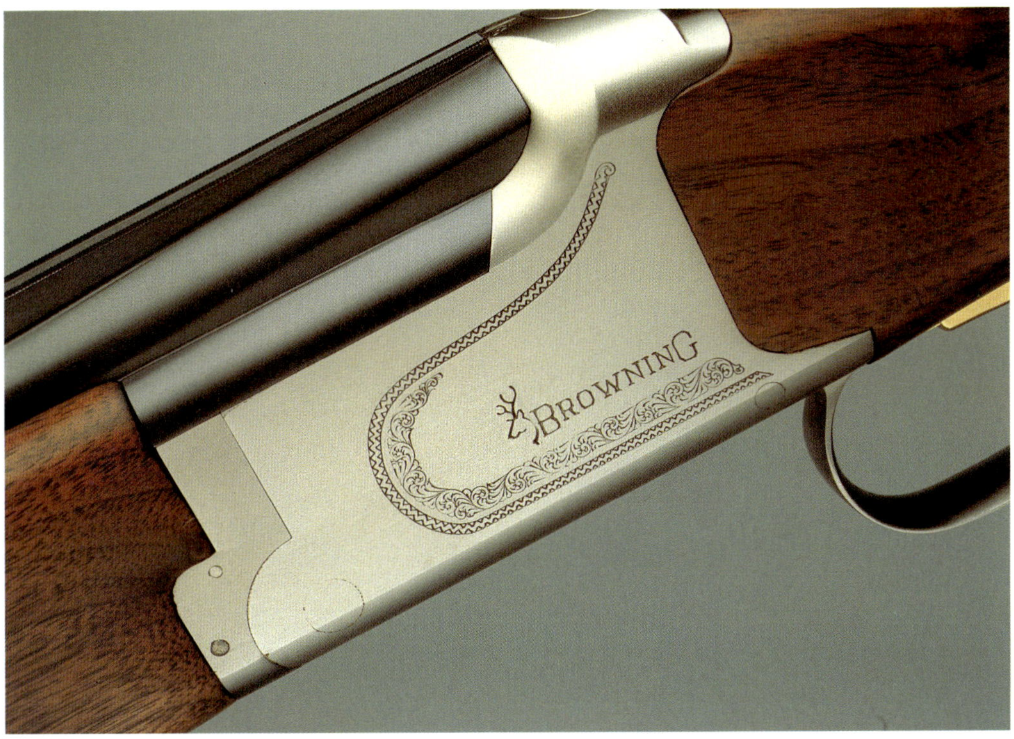

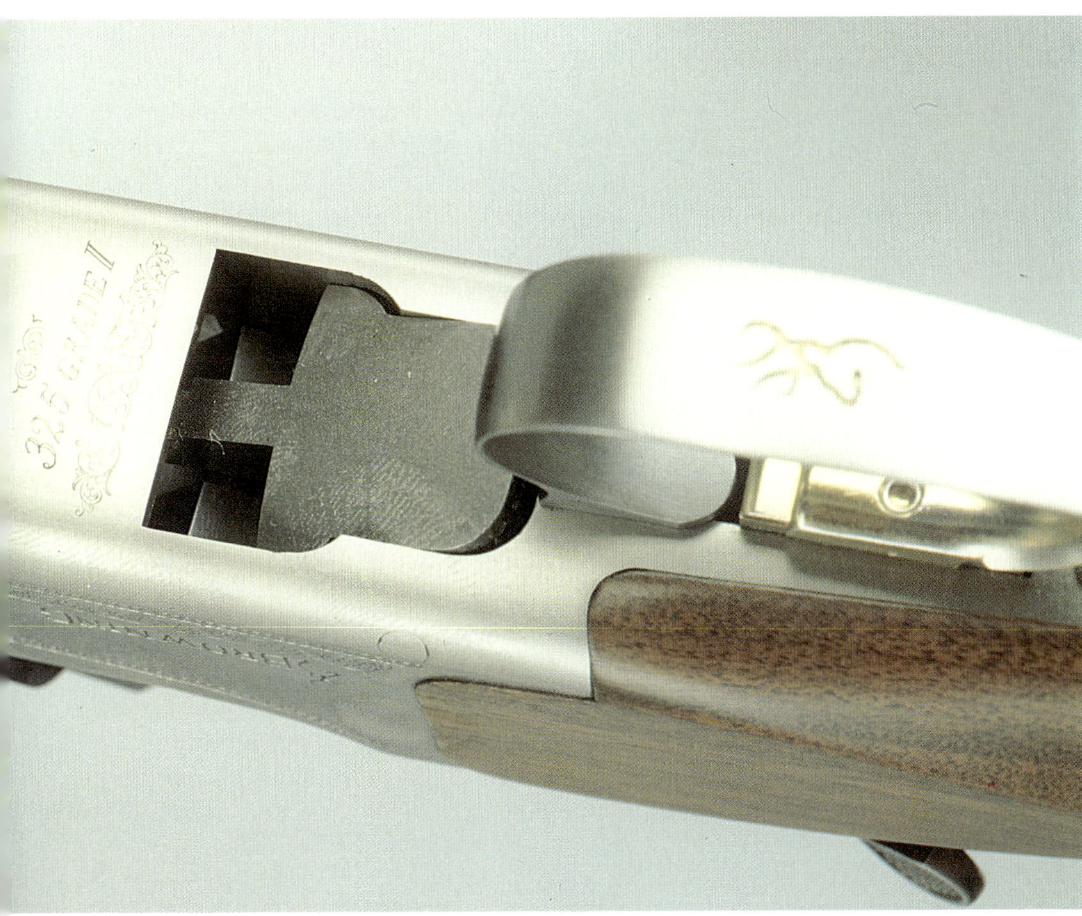

Browning ST-100 Shotgun

Manufacturer Fabrique Nationale Herstal SA, Herstal, Belgium
Type Double-barreled, superposed
Gage 12
Barrels 29.9in (760mm)
Weight 8.06lbs (3.65kg)

This is marketed as a 'Trap Gun' and in Europe is known as the 'Super Trap 80' model. It is unusual in that it is possible to vary the parallelism of the barrels so as to vary the placement of the patterns from each barrel.

The ST-100's barrels are not joined by a rib, as are most over-and-under guns, but are distinctly separated except for the breech lump and a band around the muzzles. About eight inches behind the muzzles there is a linking wedge between the barrels which can be adjusted into any one of five positions, so altering the set of the barrels and shifting the shot patterns. A table in the instruction book gives the theoretical differences, but practical tests show that while the sense of the shift follows the table, the exact distance may vary slightly.

This apart, the rest of the gun is conventional except for the ventilated rib which is attached by five supports and is capable of flexing, necessary because of the barrel adjustment feature. The single trigger is mechanically operated, rather than by inertia, to select the second barrel. The degree of choke can be selected from various options; the top barrel is always full, while the other can be had in steps from modified to full.

The gun delivers tight patterns from either barrel and the inter-barrel adjustment works well, though it needs to be checked by firing. Finish is good, and in keeping with the Browning standards of excellence.

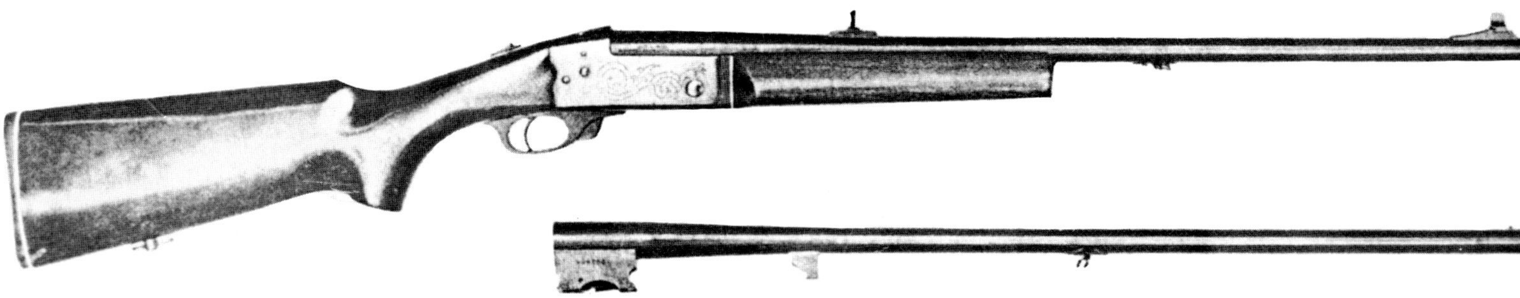

Above: The CBC Combination Gun, shown here with shot and rifle barrels.

CBC Combination Gun

Manufacturer Companhia Brasiliero de Cartouchoes, São Paulo, Brazil
Type Rifle-shotgun combination
Calibers .30-30 and 20-gage
Barrels Shotgun: 28in (711mm)
Rifle: 26in (660mm)
Weights 6.78lbs (3.07kg)
Rifle: 8.28lbs (3.75kg)

This interesting and unusual weapon is the product of a company better-known for ammunition than for firearms, though it has considerable domestic sales of shotguns to its credit. The Combination Gun is a basic action to which either a 20-gage shotgun barrel or a .30-30 rifle barrel can be quickly mounted, and it seems to be an eminently sensible working weapon for anyone living in the wilds.

The basic action is a concealed hammer, similar to that of a shotgun and carried in a simple receiver unit. To this the barrel can be attached by simply hooking the lump over the cross-pin and attaching the fore-end by means of a spring latch. The result is tight-fitting, and the action can be dropped open for loading by pressing on a catch in the front of the trigger guard.

The rifle barrel is provided with a ramp front and adjustable folding leaf rear sight, as well as having standard grooves for mounting a telescope sight. The shotgun barrel has a simple front sight bead. One advantage of this sort of action is that it suits both right- and left-handed shooters equally well.

The shotgun delivers good patterns with consistency, while the rifle barrel is as accurate as most shooters would ask, giving three-inch groups at 100 yards from rest. Altogether this is a well-thought-out combination, practical and robust, capable of adequate accuracy, and remarkably inexpensive for what it gives.

IAB Premier Skeet Shotgun

Manufacturer Industria Armi Bresciane SpA, Marcheno, Italy
Type Superposed double, single trigger
Gage 12
Barrels 26.8in (680mm)
Weight 7.68lbs (3.48kg)

The IAB company is one of the younger Italian gunmaking concerns, numbers of which have begun to prosper in northern Italy. There is a long tradition of fine metal-working and gunmaking in this region, and small companies have realized that they can aim for specialist areas of the market with high-class products and succeed where the big companies cannot compete. Over the past decade IAB have specialized in first-class competition shotguns and have won a long string of international prizes.

The appearance of the IAB Premier Skeet is impressive; oiled-finish walnut of best grade, well-executed hand checkering, fine engraving on the receiver, and a high polish and blue on the rest of the metalwork allied with meticulous fit on the parts is indicative of the care this company lavish on their products.

The mechanism uses strikers, rather than hammers, and has an inertia-operated selector on the single trigger mechanism. This is fixed to fire the lower barrel with the first pull, then the upper, and the sequence cannot be changed. The gun is opened by the usual top lever which clears a single cross-bolt; dropping the barrels cocks the strikers, and closing the gun cocks the ejectors. The safety is manually operated.

The barrels are bored with what the makers call their 'enlarged skeet choke,' a form of recessed choke in which the transition is very abrupt, with a step-form which acts as a trap for debris from the shot wads. This is not difficult to clean but it should be borne in mind, since a built-up of debris can play havoc with patterns. Patterning is extremely consistent at Skeet ranges, and there can be no doubt that this gun has earned its place in the competitive world.

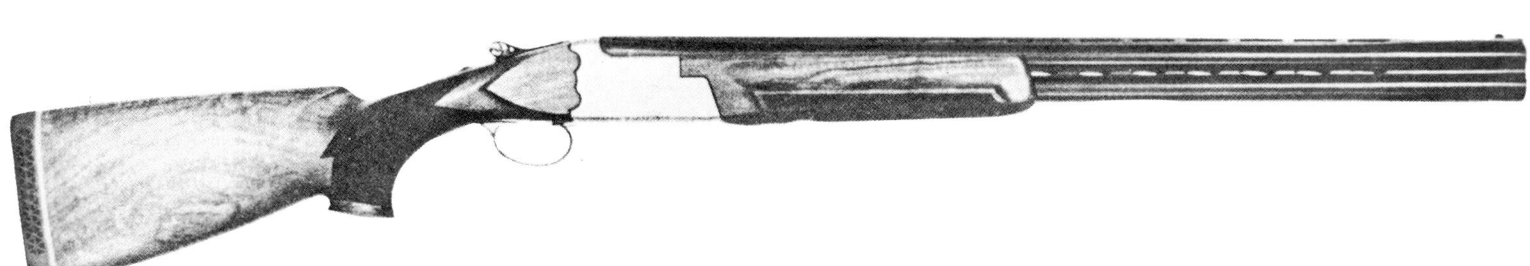

Above: The IAB Premier Skeet from Italy.

Above: The Jackhammer Mark 3-A2.
Left: The Mark 3-A1 version.

Jackhammer Combat Shotgun

Manufacturer Mark Three, Albuquerque, New Mexico, U.S.A.
Type Automatic revolver, gas-operated
Gage 12
Barrel 20.6in (525mm)
Weight 10.07lbs (4.57kg)
Magazine capacity 10 rounds
Cyclic rate of fire 240 rounds/minute

The Jackhammer is an automatic, gas-operated, 12-gage shotgun which uses a pre-loaded rotating cylinder as its magazine. The cylinder has grooves incised on its outer surface which are engaged by a stud on an operating rod, so that as the rod moves back and forth, so it rotates the cylinder. This is a very similar system to that employed in the Webley-Fosbery automatic revolver. The barrel is floating, and is driven forward by gas pressure as each shot is fired. It is then returned by a spring and gives movement to the cylinder-operating rod. This movement of the barrel also disconnects the barrel from its gas-tight seal with the cylinder, allowing the cylinder to be turned to bring the next chamber in line; on the return stroke the barrel reseals itself into the chamber mouth.

The barrel, flash eliminator, return spring and 'Autobolt' (the patented name for the cylinder operating rod) are all of high-quality steel. The rest of the weapon is almost all of synthetic material, a new material by DuPont called Rynite SST.

The cylinder, called by the makers

the 'Ammo Cassette' is also of Rynite SST, contains 10 cartridges, and is sealed with a shrink-film plastic, color-coded to indicate the type of ammunition loaded. The seal is removed by a pull-strip and the cassette slips straight into the weapon and engages the operating system. The weapon is then cocked by the sliding action of the fore-end, and is ready to fire. Once the cassette has been emptied, a simple movement of the fore-end releases it to fall clear and allow a new cassette to be loaded. It is not possible to load single cartridges into the weapon, and empty cases are not ejected while firing.

The Jackhammer's 'Ammo Cassette'.

A de-cocking lever, inside the butt-stock, allows the hammer to be safely lowered when the gun is loaded; it can then be carried quite safely. When required, the hammer can be re-cocked silently by using the same lever.

Although the chambers are for the standard shotgun cartridge, the receiver has been strengthened so that a specially-developed cartridge known as the 'Jack Shot' can be fired. This special cartridge operates at a much higher pressure than sporting ammunition and allows special loadings such as fléchettes, armor penetrators, preformed fragmenting projectiles or canister loadings, or even simply larger charges of conventional lead shot to be fired safely.

Development of the Jackhammer has now been completed, and the weapon is being studied by various official agencies. Meanwhile the company is working on more specialized ammunition options and a sound suppressor which will be relatively inexpensive and which can be discarded after a limited life.

Lanber Sporting 97LCH Shotgun

Manufacturer Armas Lanber SA, Zaldibar, Spain
Type Double-barreled, superposed
Gage 12
Barrels 28in (710mm)
Weight 7.5lbs (3.4kg)

The Lanber company of Spain has, over the past 20 years, built up a very good reputation for middle-price shotguns throughout Europe and is now beginning to export them farther afield. Their current range includes four grades of over-and-under guns (Expert, Aventura, Aventura Light, Rivaland Sporting) and three grades of semi-automatic (Victoria I, II and IV), which between them cater for practically any shooting requirement.

The Sporting 97LCH is their current 'best-seller,' particularly in the trap-shooting fraternity. The barrels are of high-grade steel and fitted into the usual monobloc breech end which carries the ejectors and locking system. The barrels are joined by a ventilated rib and the sighting rib has a slight taper and a white front beat, giving a very well-defined sight picture. The bores are somewhat loose, at 18.6mm diameter, rather unusual on a European gun, but tending to reduce recoil slightly as well as shot deformation.

The action is of steel and uses twin stud hinges, as on the Beretta system described elsewhere, rather than the more usual full-width hinge pin. One

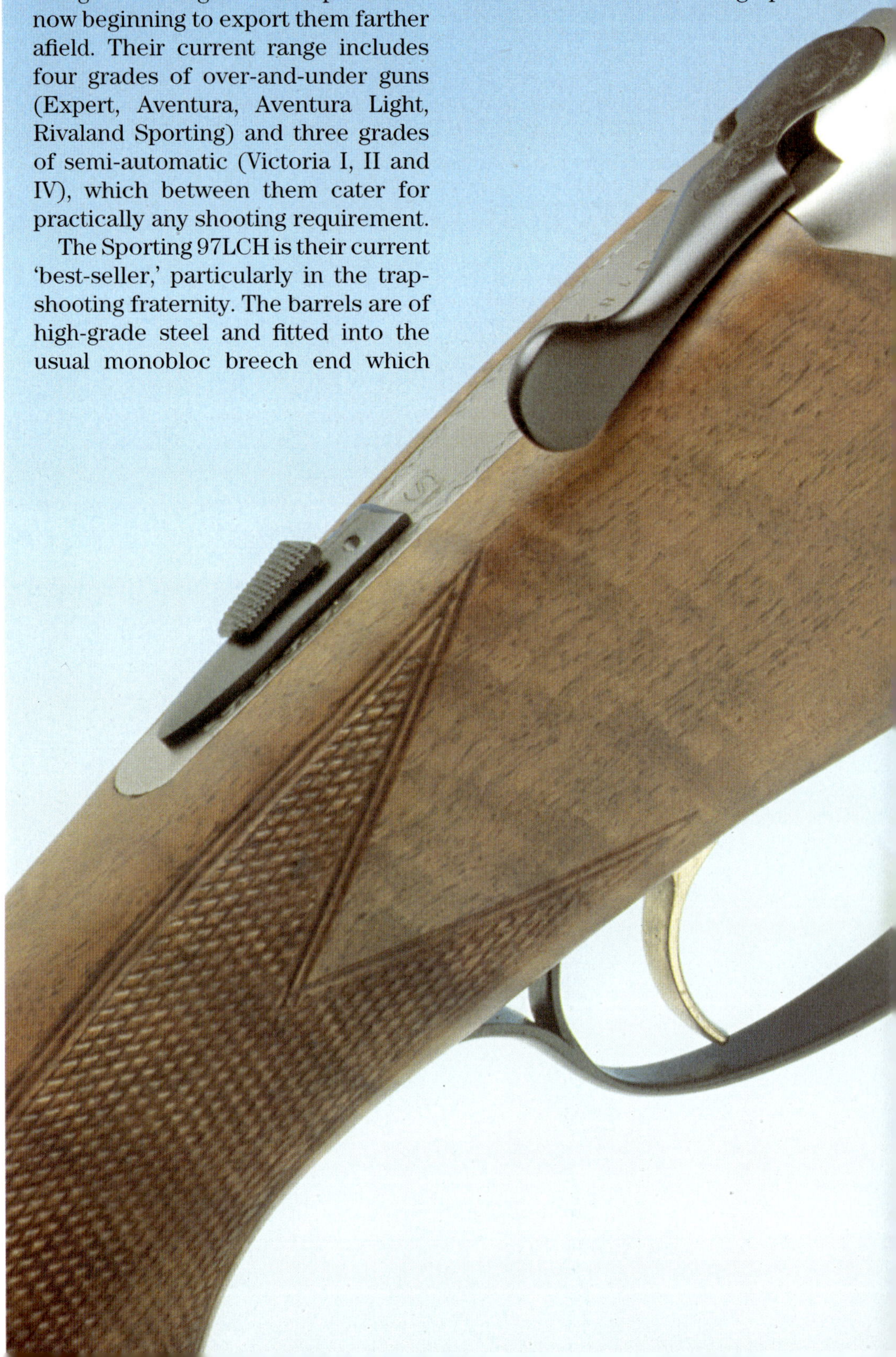

These pages: Two views of the Lanber Sporting 97LCH.

advantage of this construction is that it reduces the height of the action and gives the entire gun a sleeker appearance. A combined safety catch and barrel selector is mounted on the action backstrap, just behind the top lever. The action locks to the barrels by a full-width flat bolt which engages on a groove on the barrel block. The action side-plates are machine-engraved with a decorative pattern.

The barrels are fitted with multi-chokes, and five different chokes are provided with each gun. The multi-choke units fit unobtrusively; there is a slight enlargement of the muzzles to make room for them, but this is scarcely noticeable.

The Lanber handles well, shoots accurately and with good pattern, and well merits its popularity.

Above: The high-quality Leland Model 210.

Leland Model 210 Shotgun

Manufacturer Union Armera, Eibar, Spain
Type Side-by-side double, hammerless
Gage 12, 16, 20 or 28
Barrels 26, 27 or 28in (660, 685 or 711mm)
Weight 6.625lbs (3kg) (28in barrels)

Though made in Spain this takes its name from being imported into the U.S.A. by Leland Firearms of West Orange, NJ; it is known under the maker's name in Europe. The Union Armera has been making shotguns for very many years and has a wide domestic market for all qualities of gun. The Model 210 is a basic side-by-side modeled on the classic English 'game gun'. It is reasonably priced, fitting about half-way in the Union Armera catalog.

The gun has an elegant appearance, using the English style of straight stock and splinter fore end. The wood is good quality walnut, hand-checkered and oil-finished, while the receiver and fittings are nicely scroll-engraved and color case-hardened. The side-plates can be removed, and the interior of the lockwork is polished and engine-turned. The fit of metal to wood is very well done. The action is locked by a Purdey triple bolt, somewhat unusual nowadays, and there are automatic ejectors.

The standard gun is in 12-gage with 26-inch barrels having improved cylinder and modified choke; it is also possible to have the longer barrels with modified and full choke. The other gages noted are also available, and while the normal chamber length is 2.75 inches, 3 inch chambers can be specified at extra cost.

The Model 210 balances well, feels good, and delivers consistent patterns. The workmanship is good and most observers consider the gun represents value for money.

Luigi Franchi Model 610 Autoloader

Manufacturer Luigi Franchi SpA, Brescia, Italy
Type Gas-operated auto-loader
Gage 12
Barrel 26, 28 or 30 in (660, 710 or 760mm)
Weight around 7lbs (3.17kg)
Magazine capacity 5 rounds

The Luigi Franchi company is an old-established one with a high reputation for shotguns in Europe and elsewhere.

The Model 610 is a gas-operated auto-loader of conventional pattern, the bolt being locked to the barrel extension until freed by the action of the gas piston concealed in the fore end, along with the tubular magazine. The stock design features a flowing pistol grip which permits a rearward placement of the trigger hand, something which many shooters prefer, and the stock has rather less drop than is common. The finish is excellent, the stock and fore end in nicely-figured walnut with good hand checkering, and the aluminum receiver blacked and etched with a floral pattern.

The gun is well-balanced, allowing rapid movement when at the shoulder, and the recoil is, as usual with gas-operated weapons, damped down to an acceptable level. It delivers consistent patterns, and there is a choice of improved, modified or full choke available. For what you get, the Franchi is remarkably inexpensive, and with the company's reputation for workmanship, we would expect it to deliver flawless performance for many years. The 610 is an improvement on the earlier Model 500 and incorporates the Franchi "Variopress" system of gas regulation, which allows cartridges of varying power and length to be fixed without affecting the gas operation. A de luxe model, the 610 VS Luxe is also available.

Luigi Franchi SPAS Shotgun

Manufacturer Luigi Franchi SpA, I-25020 Fornaci, Italy
Type Automatic, combat-type
Gage 12
Barrel 19.68in (500mm)
Weight (empty) 7.05lbs (3.20kg)
Magazine capacity 8 rounds

Luigi Franchi are well-known for sporting shotguns of the highest quality, but their SPAS (Special Purpose Automatic Shotgun) series will be rather less well-known outside Italy. It was designed for police and military use and aims to be rather-more efficient in that role than conventional civil shotguns which were designed with sporting use in mind and have been 'misappropriated' to police use. The firm claim that their design gives good accuracy with little training; instant hits in all kinds of employment; great firepower; the ability to launch grenades if required; and low maintenance.

The basic SPAS Model 11 is a short-barreled semi-automatic shotgun with a folding butt which has been configured so that it can be locked under the armpit and allow the gun to be used one-handed. The receiver is of light alloy, while the barrel and gas cylinder have been hard-chromed to reduce the risk of corrosion. All the external surfaces are sand-blasted and phosphated black.

An unusual provision is for the gas cylinder to be shut off, converting the weapon to a slide-action repeater; the fore end can be unlocked to act as the reloading slide in this mode, which is designed for use with certain types of light ammunition which will not cycle the gas action reliably.

The barrel is cylinder bored and spreads a normal shot charge to about three feet at 130 feet range, reducing the need for precise aiming. The automatic action will fire about four shots per second, and at this rate of fire, with standard buckshot loadings, it is possible to put 48 pellets per second into a one-yard-square target at 130 foot range. At this range the pellets have about 50 percent more striking energy than a .32 pistol bullet.

There is a wide range of ammunition available for security use, from buckshot and solid slug to tear-gas rounds which fire a small plastic container of CS gas to 170-yards range. There is a launching attachment which fits the muzzle and which permits the firing of grenades to 150m range, and there is also a 'shot spreader' attachment which fits on the muzzle and breaks up the shot pattern to give much greater short-range spread, an option designed for indoor use.

The SPAS Model 12 differs slightly from the Model 11; it has an additional grip safety in the forward edge of the pistol grip, an improved and strengthened butt stock, and a reshaped fore end. The barrel is slightly shorter but the weapon weighs almost exactly one pound more than the Model 11.

Far left: The Luigi Franchi SPAS 12.

Below: The SPAS 12 pictured with folded butt.

Bottom: The SPAS Model 11 Riot Gun ready for use.

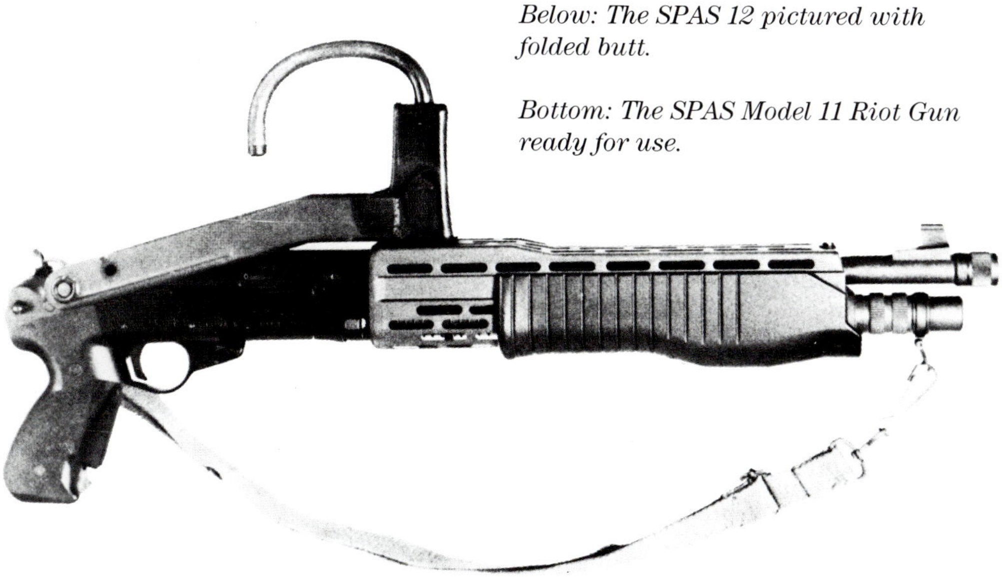

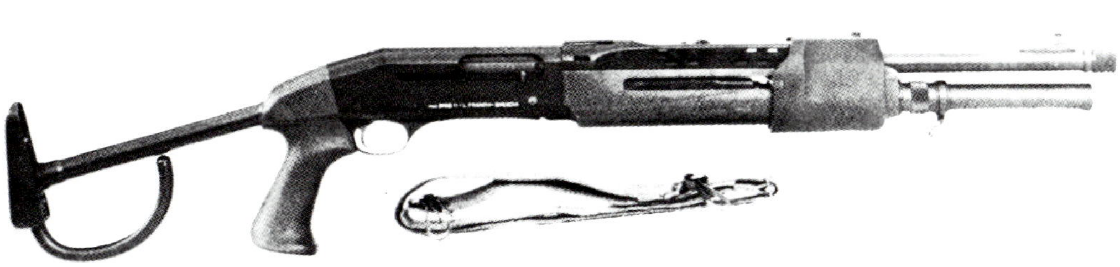

PIOTTI

Piotti Sidelock Shotgun

Manufacturer Piotti Armi, Gardone Val Trompia, Italy
Type Double-barreled, side-by-side
Gage 12
Barrels 28in (710mm)
Weight 6.6lbs (2.99kg)

The Piotti company is an old-established family firm who have a reputation for producing high-quality sporting guns at a reasonable price. Their quality is attested to by the fact that they are generally imported into other countries by top-class gunmakers rather than import-export companies.

As might be expected, the quality of fit and finish of Piotti guns is excellent. The blue is deep and lustrous, the wood fine-grained, well-figured and finished, and the fit of every part is perfect. The engraving is exceptional and covers the sideplates, bottom, trigger-guard, breeches, top strap and backstrap with ornate and tasteful designs.

The barrels are built independently, the tubes and breech lump being of the same piece of metal, and are then brazed together. There is a central rib and the barrels are choked improved and half-choke.

The action is a sidelock, with double triggers, the sideplates being silver polished, though color case-hardened plates are an available option. As usual, the second trigger breaks at a slightly higher pressure than the first, though both are very smooth and with a well-defined let-off point. For those who prefer it, a single trigger is an option.

The stock may be of straight hand-grip type or pistol grip, to choice. In either case the wood is of high quality and the finish excellent, with firm and clean checkering. As might be expected, the gun handles and shoots extremely well.

Left: The handsome Piotti sidelock. This shotgun not only looks handsome, it also handles well and shoots extremely accurately.

Remington 11-87 Premier Skeet Shotgun

Manufacturer Remington Arms, Wilmington, Delaware, U.S.A.
Type Automatic, gas-operated
Gage 12
Barrel 25.5in (648mm)
Weight 7.5lbs (3.4kg)

Introduced in 1987, the 11-87 Premier Skeet is intended, as the name implies, for clay pigeon shooting, and it has gained a good reputation in this field for its accuracy, handiness and low recoil.

Remington automatic shotguns are gas-operated, tapping off a proportion of the propellant gas to drive a piston rearwards and so operate the bolt and reloading mechanism. In most of the Remington 11-87 series, the gas is self-regulating, so that virtually any cartridge capable of fitting inside the chamber will operate the action satisfactorily. The Premier Skeet mode, however, is regulated for 70mm cartridges only, and firing smaller charges may not result in successful reloading. This might be a disadvantage in field shooting, but since this gun is purely for one type of sport using one type of cartridge, it is an acceptable restriction and it does allow the gas system to be easily 'tuned' for the most trouble-free, reliable and consistent performance.

The barrel is fitted for a multi-choke, and three are supplied with the gun, allowing the owner to set the shot pattern to his preference. The mechanism cycles smoothly; pulling back the cocking handle locks the action open until released by a carrier release catch on the loading ramp. With the chamber loaded, the magazine can then have two cartridges fed in from underneath the action.

The stock is a full pistol-grip with cut checkering. It is of standard 'skeet' length, just short of 14 inches (350mm) and with an average amount of drop. There is no form of adjustment, and no options, but most shooters are happy with this length. There is a rubber recoil pad, and a synthetic protective coating to the wood. Metal parts are in a black satin finish.

Altogether, the 11-87 Premier Skeet is a sound, no-nonsense tool for competition shooting, and is particularly recommended for beginners in the game.

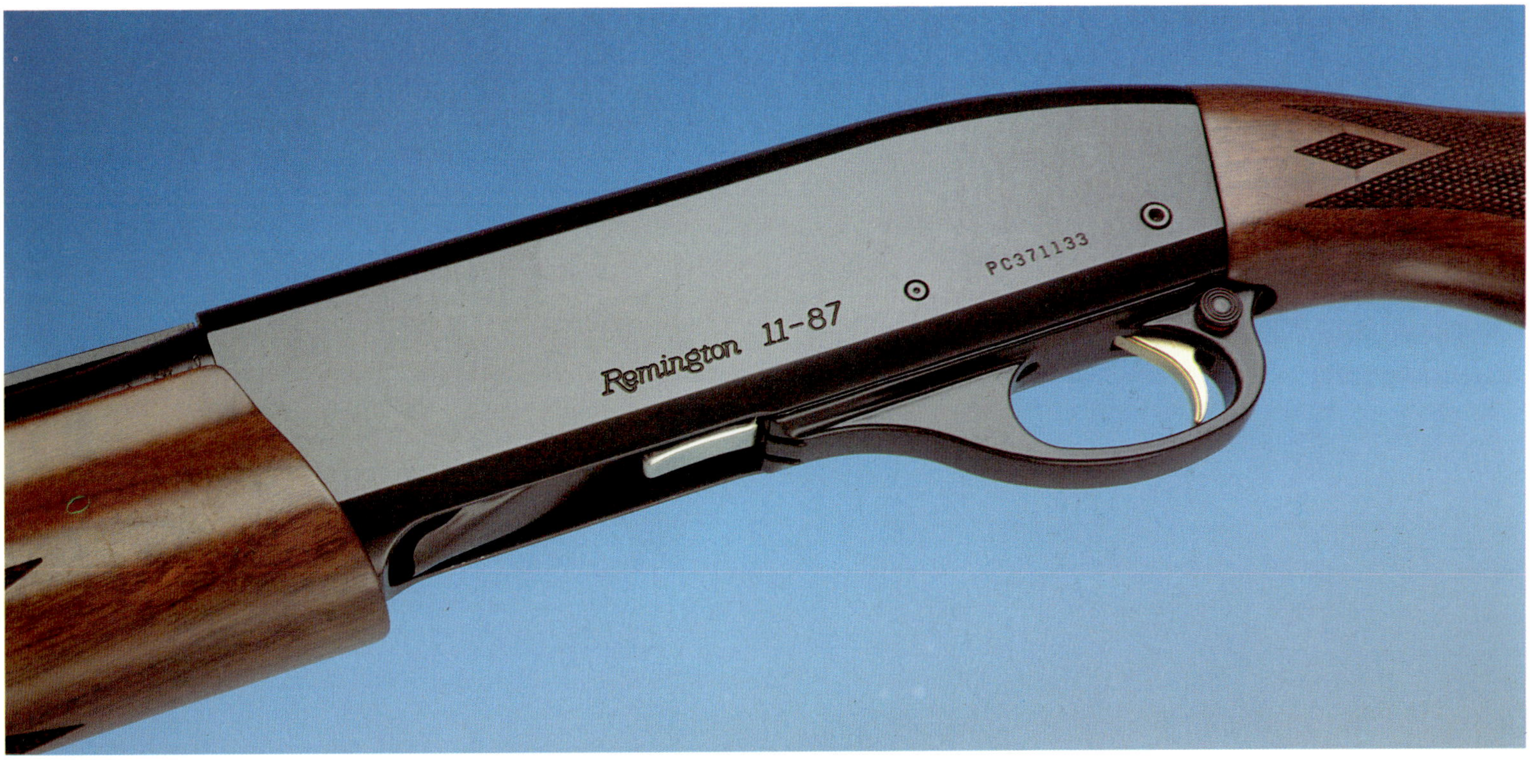

Above and left: The Remington 11-87 Premier Skeet, a sound and reliable shotgun for competition shooting.

Rizzini Multichoke Shotgun

Manufacturer B. Rizzini, Marcheno, Italy
Type Double-barreled, superposed
Gage 12
Barrels 28in (710mm)
Weight 8lbs (3.62kg)

The Rizzini company is another of those old-established family firms operating in the traditional gun-making area around Brescia in northern Italy. Most such firms tend to aim at one particular area of the shooting market, but Rizzini covers the entire range of quality, making on the one hand entry-level economy guns for practical shooters, and on the other hand, luxurious hand-crafted, custom-built guns. Their wide rfange of products has ensured their survival in an area where small firms must fight for their living.

The Multichoke is one of the inexpensive guns, but there is nothing cheap or shoddy about it. The barrels are of best steel, built on the monobloc system in which the two barrels are inserted into a chamber block. They are separated by a ventilated rib, with another ventilated rib above the barrel carrying a translucent red bead foresight and a white bead center sight. They are prepared for multichokes, four of which are supplied with the gun, together with a key for unscrewing and replacing them.

The action uses coil springs, common with Italian guns, and a recoil-operated single trigger which tends to be on the light side. A barrel selector-cum-safety catch lies on the backstrap. Locking is done by the usual bolt engaging in a slot, but into the monobloc below the lower barrel, and the barrels are hinged on side pins rather than on a full-width hinge pin. The sideplates and under surface are machine engraved with a traditional sporting motif.

The stock is of average drop, protected by a synthetic finish, and the fore-end is a hand-filling design with finger grooves. As a basic beginner's gun the Rizzini represents good value.

Above and left: Two views of the Rizzini Multichoke, a basic beginner's gun representing excellent value.

Right: A close-up shot of the barrels of the Multichoke.

Rossi 'Squire' Shotgun

Manufacturer Amadeo Rossi SA, São Paulo, Brazil
Type Side-by-side double, hammerless
Gage 12, 20 or .410
Barrels 26in (660mm) or 28in (711mm)
Weight 7.75lbs (3.51kg) (12-ga)

Amadeo Rossi are a Brazilian company who, over the past 20 or 50 years have built up something of an export trade, particularly in revolvers. This hammerless shotgun first appeared in the 1960s and has recently been improved.

The 'Squire' is an unpretentious gun, designed to be used rather than admired. The stock and fore-end are of some local hardwood, plainly finished to resemble walnut and without checkering or decoration. The metal is well polished and blued, and the fit, though not to the highest standards, is perfectly serviceable. The mechanism of the lock is robust and the manufacturer's aim has been to produce a design capable of machine production and using as many interchangeable parts as possible. This at least has the virtue of delivering a sound gun at a reasonable price.

The 12- and 20-gage guns are well balanced full-sized weapons; the .410, as might be expected, is on a reduced scale and weighs rather less. We are, in fact, rather surprised that Rossi find it profitable to make a .410 gun since the current fashion appears to be moving away to the 29-gage when a light weapon is required. Nevertheless, at whatever gage is chosen the Rossi functions reliably and shoots well, delivering consistent patterns to the point of aim.

Rottweil Super Trap Combination Gun

Manufacturer Deutsche Jagdpatronenfabrik GmbH, Rottweil, Germany
Type Combination single or superposed
Gage 12
Barrels Single: 34in (864mm); double: 32in (812mm)
Weight 8.75lbs (3.96kg)

The phrase 'combination gun' means different things to different people; to workaday farmers it can mean interchangeable rifle and shotgun barrels, to upland shooters it can mean simple interchangeable barrels with different degrees of choke. But to International Trap competition shooters it means a gun which is specifically designed for their peculiar requirements and which can shift from a double over-and-under to a single barrel on call, so as to fit the various types of contest. On the face of it this sounds easy, but a look at this Rottweil gun shows that some careful thought and ingenious design is necessary to make a success of it.

The basic stock and receiver is no more than that; to it must be added first the barrel of choice and then the appropriate trigger unit. With the single barrel, there is (obviously) a single trigger; with the over-and-under set there is a selective single trigger, inertia operated and with a button which allows selection of the first barrel. The trigger units slip in and out and exhibit precise workmanship; the hammer coil springs are encased in telescoping steel tubes for alignment and protection, and all metal surfaces are polished clean of tool marks.

Each barrel set has a ventilated rib which stands well clear to avoid heat mirages, and the single barrel has a short balance tube beneath it so that whichever barrel is fitted the gun always weighs and balances the same. The same fore end will fit either barrel set. The stock and fore end are in satin-finished French walnut with excellent hand-checkering, while every metal surface is immaculately finished. The bores are hand-honed, test-fired, and re-worked if necessary at the factory in order to produce absolutely flawless patterns. The result of this careful hand-fitting shows up in its performance, which is beyond criticism; it also shows up in the price, which reflects the excellence of this product.

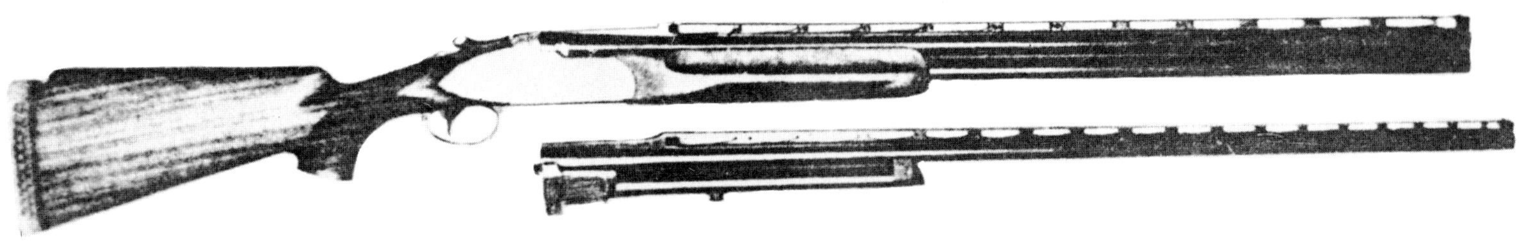

Above: The Rottweil 'Super Trap' allows the use of single or superposed double barrels.

Left: The Rossi 'Squire,' shoots well, delivering consistent patterns.

Ruger Red Label Shotgun

Manufacturer Sturm Ruger & Co. Inc., Southport, Connecticut, U.S.A.
Type Double-barreled, superposed
Gage 12 or 20
Barrels 26 or 28in (660 or 710mm)
Weight 7.5lbs (3.4kg) in 12-ga.

Sturm Ruger have been well-known for their handguns since the late 1940s; in the late 1960s they began work on a shotgun design. First shown in prototype form in 1971, it was progressively developed and perfected, and went on sale in 20-gage in 1978. A 12-gage was added in 1982, and although the basic design has remained unchanged, there have been a number of small improvements from time to time as refinements have been added.

The Ruger uses some patented design features, notably the positioning of the locking bolt between the bores so as to obtain a low-set profile, and the inertia-locking single-trigger mechanism which can be set to fire either the upper or lower barrel firs. There are rebounding hammers and a hammer interruptor to guard against accidental discharge when the gun is cocked and set to safe; when set to fire, the interruptor is only moved by positive action of the trigger. The action body may be of blued or stainless steel to choice.

Below: The open breech of the Ruger 12-gage.

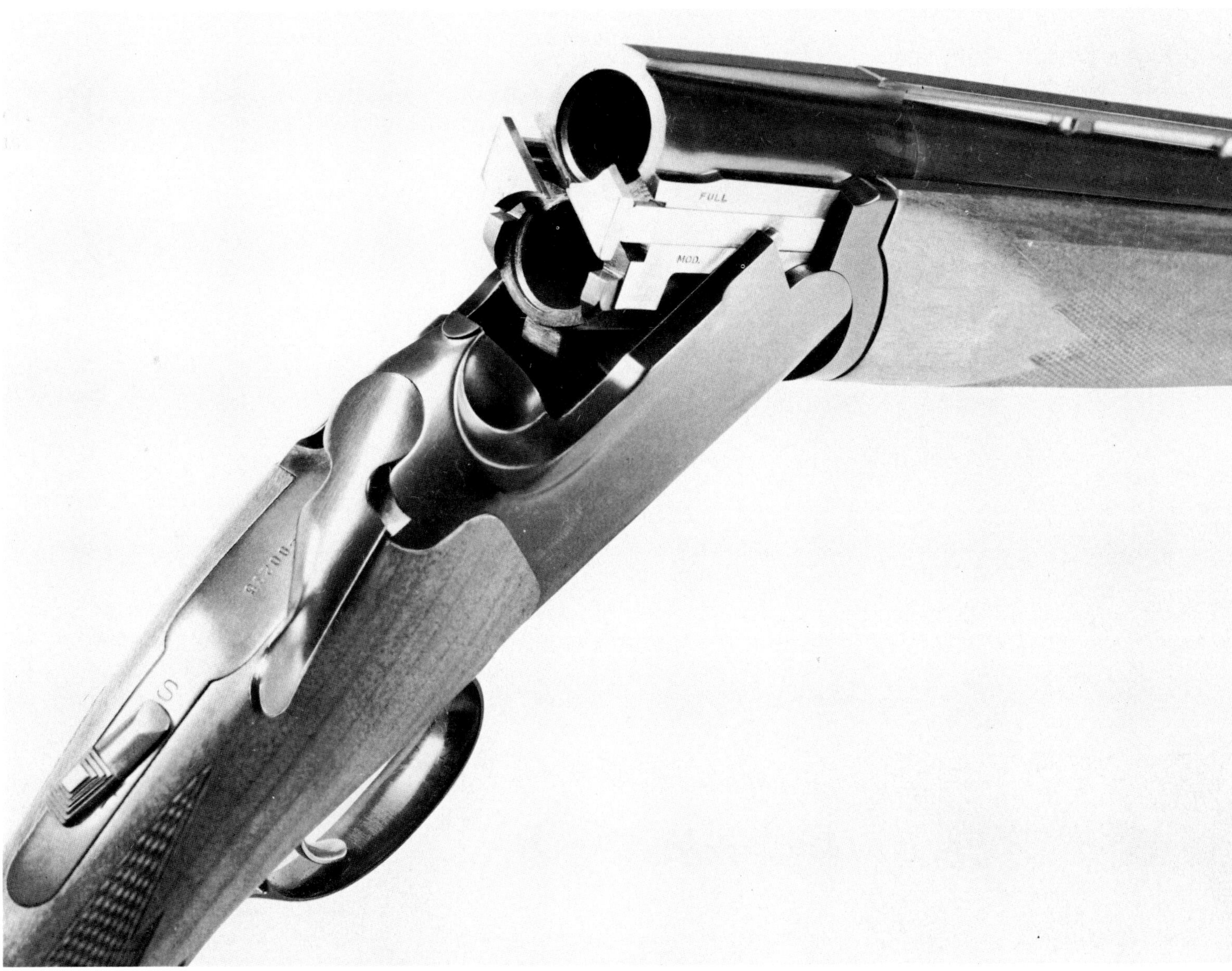

The hammer-forged Cr-Mo steel barrels are silver-soldered into the breech end monobloc, into which go the ejector mechanism and the trunnion pins which form the barrel pivot. There is a ventilated rub with glare-free top and a brass foresight bead. Stock and fore end are of American walnut, well-figured and neatly hand-checkered. The muzzles are fitted for multi-chokes, five of which are supplied with the gun, together with a key for fitting and removing them.

In the field the Red Label is a well-balanced, accurate gun with light, but not too sensitive, trigger and moderate recoil. It can be used equally well for game or competition shooting, and for the person restricted to using one gun, the Ruger should cover every eventuality.

These pages: Two views of the Ruger Red Label, a well-balanced and accurate shotgun that can be used in many different types of competition shooting.

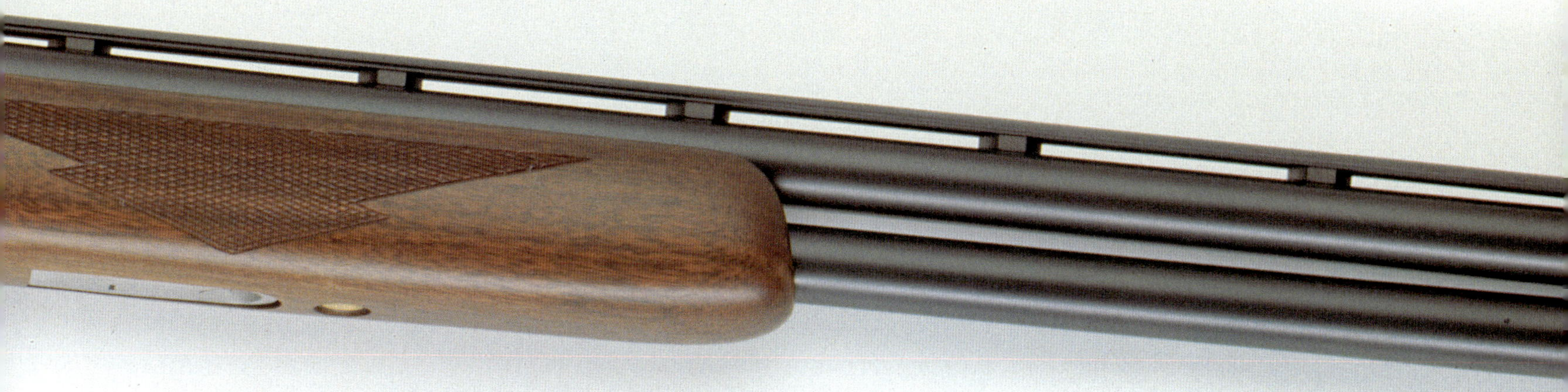

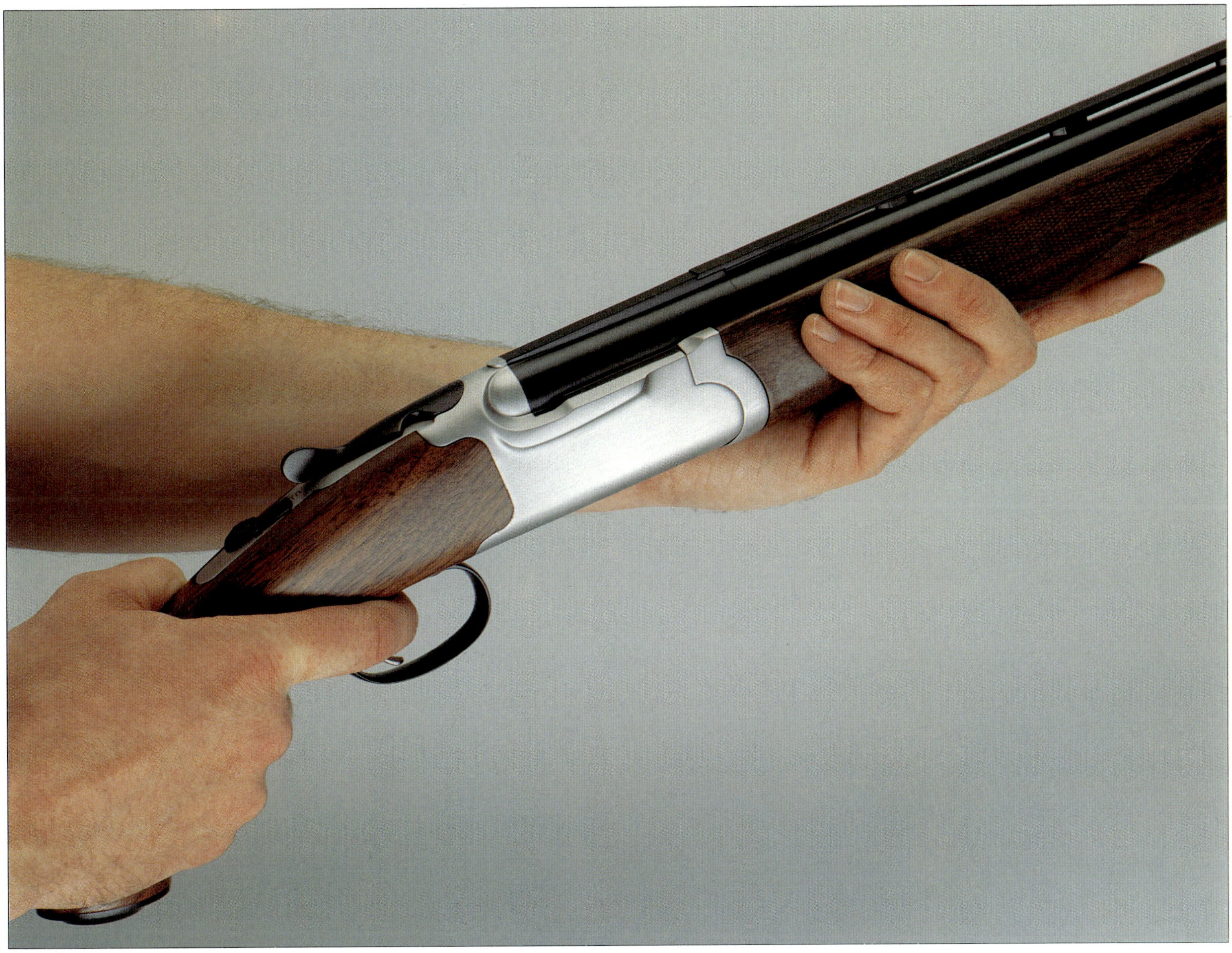

S.A.B. 'London' Shotgun

Manufacturer Societe Armi Bresciane Srl., Gardone Val Trompia, Italy
Type Side-by-side double, automatic ejector
Gage 12 or 20
Barrels 26.7in (680mm) or 27.5in (700mm)
Weight 6.62lbs (3kg) (26in barrels)

S.A.B. build a number of grades of shotgun and the 'London' model is their top line; as the name implies, it sets out to duplicate the type and quality made famous by the London gunmakers, and it achieves this very well.

The 'London' comes in a traditional gun case, leather-covered and baize-lined, into which the dismantled gun and its cleaning gear fit neatly. The gun itself is elegantly finished with an English-style straight stock in European walnut, oil-finished, the case-hardened receiver is neatly engraved, as are the trigger guard, top lever and other components, the barrels are well polished and blued, and the fitting of metal to wood is excellent. The front trigger is hinged so as not to trap the finger on the second trigger during recoil, the firing pin holes are bushed, and the matted top rib is finished by a white metal front bead.

The stock has a slight cast-off and little drop, making it perhaps best suited to those small of stature. Fired with light loadings it is comfortable to shoot, but heavier loadings tend to punish the firer due to the low weight of the gun. Nevertheless, this low weight has its advantages when carrying the gun all day, and it is quick and accurate in coming to the shoulder and pointing.

Viking Arms SOS Shotgun

Manufacturer Viking Arms Ltd., Harrogate, England
Type Slide action repeater
Gage 12
Barrel 24.25in (616mm)
Weight 7.43lbs (3.37kg)
Magazine capacity 7 rounds

The shotgun has evolved into certain well-known shapes over the years, and the appearance of something new comes as a shock to most people. The Viking gun is designed along the lines of the modern assault rifle, with a 'straight-line' stock and a carrying-handle-cum-sight unit which requires an equally high-set foresight. The makers suggest it as a 'defense' gun rather than as a purely sporting gun, and I have little doubt that the appearance of this weapon on some European shoots would result in a rapid request for the bearer to leave.

But leaving visual impressions aside, the Viking is a well-made weapon with certain definite 'plus' points. It has an unusually large magazine for a slide-action gun, and since the barrel is cylinder-bored it makes a good gun for firing solid slugs. The sights assist in this, though they are not capable of being adjusted without the aid of a gunsmith. As a trap gun or as a sporting gun the shape takes some getting used to, and it does not come to the shoulder as easily as a traditional shape, though doubtless practice would improve this.

The straight-line configuration helps to control recoil, the gun appearing to jump less and be rapidly recovered, though this is only of value when firing against an immobile target. There is the possibility that the gun would be attractive to police or security forces; it is certainly reliable and accurate, simple to dismantle and maintain, all features making it attractive for service use, and it is comparatively inexpensive. An optional butt of conventional form will be available in the near future so that it will be possible to convert it into a more normal-looking pump gun for 'social' occasions.

Viking Suhl Shotgun

Manufacturer Viking Arms Ltd., Harrogate, England
Type Side-by-side double, non-ejector
Gage 12
Barrels 28in (711mm)
Weight 6.56lbs (2.97kg)

Suhl, in Thuringia, was once the heart of the German gunmaking industry, but when Germany was divided in 1945 it vanished behind the Iron Curtain and the independent gunsmiths were amalgamated into impersonal state-controlled cooperatives. The quality was still apparent, but the individuality of different makers vanished. The Viking shotgun was one of these products. Since the reformation of Germany, the various state organizations are being slowly dismantled, but at the time of writing it is not entirely clear how the former Ernst Thalmann Gunmaking Cooperative is being split up, and therefore we list the gun under the name of the British importer.

In an age when manufacturers vie with each other to make more and more luxurious products at higher

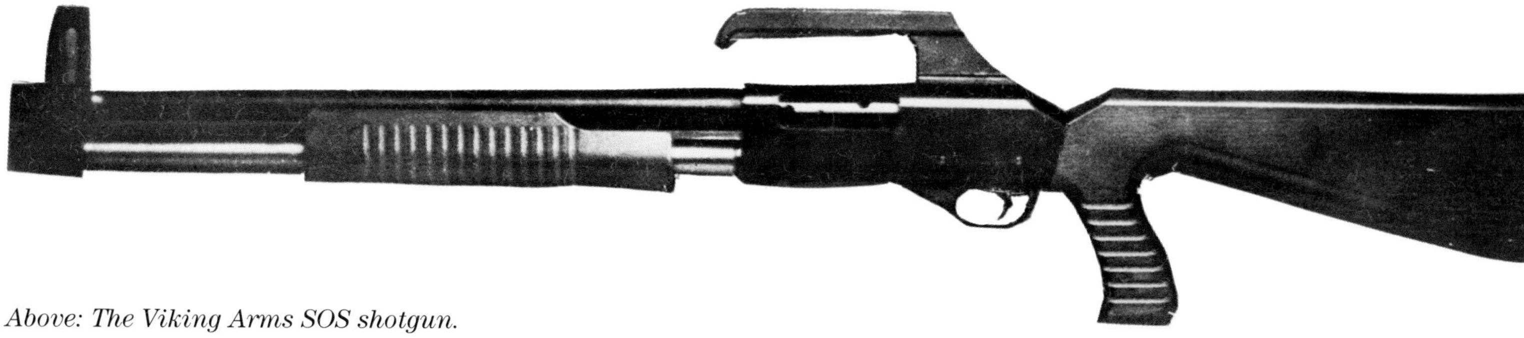

Above: The Viking Arms SOS shotgun.

and higher prices, the Suhl shotgun comes as a welcome surprise; it is an unpretentious 'working gun', with no concessions to elegance. The walnut stock has a half-pistol grip, the fore end is machine-checkered, but the finish is good and the fit of the gun to the stock is excellent. The action is a double-bolted box-lock, color case-hardened and without decoration, but it works smoothly, the trigger pull is crisp and consistent, and the whole action is tight and sound.

The barrels are bored quarter and three-quarter choke on Continental standards, closer to half and full-choke to western ideas, but the patterns are good and consistent. It handles well, the stock being cast-off for right-handed shooting, and gives the impression of a no-nonsense gun which will stand years of hard use.

This page: The Ruger 12 gauge shotgun.

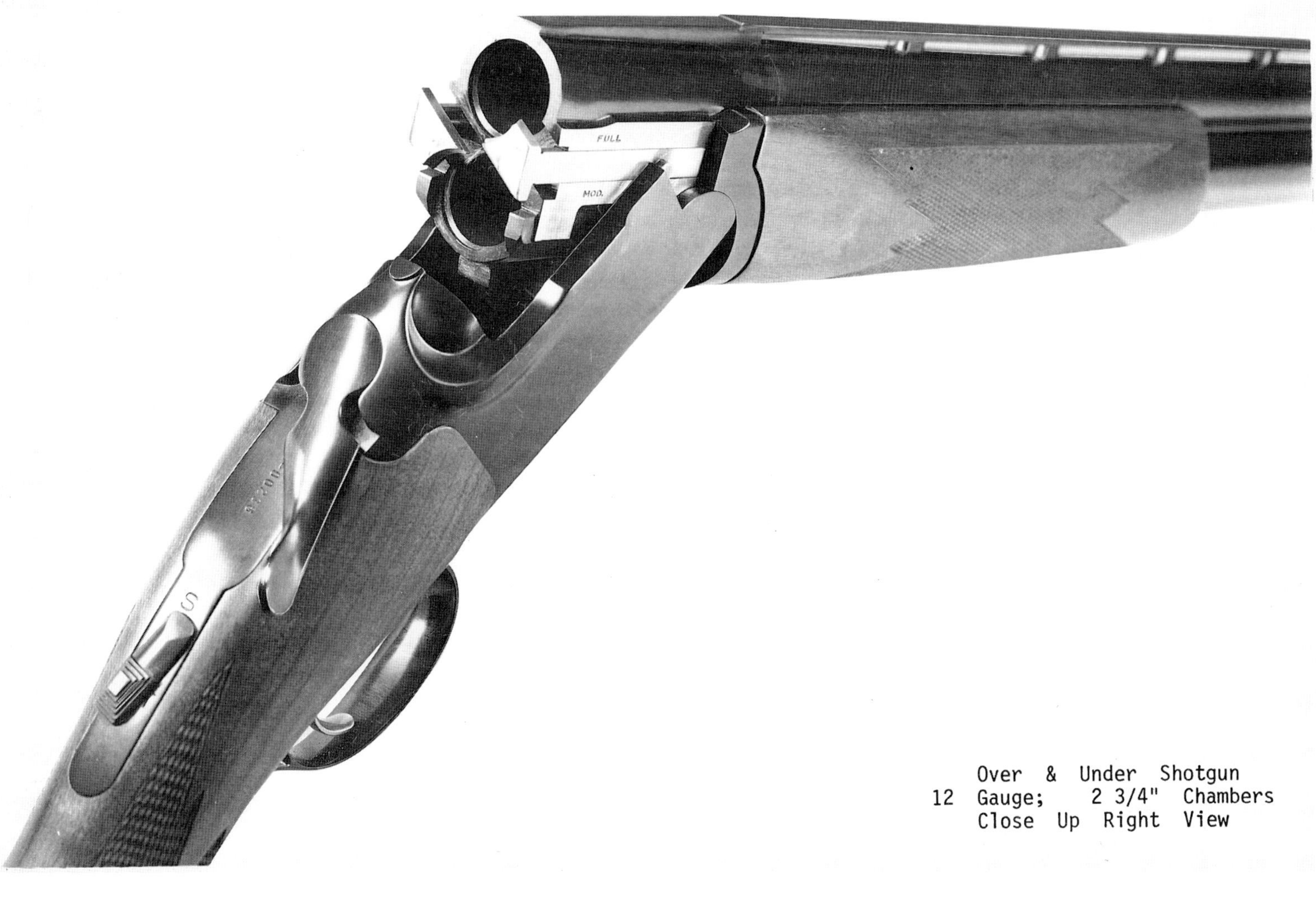

Acknowledgments

The author and publisher would like to thank Design 23, Susan Brown for production, and Judith Millidge the editor, for their help in the preparation of this book. Most of the photographs are from the author's collection or have been supplied by the manufacturers and our thanks are due to them. Additional material was provided by the individuals and organizations listed below.

BPL: 77

Guns and Shooting Magazine/Dave Page: 138-139, 140-141 (all 3), 144-145 (both), 148-149, 150, 151, 152-153 (all 3), 155, 156-157 (both)

Jacques Lenaerts: 61 below, 69 below

Reuters/Bettmann: 9 top

The Research House: 1, 2-3, 6-7, 8, 10 (below) 12, 21, 28, 50-51, 72, 85

H P White Laboratory: 143 (both), 144